The Sherlock Holmes Cookbook

Other Books by Fanny Cradock

Fiction

The Lormes of Castle Rising
Shadows over Castle Rising
Scorpion's Suicide
My Seed Thy Harvest
The Rags of Time
O Daughter of Babylon
The Echo in the Cup
Gateway to Remembrance
The Eternal Echo
The Land Is In Good Heart
Women Must Wait
Dark Reflection
Shadow of Heaven

Children's Books

When Michael Was Three
When Michael Was Six
Always
The Dryad and The Toad
The Story of Joseph and Pharoah
Naughty Red Lion
Naughty Red Lion Beware
Fish Knight-Sea Maiden
The Gooseyplums of Duckpond In The Dip
Brigadier Gooseyplum Goes To War
The Gooseyplums By The Sea

Cookery and Travel. By Fanny and Johnnie Cradock

The Practical Cook
The Ambitious Cook
The Daily Express Cookery Book
Bon Voyage
Bon Viveur in London
Around Britain With Bon Viveur
Bon Viveur's London and The British Isles
Bon Viveur in The Austrian Tyrol
Bon Viveur in Barcelona and The Balearics
Bon Viveur in Belgium
Bon Viveur in Denmark
Bon Viveur In Holland
Holiday On The French Riviera
Bon Viveur In Sweden
Holiday In The Touraine
Bon Viveur's Guide to Holidays In Europe
Cooking with Bon Viveur
Bon Viveur Request Cookery Book
Wining and Dining In France With Bon Viveur
Beginning to Cook with Fanny and Johnnie
Children's Outdoor Cookery with Fanny and Johnnie
The Young Chef with Fanny and Johnnie
Children's Party Cookery by Fanny and Johnnie
Veg and Vim
Cabbages and Things
The Daily Mail Cookery Book
The Cook's Book
The Sociable Cook's Book
The Cook Hostess's Book
Common Market Cookery—France
Common Market Cookery—Italy
Three Hundred and Sixty Five Puddings
Three Hundred and Sixty Five Soups and Their Accompaniments
Home Cooking
Problem Cooking
Giving a Dinner Party
Colourful Cookery
Fanny Cradock Invites
Eight Special Menus
Modest but Delicious

THE SHERLOCK HOLMES COOKBOOK

by Mrs Hudson

compiled by
FANNY CRADOCK

Illustrations by Val Biro

W.H. ALLEN · LONDON
A Howard & Wyndham Company
1976

Copyright © Fanny Cradock 1976

*This book or parts thereof may not be
reproduced in any form whatsoever
without permission in writing
Printed and bound in Great Britain
by Richard Clay (The Chaucer Press) Ltd,
Bungay, Suffolk
for the Publishers, W. H. Allen & Co. Ltd,
44 Hill Street, London W1X 8LB*

ISBN 0 491 01947 5

Contents

Author's Foreword	7
Mrs Hudson introduces herself	9
My household hints	15
including a few simple facts to aid the beginner	17
and	
a little practical nursing advice and receipts for the sickroom	24
Breakfasts	29
Soups	43
Fish	55
Poultry and game	75
Meat	93
Offal	113
Vegetables	127
Cheese dishes	137
Puddings	145
Afternoon tea receipts	171
Savouries	193
Beverages	205
Esteemed sundries	215
Preserves	227
On writing this little book	243
Index	249

Author's Foreword

The idea for this book is not mine, but had, as I understand it, been mooted by several people, according to the trustees of the Conan Doyle estate. Eventually I came to hear of it and became fascinated by it.

Here was this character, Mrs Hudson, cooking for two men during the heyday of the Victorian era, an era which already contained special appeal for me since it gave to us the woman who wrote everything contained in *Escoffier's Guide to Modern Cookery* some years before this masterpiece of his was published.

The name of this lady was Agnes Bertha Marshall. Her story will be told in another book upon which I am still working *The Great Marshall Mystery*, and it is a mystery, since this beautiful, socially eminent cook was, to imitate Mrs Hudson's style – A Most Remarkable Woman whose origins (and demise) are wrapped in deepest mystery!

I have borrowed from her writings and associated her in the most tenuous terms with Mrs Hudson. I have also drawn upon my own family recipe books and accredited many of the recipes contained in my old records to Mrs Hudson. In short I have hunted through all Sir Arthur Conan Doyle's 'Sherlock Holmes' stories, gleaned every quote I could find and upon this slender framework, built *The Sherlock Holmes Cookbook*! It has been the greatest fun to write. It has given me immense pleasure. It has also driven my little cookery team to the brink of Total Exhaustion, checking and testing every single published recipe, since I will never, in any circumstances, depart from my husband's and my chosen slogan 'nothing published which has not been tested, tasted and found worthy of inclusion'.

If it gives a few moments of pleasure to our friends who are also our readers my work will indeed have been totally rewarding.

Fanny Cradock (8 April, 1975)

Mrs Hudson Introduces Herself

MY dear father always bade me 'keep yourself to yourself my child' and I have always obeyed him.

Never was it more necessary than during the long years when I was housekeeper to Mr Sherlock Holmes at 221b Baker Street; where I was housekeeper to *two* gentlemen, for, despite his marriage, Dr Watson was so frequent a visitor as to be of prime consideration in the matter of meals.

Now that I am retired and living in tranquillity, thanks to the very generous and totally unexpected pension given me by Mr Holmes, I have no more to do with my time than keep my cottage in trim and tend my little garden.

It was after I had been settled here for about a year – the exact date escapes me – that a chance remark from my late sister's son, my only surviving relative, set me to thinking that perhaps other Cook House-keepers to single gentlemen could just possibly benefit from my experiences.

I should explain that my nephew Septimus Coke had already entered the trade of journalism and was in fact very excited by his prospects since he was actually employed by the *London Mail*.

He chanced to ask if I had kept any record of Mr Holmes' (and Dr Watson's) favourite dishes, to which of course I replied by showing him my books. Bringing these out took me back very clearly to the long hours spent, writing by candlelight, awaiting the return of my gentlemen from one or other of their often perilous exhibitions. Then I had nothing more to do than keep an eye upon the state of their food and ensure that it did not deteriorate through being kept waiting, often for many hours past the appointed time. So I entered my receipts and advice notes, my personal reminders and any other facts which might prove useful to me as reference upon future occasions. Septimus became very excited as he studied these.

'You know, Aunt Sarah,' he said, his rather pale blue eyes gleaming behind their spectacles, 'you should make these into a book. Indeed it is not beyond the bounds of possibility that I could persuade my Editor on the *London Mail* to accept some of them – extracts of course – and I would be pleased to edit them for you.'

At the time I brushed the idea aside as far too fancy for a person of my station; but it kept coming back as I cut and bunched my Herbs, planted my Gilly-flowers or took cuttings of my Pinks.

I remember, one hot August day, coming into the cool of my little sitting-room with all its treasured mementoes of those years in service with my dear gentlemen; when I realised the whole idea had so taken possession of my mind that I could no longer concentrate upon my gardening.

I began to look through my 'Specifics Book', my 'Pickling Receipts', (Dr Watson was always very partial to a good side-dish of chutnee or a good jar of strong pickles) my 'Pudding Records', (Mr Holmes was fond of a good slice of Plum Duff on a cold winter's day) and saying, out loud to myself 'Sarah Hudson, sometimes old heads may be found upon young shoulders, you *shall* take your nephew's advice!'

There and then I put on my bonnet and, securing the door behind me – old habits die hard although one might well leave all portals open in *this* village – I went down the lane to Mrs Peetie the postmistress in whose shop I purchased a ream of long paper which she named 'foolscap'. I chose it because I had once glimpsed my Great Ideal, Mrs Agnes Bertha Marshall, writing upon precisely such paper in her little office when I visited her School of Cookery in Great Mortimer Street to make a small purchase. This foolscap cost me 4s. 4d. I further added to my Capital Expenditure by purchasing a new penholder for $\frac{1}{2}$d and a box of one dozen fine-pointed 'Ledger' pens for $4\frac{1}{2}$d. Thus did I embark upon my venture having laid out in initial, and, as it transpired, total capital – four shillings and ninepence.

Now being, by my dear father's early training, a methodical person I soon realised that if I did not grasp the helm firmly of my little ship, which I called My Great Writing Adventure, I should quickly find myself in Troubled Waters, so I set myself a stern pattern of labour from which I never deviated thereafter.

At this juncture, you may ask how it is that a woman of my station had acquired sufficient education to write at all.

I was born in Hoxton. My father was apprenticed at the age of ten to a Mr Smith who was a cabinet maker of great skill. My father stayed with Mr Smith until he died, by which time my father learned his trade well and showed a great aptitude himself for cabinet making. Eventually, he became a partner with Mr Smith's son Joe. I had little or no schooling; but when eleven years of age I was taken into the

Mrs Hudson introduces herself

household of a family in Upper Grosvenor Street as a junior nursery-maid. This was of the greatest good fortune to me for the Nanny of the household, on finding I could scarcely read or write, obtained the permission of the Lady to include me in the first lessons given to the children. The Lady and Nanny between them (it is not proper to give you the names of these good, private persons) insisted on the schooling being continued even when the children were given their lessons by a Governess. Thus it was that by the time Nanny had spotted my great interest in All Forms of Cookery and sent me below stairs to learn a little from Cook, I was able to write down what I learned, from the proper way to pattern a mushroom; which Cook called 'turning', to the most beautiful receipt I have ever known for Real Lemon Curd. After two years more I found myself permanently 'below stairs' as assistant cook to Cook who was by this time getting on in years and endeavouring to conceal the fact. So it was not long after that I did the majority of the cooking and Cook from her rocking chair, suffering cruelly from the rheumatics, only directed operations.

When I was thirty, Cook retired. Then I became official Cook to the Family; but found myself without a situation when my Lady was widowed and forced to retire to the country in Considerably Straitened Circumstances.

It was then that I read an advertisement in *The Times*. 'Cook Housekeeper required by single gentleman living in rooms in Baker Street'.

I answered it and, here my conscience forces me to confess to the One Untruth of My Entire Life. I gave my age as forty when in truth I was but thirty! I signed myself Sarah Hudson (Mrs) and thus I obtained the post. Having so done I suffered many pangs of conscience over the ensuing years and after Mr Holmes' return, (readers will recall the story of his alleged, tragic demise) I confessed All to him. You may imagine my surprise and relief when Mr Holmes laughed at my revelation. In fact he said, when he had done laughing, 'What a great relief Mrs Hudson, now I know that I may enjoy ten more years of your good care than I had thought possible,' and so dismissed the matter. A lesson to us all on how conscience exacts its own, oft-times needless, but even so deserved miseries.

I need only add that my receipts and specifics as contained in this book were all at one time or another served to and approved by Mr Holmes, Dr Watson and their many divergent guests.

signed   *Sarah Hudson* (*in her seventy-second year*)

My Household Hints

A FEW HOUSEHOLD HINTS I HAVE FOUND TO BE HIGHLY EFFICACIOUS

AID TO COOKERY

Since it is a fault in many cooks that their last batch of baking is overlooked through the attention being turned elsewhere at this juncture, I venture to pass on my Infallible Hint. Before closing the door of the oven put a large piece of paper just inside it and pull out so that it hangs like a white flag outside the fastened door. This way your attention is constantly drawn to the oven. Do it always while baking and you will have no burned items to your chagrin.

TO KEEP BUTTER COOL

Dissolve 1 oz of saltpetre in 1 pint of water. When it is completely blended stand the butter dish within the vessel, so that the saltpetre-water comes well up its sides. Place a wet cloth over the butter dish so that the ends may rest in the saltpetre-water and the butter inside will keep constantly moist. This is nigh on as efficacious as putting ice about it!

TO SWEETEN RANCID BUTTER

Cut as much as you require, place in a bowl. Then make up a mixture composed of 1 pint cold water to 1 extremely generous pinch of carbonate of soda. Stir well, pour over the butter, leave for at least twenty-four hours when the butter will be found to be as sweet as ever it was when first churned.

TO KEEP A CUT HAM MOIST

Particularly at the Festive Season, when families invest in such a very large ham to accompany the Christmas Turkey, cooks are made anxious by the drying out which occurs *at the cut* end once the ham has been broached. IF you spread, like jam, a goodly layer of slightly warmed mutton fat over the cut part and a layer of paper over this, you may remove both easily before returning to table. If not wishing to be economical, then slightly warmed butter may be used in this manner.

MUSTARD – WASTE NOT

If the mustard pot be half filled when taken from the table, then smooth over the top of the contents in so far as is possible and pour a very small quantity of olive oil across the back of a teaspoon to form a skin over the mustard. Thus it may be kept to serve again. Merely pour off the oil, stir the mustard and it will be found to be improved by the particles which remain and are stirred in. IF of a frugal turn of mind, conserve the little drops of mustard oil in a small bottle with a cork. When there be plenty, make Oxford Sauce with it (see p. 241) which as it keeps for one year at least on a dry goods shelf may be made when the fancy pleases.

TO PRESERVE LEMONS

Coat them all over with raw unbeaten egg white. Let them dry and repeat twice more thus ensuring that the lemons will keep for many weeks, even in the hottest weather. The albumen locks in the precious lemon oil which IS the vitality of the lemon or the real significance of the term 'zest of lemon'.

MY BROWNING FOR SOUPS AND GRAVIES

Place 1 lb of granulated sugar all alone in your thickest, small stew pan and set it upon the very rim of your stove where the heat is passing gentle and then wait, watching it very carefully until a dark bubble breaks at centre. Shake the pan a little and set it down. Then wait again until the bubble re-rises, others join it and the central brown spot of syrup breaks all over the rest. Take up a wooden spoon and stir slowly until all be perfectly black. Stir in 1 pint of cold water; but pray do not do so without a stout glove drawn well over your stirring hand. The hot sugar syrup will erupt at each addition and nothing be more painful nor penetrating than a sugar burn. Boil on until all is dark and smooth. Bottle, cork down when cold and store for future use.

HOW TO CLEAN DIRTY DRIPPING

There is nothing more eloquent of a dirty cook than one of those terrible jars of dripping which has been allowed to accumulate month after month in layers, with what insects entrapped therein in summer the mind positively refuses to contemplate! Here is a simple way to keep it clean and fit to use.

Place the dripping in a very roomy bowl. Take up a kettleful of absolutely boiling water and pour it thereon. Now leave it be until the

My household hints

water be quite cold. I usually clean my dripping the last thing at night before damping down my range ready for drawing again in the morning. Then you will discover that the dripping has all risen to the top and formed a thick layer. If you cut this away in wedges and turn it over to its under-side, you will find that all the impurities have clung to it and so may be easily and quickly scraped away with a knife.

HOW TO DRY RASPBERRY LEAVES

For town-dwellers I append the reminder that all punnets of raspberries, as sold by respectable greengrocers have their punnets lined out with raspberry leaves before the fruit is placed therein.

Country dwellers will only need to go out and take theirs from the canes in the fruit cage, or from beneath their bird-safeguarded canes which have been frugally enveloped in old, lace curtains. In either case wash the leaves thoroughly. Wipe them dry, then lay leaf over leaf until you have a fat bunch. Tie this securely with thin string in which you make a strong loop that the completed bunches may dangle from a hook and so become perfectly dried in a warm airy place. When dry, take up the bunches and wrap them close in black tissue paper then no dust may collect upon them (*polythene bag, F.C.*). Then when you are confronted with a piece of Gammon, you may first boil it as usual and then complete your cookery of this item by baking it in paste with dried raspberry leaves (p. 40).

TO MAKE LACE STRING-COLOURED

Take 2 tablespoons of soot, cover with 1 quart of boiling water, leave standing for one half an hour, then strain through muslin. After washing the lace, dip it in this, stretch it out upon a covered board to dry and it will be perfect.

JAVELLE-WATER FOR REMOVING STAINS

Dissolve 1 lb common soda in 1 quart boiling water, then stir in $1\frac{1}{4}$ lb chloride of lime and let it stand until quite cold. This may also be used as a bleach. Put a small quantity into a tub of water, put in white garments overnight which have lost their whiteness sadly. In the morning use blue bag and rinse as usual and they will look as if they have been grass-bleached!

TO REMOVE GREASE FROM A CARPET

Blend 4 tablespoons of ammonia with 1 pint of hot water. Use a very clean, small brush, and with this solution brush the grease spots. Then rub dry immediately using a clean, soft cloth. Now make a paste of Fuller's earth and cold water and spread this over the stains or spots. Leave until quite dry. Then brush off. If very old grease stains then the Fuller's earth treatment may require repeating.

MY SCORCH MARK MIXTURE

Boil half a pint of Malt Vinegar with 2 oz common soda, 2 oz Fuller's earth and one 4 oz onion (in skin) chopped fine. Strain and when cold spread over the mark and allow to dry, then the mark will be found to have vanished!

MY FURNITURE POLISH

ASSEMBLY

1 oz beeswax; 1 oz white wax; ½ oz Castile soap; half a pint turpentine; boiling water; and ½ fluid oz methylated spirits.

PROCEDURE

Shred the wax and soap very fine. Add just enough boiling water to dissolve them, and produce a smooth, slithery paste. Stir in the turpentine and methylated spirits.

MY SILVER CLEANER

Take a bar of good soap (2 *square tablets of Fairy, F.C.*), cut all up and stir with 1½ pints boiling water so that it makes a jelly when cold. To this add powdered whitening and beat well until the mixture is like whipped cream. Store in a jar with a tied down parchment for a lid. (*Any screw-topped or bottling jar will do, F.C.*). Plunge a damp flannel into the mixture and rub the silver all over. Then rinse well in warm water, wipe and leave to dry. When polished with a shammy leather there will be a brilliant polish equal to new. This is a great improvement upon purchased materials and leaves no trace of whitening in any crest or engraved part.

Author's Note

We have given up buying silver and furniture polishes and make these up regularly instead. They are marvellous. *F.C.*

HOW TO CLEAN WINDOWS AND DISPOSE OF FLIES SETTLING THEREON IN SUMMER

Dip a soft cloth into paraffin until it is thoroughly impregnated. Work this vigorously over the windows and then polish with a clean, dry cloth. Not only will the windows shine but flies will NOT settle upon them. This is also the Quickest Way!

TO BANISH SLUGS IN YOUR GARDEN

Place a small container such as an old tin or jam pot in the soil up to its rim and fill it with milk. Slugs find this – and indeed Stout also! – irresistible. They drink of it greedily, and at length fall in and are drowned! I have captured as many as forty-five slugs in one night with this simple device.

A FEW SIMPLE FACTS TO AID THE BEGINNER

A plucked fowl or game bird, still retaining some very small feathers and those long hair-line threads, called pin feathers, which depend from the skin, may be cleared in an instant if revolved upon a napkin-wrapped poker over the maw of your coal stove. Wrap the poker around and around in a tea cloth and thrust inside the bird. Thus may the hand which holds the poker stay clear of the fierce heat. I am assured on the Very Best Authority that an open gas flame will perform the same function with as much speed and ease.

A Handful of Common Salt scattered over a dull-looking kitchen table will bring the wooden surface up bright and almost white if it be scrubbed hard with a scrub-brush and cold water.

A Pinch of Common Soda in vegetable water will turn greens bright green – certainly – but equally successfully will destroy all their goodness and flavour. Pray never be tempted to try this sinful treatment.

If the Lady of the Household has chanced to receive and wear a corsage of fresh violets, which wilt when detached from her gown by her maid, these may be speedily and lastingly refreshed if they are placed faces downwards in a bowl of fresh, cold water. Thus they do drink and are invigorated so as to be worn again the next day.

A small piece of charcoal, if placed in a jar of cold, sweet water will refresh a flabby cucumber miraculously.

If sausage meat is required speedily and Cook has only sausages in the larder this may be quickly settled by pouring boiling water over the unwound sausages in string. Do this in the kitchen sink. Let the water run away immediately. Then tear an opening in the skin of the first sausage which will come from its skin entire, and so proceed down the string thus obtaining the desired sausage meat without a vestige of wastage.

If you wish to make your puff paste rise high while baking desist from flouring the tin upon which it is baked. Instead rinse this under the cold water tap, shake off all but a few drops. Lay the pastry upon the wetted tin and, very lightly, lay a buttered paper over the item or items for two-thirds of the complete, given cooking time. Thus the paper cover *draws*, and the moist base *thrusts upwards by steaming*, and the twin method combines to make a far lighter, far more impressive risen pastry.

If you should fear that any pan might burn milk while this is being boiled, place a child's marble within the pan first. Then pour on the milk and all will be very well indeed.

If you wish to avoid crusting on the top surface of any sauce to be stored overnight or longer, just heat a tablespoon in boiling water. When this is hot, wipe and pass the base of the hot spoon over butter and then over the top of the sauce. Thus may it be protected from any crusting whatsoever.

Soft brown (pieces) sugar absorbs the natural humidity in our atmosphere very rapidly. Then should warm dry weather follow, it forms great lumps. To obviate both these difficulties make a habit of spreading a newly-purchased bag out over a baking sheet and putting high above your stove that it may dry out. Then rub down and store in an earthen container with a very close-fitting lid.

Meringues go soft if exposed to our natural humidity. As soon as they be dried out in the oven just give them time to cool upon a rack and then pack them into a glass jar with a well-fitting glass stopper. Thus will you keep them crisp and good.

If sugar be dampened before it is spread very evenly upon the top of a cake or pudding, then to be caramelised by salamander (*under a strong grill*, F.C.) it will crust much better and more evenly in texture.

If a cake sticks in its tin after baking, lay it upon very damp cloths for a moment or two and this will cause it to ease away.

My household hints

If a cream or jelly sticks to its mould and refuses to come away, wring out a cloth in boiling water and lay the container upon this. Be careful not to do so for more than a few moments at a time or the pattern of the tin will be despoiled by the melting of the mixture therein.

If a panful of hot water be placed upon the floor of the oven while bread-baking is in progress the bread will be the much more light and aerated thereby. (*No change 1975, F.C.*).

If all bacon rinds are carefully put by after cutting them from bacon rashers, then a few of these thrown into a stock or soup or brown sauce will add considerably to the flavour. Just remember, if the bacon does have a tendency to saltiness, to taste the simmered liquor thereafter before adding more salt!

If mussels when bought and brought home are placed, un-bearded and un-scrubbed into a roomy bucket and then sprinkled all over very liberally indeed with coarse oatmeal – provided you put them into a dark cupboard thereafter – the mussels will feed upon the oatmeal overnight thus cleaning and fattening themselves before they are cleaned and cooked.

When putting down new-laid eggs for winter use put into a solution of water-glass, make sure that this preparation is allowed to come a clear two inches above the so-stored eggs.

Do not throw lemon or orange peel away. Lay both or either upon a baking sheet and set this upon the floor of your cooling oven. Thus they will dry out and become perfectly crisp. Then you may add them to a muslin bag of tied herbs to great enhancement of flavour.

If through over-vigorous beating your glacé or royal icing when laid upon a cake shows little air bubbles breaking upon the surface, take a stout darning needle and prick each one carefully. This will cause them all to subside and disappear. Just remember the next time to stir very thoroughly, but do abstain from any more vigorous beatings.

If the key of a sardine tin breaks midway do not, at risk to hand and contents, dig away with a fork to excavate the little fishes, but take up an ordinary pair of pliers, grip the key handle and turn away with ease until the whole top be exposed.

If you have over-browned a meringue top to a pudding do not despair. Take a very slim, very sharp knife which has recently been through the knife-cleaning machine – which sharpens as well as cleans it – and with this knife cut the offending dark brown layer away. Dust all over with sifted icing sugar and re-salamander (*Grill, F.C.*) more gently this time. (*The same applies when browning under a grill, F.C.*).

If you read in one of my receipts the directions to use crushed loaf sugar you may think, should you be an inexperienced cook, that this presents difficulties. I will therefore explain the easy way of it. Take a stout piece of brown paper. Lay the loaf sugar along inside a double fold. Bring the upper double fold over both. Then take a rolling pin and roll/press over the paper that all inside will be crushed easily and well.

A LITTLE PRACTICAL NURSING ADVICE AND RECEIPTS FOR THE SICKROOM

FOOT'S BED TABLE

You may distinguish this purchase by the special name 'The Adapter'. It may be obtained from Foot's shop at 171 New Bond Street. This invalid table can be raised, lowered, revolved or inclined and is the Very Best for serving meals to invalids. There are four styles. This remarkable table cannot overbalance; but it is a costly item so should be regarded as an *investment* by any Housekeeper who anticipates that Caring for the Sick will be among her duties. I personally recommend No. 3 with 'Very Superior Finish' which will call for the somewhat large outlay of £2 5s. 0d. (*Try John Bell and Croyden, but expect to pay rather more! F.C.*).

FOR GENERAL LAUNDRY PURPOSES

There is nothing to beat John Bond's Crystal Palace Marking Ink, this being indelible and never in the slightest way harmful to any fabric. A small bottle will cost 4d., which is a very small outlay for ensuring that you receive back from your laundry those items which you send, and do not receive others instead which are (a) not your property, (b) generally of inferior quality, laundries being what they are today. (*And more so today. F.C.*).

A GENTLE LOOSENING DOSE

A spoonful of Fowler Lee's Black Treacle may be administered, even to very small children when the stoppage of bowel movements are

My household hints

observed. It is mild but efficacious in action and the dosages are herein set out for your guidance.

Under *5 years*   1 teaspoon
Under *18 years* 1 dessertspoon
Adults   1 generous tablespoon

Administer after a hot beverage and in the morning hours.

SLIPPING DOWN IN BED

When Mr Holmes was incapacitated by a Bronchial Congestion and Dr Watson, after some High Words, had succeeded in confining him to his bed, he informed me in no uncertain terms that the patient was NOT to be permitted to Lie Down. Happily I knew what to do and just as well I did, for, having left the sick room in order to obtain my equipment I saw that immediately my back was turned, Mr Holmes had slipped down in the bed and was wheezing sombrely with his great nose buried in the bedlinen. Exhorting him to pull himself back up into a sitting position, and gaining my objective after sundry 'Pshaws' on his part, I then handed him a large bolster tied strongly with two tapes at each end. 'Now pray assist me Mr Holmes,' I said firmly, 'by inserting this bolster under your knees.' With some reluctance he did so and left the tapes hanging down at either side. Thus I was able to tie the bolster to the iron uprights of his bed and secure them, thereby holding him up even though he should drop off to sleep – which I sincerely hoped would be the case. Admittedly I was pursued from the room by his remonstrances on 'being trussed up like a turkey cock', but nevertheless it worked and Dr Watson on his return was pleased to congratulate me on a 'capital idea'.

HOW TO MAKE PROPER BARLEY WATER

When Mr Holmes first brought That Boy to the house I discovered, by what means it is indelicate to explain here, that he was suffering from a mild chill upon the kidneys. I therefore dosed him twice daily with this, my barley water, which after three weeks quite dispelled the condition as I took pains to ascertain myself.

ASSEMBLY

$1\frac{1}{2}$ oz pearl barley (Robinsons I have always found to be the best); $1\frac{1}{2}$ pints water; $\frac{1}{2}$ a good-sized lemon; Barbados sugar to taste.

PROCEDURE

Place the barley in a clean cloth lined into a colander and let it be well-rinsed under the cold tap or kitchen pump. Now blanch it in cold water in a cooking pan and let it come fast to the boil. Strain it in clean cloth likewise lined out into a colander. Place barley back into pan, cover with given quantity of cold water to which you have added the very thinly peeled rind of the half lemon, and allow all to simmer very gently for one hour at the side of your stove. Strain through a tammy cloth and sweeten very sparingly.

BEEF TEA

Mr Holmes displayed no interest in my dosage of That Boy with Barley Water but he did order me to make him Beef Tea*, saying, 'The lad's skin and bone which is no good to me, so feed him up Mrs Hudson and let him have a mug of beef tea every morning for a month. Then we will see what he is made of in the matter of running commissions for me at speed.'

Beef tea may be very simply made if there so happens to be an empty champagne bottle in the house. First it is necessary to take 1 lb of lean rump steak, in which there is more flavour than ever to be found in fillet! Scrape it upon a board with a well-sharpened knife and be sure to discard all skin particles and scraps of gristle and fat. Push down into the neck of the champagne bottle so that it falls to the base and when all is so inserted, place in 1 gill of carefully boiled rainwater. Cork down securely, tie up in thick cloths with a binding about the bottle of twine and sink into a deep container like a great stockpot or iron cauldron so that it may stand upright, but rest not upon the pan base, but upon a piece of wood which will offset the danger of the bottle cracking. Cover all over and draw to a corner of the stove. There let it simmer with the merest bubble of lazy movement for all of twenty-four hours. After this time, when the bottle be unwound and the contents poured very carefully through a tammy cloth and equally carefully wrung out, it will be found that the shards of beef are almost white in colour and totally purged of all their flavour. IF the resultant liquor be divided into two parts and the second part stored under a piece of butter muslin in the cold larder there will be sufficient for one portion to be served each day; by which time a further supply may be obtained by the same method and so on for as long as may be deemed necessary.

* See also Beef Jelly for Invalids p. 54.
Note Dosage for a Sick Dog, 1 teaspoon *per diem*.

MY REMARKABLE THROAT CURE

That Mr Holmes was from time to time a positive bundle of nerves was indisputable. Some said it was due to those terrible injections. I incline more towards the conviction that all great men are of such fine-drawn temperament, by their very nature, that their nerves suffer for it more than do we ordinary folk.

However, be that as it may, there came an evening in winter, some years ago now when Mr Holmes came in out of the fog possessed of no more voice than a mere whisper.

'Here's a fine state of affairs,' he croaked divesting himself in the hallway of his deerstalker and ulster. 'What do you do about this Mrs Hudson?'

'What exactly do you require me do sir?' I asked of him.

'Why,' even in a whisper his voice was impatient, 'restore to me my speaking voice. I have to address a most learned Society tomorrow evening upon certain aspects of criminology as I have discovered them.'

'Then sir,' I replied, with equanimity, 'pray cease attempting to speak any more this night. Be so obliging as to write down any instructions you may have for me or That Boy and permit me to give you a glass of something to sip, as hot as possible, when you have retired for the night.'

I further enjoined my master, that the beverage must be taken only *after* he was safely ensconced between the sheets.

Surprisingly enough he agreed, though I was not surprised to receive a somewhat petulant note from him concerning 'pap food' when I served him with hot Broth (p. 46), followed by a soft dish of poached eggs and spinach which years later I learned from Mrs Marshall was properly called *Eggs Florentine* (p. 34). He then partook fairly liberally of a soft cheese concoction which I again learned later was called a *Cheese Fondue* (p. 142), after which he expressed himself satisfied and was content to sip only a glass or two of port wine, while conducting one of his incessant Experiments.

In due course I rapped upon his door and on receiving the invitation to 'come in Mrs Hudson I am abed', I entered with my cure upon a tray. Mr Holmes was indeed abed, his famous dressing-gown about his shoulders, a book propped upon his knees and his nightcap firmly, but askew, fixed upon his head.

In the morning a roar of indignation from the breakfast table gave me all the confirmation I needed that my prescription had again succeeded.

THE CURE
Take a tall tumbler (*8 fluid oz, F.C.*) and into it place 2 very generously heaped tablespoons of home-made black currant jam. Add the squeezed, strained juice of 1 medium lemon, a walnut-sized piece of butter and then pour on boiling water until the glass is filled. Stir until the currants in the jam have become pallid. Allow these to settle at the base and see that the fluid is sipped while still extremely hot.

HOW TO EASE THE TOOTHACHE
Purchase from a chemist one dried seed-head from a large poppy. Place the head in a roomy square of flannel. Immerse all into boiling water. Wring out the flannel when the poppy seed-head has become soft. As soon as heat is bearable place against the affected part of the face and there let it lie until it is absolutely cold. Repeat as often as is necessary to ease the toothache. If doubting the sensibility of this receipt, pray bear in mind that poppies contain *opium*!

TO DRAW AN ABSCESS
Purchase a fair-sized parsnip. Peel and boil to a pulp. Squeeze out in a tammy cloth (*sieve, F.C.*), bathe the affected part with the conserved parsnip water. Then apply the pulp as a poultice using it as hot as the sufferer may bear it.

BREAKFASTS

Breakfasts

Grilled Bloaters
My Hot Breakfast Cakes
A Delicate Fricassée of Eggs
Boiled Eggs
Eggs Florentine
Egg and Tomato Ramekins
Hominy with Cheese
My Kedgeree
Cold Fowl Kedgeree
Scrambled Eggs with Rice
Properly Cooked Sausages which Never Burst
Oatcakes
Devilled Chicken
My Devil
Devilled Chickens' Legs
Baked Gammon with Raspberry Leaves

BREAKFASTS

A fad which has been introduced among some foolish persons is that of abstaining from partaking of a proper breakfast, and instead, of sipping at a single cup of coffee and nibbling at a single piece of toast. Few people tried this novel experiment however and those who were foolish enough so to do, very quickly returned to their former custom of partaking of a proper, hearty meal at the beginning of each day. Whatever the opinion of a handful of 'faddists', the great majority will understand and appreciate that breakfast is the most indispensable and most necessary repast of the day.

A good breakfast may well consist of the following items: Porridge with Cream. Stewed Figs or Prunes. Kedgeree or Grilled Bloaters or Curried Oysters. Grilled Mushrooms, Beef Rissoles or Cutlets Reform. Scrambled Eggs or Eggs and Bacon, or Grilled Sausages and Bacon, Grilled Mushrooms, Scotch Eggs, Devilled Kidneys. Oat Cakes, Scones, Baps, Toast, Crumpets, Muffins, Milk Rolls. Jam, Marmalade, Honey. Tea and Coffee.

Upon the Sideboard: Cold cuts of meat, Game Pies, a Ham, a Tongue. Cold Game in Season. Beefsteak and Kidney Pies. Veal and Ham Pies. Fresh Fruits in Pyramids.

A cross-section of the above* was always offered in my Lady's household. We kept less state when I worked for Mr Holmes.

This Breakfast Bill of Fare presents only the bare bones of the matter so now I will particularise somewhat.

---

* I unrepentantly and adamantly insist that such a breakfast as Mrs Hudson advocates is calculated to slay the taste buds and ruin the palate for the rest of the day, though the late Mr W. Somerset Maugham did remark to my husband and me some years ago that 'to eat well in England it is necessary to eat three breakfasts daily!' F.C.

GRILLED BLOATERS

There is a special way with them and it should at all times be adhered to. Begin by removing the heads. Then split each bloater down the back and remove both the roes and the spinebone. Lay the fish inside down upon a gridiron and cook over only a medium fire until they are nicely browned, then turn them over carefully and repeat upon the other sides. While this is in progress take a small iron skillet and melt therein a knob of butter and in this fry the roes that they may be dished with the bloaters upon a clean napkin and sent to table with a sprig of Fried Parsley and some cut lemon.

MY HOT BREAKFAST CAKES

These must be eaten hot from the oven and That Boy and I between us would send up a half dozen for the gentlemen and then set about another half dozen at five minute intervals, so that all were eaten at their peak.

ASSEMBLY

1 lb self-raising flour; 1 generous pinch salt; 4 oz good butter or better still 4 oz of rendered down, strained, firmed chicken's fat; a little buttermilk.

PROCEDURE

Sift the flour carefully into a roomy basin with the salt. Take up the butter and cut it into the flour ever dipping it in that the knife do not get greasy. Then rub the butter finely through the fingers until it resembles oatmeal. Bind it with buttermilk to make a smooth rolling dough. Turn it instantly upon a lightly floured surface, press it lightly with the rolling pin to $\frac{1}{4}$-inch-thick rounds. Stamp out into 2-inch rounds, place on a buttered baking sheet and bake in a moderate oven (*Gas Mark 4, one shelf above centre, F.C.*) for a mere eight-to-ten minutes. Remove immediately, butter both sides liberally and send up at once to table in a folded napkin that they may be still piping hot.

A DELICATE FRICASSÉE OF EGGS

ASSEMBLY

6 hard-boiled eggs; $\frac{1}{2}$ pint freshly-made creamy white sauce; salt; pepper; grated nutmeg; $\frac{1}{2}$ oz sweet butter; 2 oz thick cream; 1

Breakfasts

dessertspoon fine-chopped parsley; properly creamed potato for the border.

PROCEDURE

Slice the eggs across into rather thick slices. Season the white sauce with salt, pepper and nutmeg to taste. Impart to it a final sheen with the butter stirred in while it still be hot. Place half in a small chafing dish. (*Any heat resistant container, F.C.*). Lay down the eggs upon it. Cover with the remaining sauce into which you have blended the cream. Scatter parsley overall and border neatly with creamed potato forked up with evenness and care.

BOILED EGGS

A very serious matter and not one to be undertaken lightly. Hence the foolishness of the claim that 'anyone can boil an egg'.

For boiling, it must be accepted that eggs cannot be too fresh and therefore the nonpareil of boiled eggs must be those which are perfectly cooked *after being taken warm from the nests*. Here too there can be a pitfall, for a half minute longer should be allowed for the cooking of such a one against an egg which is three to four days old, the age for which these instructions are intended.

PROCEDURE

Have ready a saucepan of boiling water. Put each egg into a tablespoon and lower gently into the boiling water, being very careful to ensure that the spoon touches the bottom of the saucepan before it is withdrawn to avoid cracking the shell. If a shell be cracked it is always safe to credit its state to the foolishness of the cook! For those who prefer an egg very lightly boiled allow three to three and a half minutes. Four minutes boiling will coagulate the white and five minutes will set it firmly. When you desire cold, hard boiled eggs, eight minutes always is sufficient, after which the eggs should be plunged into cold water, tapped against the sides of the pan therein until the shell be cracked all over, and then peeled under a very thin stream of cold tap water. The water thus forces itself through the shell and inner skin and enables the peeler to remove the shell in two pieces without blemishing the smooth surface – unlike those scarred and nicked objects which bring shame upon the producer. If the shelled egg be allowed to remain in cold water until it is completely cold, this prevents a dark rim forming around the yolk between yolk and white.

EGGS FLORENTINE

ASSEMBLY

4 good-sized eggs (*standard, F.C.*); salt; black pepper; nutmeg; grated Parmesan cheese; 4 tablespoons thick cream; 1 small nut of butter; $1\frac{1}{4}$ lb fresh spinach; wine vinegar.

PROCEDURE

Spinach being a vegetable of particular distinction it is demanding of careful treatment. It has much iron in it and more water, therefore must always be cooked quite dry. Pick over the leaves, discard any browned ones, remove all stems, rinse under cold running water and place in a thick pan over a low heat. Stir with a wooden spoon until the juices run freely and then cook for a maximum seven minutes. Rub through a fine sieve into a basin, blend in a seasoning of salt and black pepper, add thereto a pinch or two of nutmeg and 1 rounded tablespoon of fine-grated Parmesan. Stir all well, add 2 of the 4 stated tablespoons of cream and rub a smallish chafing dish (*7-inch diameter heat resistant, shallow container, F.C.*) with the given butter. Turn in the prepared spinach purée, level off neatly and then, with the aid of a tablespoon dipped into boiling water make four deep-ish indents to receive the eggs, poached as follows.

Pour a 1-inch depth of boiling water into a shallow fry pan. Add to this 2 tablespoons of wine vinegar. Place over the lowest possible heat. Break the eggs, singly, into a saucer and slide each extremely gently into the water vinegar mixture. Allow eggs to set slowly, flicking a little fluid over them to make a fine film on top. When eggs are set (the vinegar in the water prevents their sticking), lift each one out on a metal slice and rest for a moment or two, still on the slice, on a clean, folded cloth so that surplus moisture may be taken up by it. Place each egg in a pre-prepared indent in the spinach. Spread the remaining cream gently over the eggs. Scatter grated Parmesan cheese lightly overall and slip for a moment under a fierce grill or pass a red-hot salamander over the surface to bubble and brown the cheese and give heat to the cream.

EGG AND TOMATO RAMEKINS

Having been given such a reputation for good breakfasts by my Great Employer I have selected (for inclusion in my book) only the ones which he and Mr Holmes favoured most. High on my list therefore

Breakfasts

must come *EGG AND TOMATO RAMEKINS* to which they were particularly partial.

ASSEMBLY
6 small china ramekin cases (*or individual soufflé moulds, F.C.*); butter for rubbing their interiors; 4 oz chopped, cooked, lean ham; 2 rounded tablespoons fine-chopped parsley; 6 eggs (*standard, F.C.*); 6 thinly-sliced back bacon rashers (*No. 5 cut, F.C.*); 3 good-sized, firm tomatoes; salt; pepper; 3 crustless slices of bread cut ½-inch thick.

PROCEDURE
Butter the interiors of all ramekin moulds. Divide the ham between them and scatter over the bases. Sprinkle thereon the evenly divided parsley, then break one egg into each. Season lightly, place in a shallow pan with boiling water therein to come half-way up the sides of the moulds, cover all with one circle of butter paper and place in a strong oven (*Gas Mark 6, one shelf above centre, F.C.*). Poach until the whites are just set *but no more*. During the cooking time, de-rind and dry-fry, over the rinds, the bacon rashers until they are wavy but not crisp. Split the tomatoes centrally. Cut across these lightly with a very sharp knife just to cut the skins N.S.E. and W. which stops them bursting. Fry face-downwards in the bacon fat with as much butter added as is judged to be necessary, using only a mild top heat on your stove. While these are frying, toast the bread and divide each piece in halves. Lay a soft-fried tomato upon each, cut side uppermost. Season lightly with salt and pepper. Run a knife or teaspoon handle around each steamed/baked egg and invert each one over the tomato on each piece of toast. Lay a curly rasher of bacon upon each and send to table.

HOMINY WITH CHEESE

If you have gentlemen who, in mid-winter, are forced to face inclement weather and possibly stand about in it all day, then there is nothing better for them than this dish which warms the stomach. It is well known to everyone that a well-warmed stomach ensures the circulation flows freely throughout the body. With this both *my* gentlemen concurred.

ASSEMBLY
½ pint milk; 1 oz butter; 1 gill water; 2 oz hominy (*maize flour, F.C.*); 1½ oz fine-grated hard cheese; salt; pepper; 1 extra oz grated hard cheese; melted butter.

PROCEDURE

Place milk, water and 1 oz butter in a pan and bring to the boil. Scatter over it the hominy and stir with a wooden spoon until mixture is very thick indeed. Season to taste with salt and pepper, then stir in the 1½ oz of prepared cheese. Butter the interior of a small to medium pie dish. Turn in the hominy and spread him about evenly. Scatter the remaining 1 oz cheese on top. Moisten with little drips of the melted butter and bake in a sharp oven (*Gas Mark 7, one shelf above centre, F.C.*) until well browned on the top.

MY KEDGEREE

We will speak about Mr Holmes' perfect rulings for the cooking of rice on p. 37. It is advisable to refer to this passage before proceeding direct with the receipt.

ASSEMBLY

½ lb Patna rice, cooked; 4 hard-boiled eggs; 4 heaped dessertspoons freshly chopped parsley; salt; pepper; 1 lb of either steamed, skinned and flaked salmon or smoked Finnan haddie; 5 oz good sweet butter.

PROCEDURE

Turn the cooked, strained rice into a roomy mixing bowl and add thereto the chosen fish, the parsley and a seasoning of pepper only for Finnan haddie, salt and pepper for salmon. Shell the hard eggs, remove the whites from the yolks and chop both up quite separate and very fine. Season with salt and pepper. Melt the butter very slowly in a pan immersed in an outer pan of boiling water, so see that your kettle be singing upon the hob before embarking upon this receipt. Work all together the contents of the bowl. Turn on to a heated dish. Then, with a fork held in each hand work up into a neat panel, fairly high and rising to a central ridge. Take up the hard, chopped egg yolks and use them to form a narrow border all around the base of the Kedgeree. Take up the whites and do likewise around the outside of the yolks.

It is then a pleasing fancy to have ready eighteen carefully shelled prawns with their heads left on. Before using these pour the melted butter slowly and evenly over and throughout the Kedgeree. Finally arrange the prawns, heads erect down the 'spine' of the Kedgeree and send thus to the table, remembering to provide finger bowls of lukewarm water so that the fingers which come into contact with the prawns may be dipped therein and wiped dry upon a napkin.

COLD FOWL KEDGEREE

You will require forethought for this dish which is immensely popular with the gentlemen. You must first be prudent enough to send in a dish of Devilled Drumsticks (p. 40) for breakfast on the preceding morning. You must further cook more than you know will be required and thus be enabled to set aside four drumsticks for your kedgeree. Marry to these six chickens' livers and you may proceed to make this most popular club-men's breakfast dish following the exact procedure as outlined in both Assembly and Procedure for MY KEDGEREE on p. 36. Just omit the fish. See that your chosen drumsticks are liberally coated with their *Devil* (p. 39) and further see to it that you fry your chickens' livers, before commencing, in melted butter and oil in equal parts of 1 oz each. Thereafter you merely chop the flesh of both livers and drumsticks, (consigning the bones to your poultry stock pot) and proceed as already explained.

SCRAMBLED EGGS WITH RICE

Of this dainty Mr Holmes was wont to say very firmly, 'nothing could be more difficult! There is not a cook in five hundred who can scramble eggs to perfection nor cook rice properly'. Mr Holmes ruled that eleven and a half minutes over the open stove in fast-boiling salted water was the exact time for rice-cooking. Then, he insisted, all was flung fast into a strainer that every drop of starch-water should be drained away. 'And that,' he would add, 'requires a very large quantity of water to a very small quantity of rice.' He was of course, as always, perfectly correct in these asseverations.

ASSEMBLY

6 eggs; 6 tablespoons of the very richest, sweet, new milk (*sic, F.C!*) or in default of this 4 tablespoons of thin cream and 2 of somewhat inferior milk; salt and pepper to season; 2 very small shallots; 1 heaped tablespoon fine-chopped parsley; 2 oz butter; $\frac{1}{2}$ fluid oz olive oil; 4 tablespoons cooked rice; 2 thick slices buttered toast.

PROCEDURE

Place 1 oz of the butter with the olive oil into a smallish thick pan and allow to heat and melt together. Meanwhile, peel and fine-chop the shallots. When pan contents 'sing' scrape in the shallots and turn and fry these very gently until they are soft and golden. Add the remaining butter. Beat up the eggs with milk or milk and cream, season lightly, pour into the pan. Begin stirring. Now this is an exception to the general rule that all things should be stirred with a wooden spoon. The edge is not sharp enough for properly scrambled eggs and a metal spoon must be used. This must be drag-stirred round the base edges, and across the base with steady and unceasing regularity until the mixture begins to come up on the spoon in fat blobs. At this point incorporate both rice and parsley and continue drag-stirring until mixture is just too loose and moist. This is most important, since eggs go on cooking in a warmed pan – off the stove – even as they continue cooking on a warmed plate. Therefore in the time it takes to spoon the mixture on to two $\frac{1}{2}$-inch-thick slices of buttered toast the mixture will have had time to come to the proper creaminess without a hint of dryness, which is the hallmark of well made scrambled eggs. Serve immediately, for such a dish ranks with some of the greatest – like perfect omelettes for example. It may *not* be kept waiting, the person for whom it is intended *may* however.

PROPERLY COOKED SAUSAGES WHICH NEVER BURST

Pray desist from the malpractice of pricking sausages. This assists them to burst out of their skins during cooking. Instead – unwind one or more pounds. Melt down sufficient clean dripping (there is nothing more shameful than dirty dripping) to coat the base of a baking tin to a depth of a quarter of an inch. Then tow the strings of sausages through the melted fat, making sure that they are coated all over. Place them in a moderate oven (*Gas Mark 4, mid-shelf, F.C.*) for twenty minutes. Remove, turn over, return to oven and brown as much as may be considered desirable. *They will never burst.*

OATCAKES

Mr Holmes, who always approved mightily of my breakfasts, was capable of demolishing an extraordinary number of my oatcakes. More especially so when he had been out on a case all night. Instead of being exhausted, he would come to the breakfast table rubbing those long hands of his and exclaiming 'capital, capital' and reaching for a first one. When he discovered this to be fresh from my stove, he would exclaim, 'Ah ha! just as I like them.' Then he would split them open and put a considerable amount of butter between.

ASSEMBLY

8 oz medium oatmeal; 3 oz sifted self-raising flour; 1 flat coffeespoon soda-bicarbonate; 3 oz pure lard; 1 flat teaspoon castor sugar; boiling water.

PROCEDURE

Mix oatmeal, flour and soda-bicarbonate very thoroughly. Rub in the lard until very fine-grained. Sift in the sugar, also through the fingers, then take up a small table knife and pouring with restraint, gradually work up this with the boiling water until a firm dough be obtained. Sift a little flour upon the table. Roll out the dough to a ¾-inch thickness. Cut into 4-inch squares. Divide diagonally into triangles. Bake in a moderate to brisk oven (*Gas Mark 6, mid-shelf, F.C.*) for approximately fifteen minutes. Wrap immediately in a napkin, (remembering to scrape the base of each one lest some flour adhere thereto) place in a basket and bear at once to table.

DEVILLED CHICKEN

I chanced to hear, when carrying in the coffee pot, a comment made by Mr Holmes upon my breakfasts. He said, 'Mrs Hudson has as good an idea of breakfast as any Scotswoman.' As I observed, upon entering the room, he was examining a dish of devilled chicken as he spoke. Now there are many forms of 'devils' and the one which both gentlemen preferred is the one I have given here. It should be borne in mind that 'drumsticks' are not considered elegant for dinner service but may be used up in this manner. The drumsticks should be roasted with any fowls, removed before service and then the remainder of the bird cut up properly for easy table service. It has also been my practice to remove the 'oysters' as the two oyster-shaped pieces of particularly succulent flesh have been named. These lie beneath the fowls in their two oyster-shaped bone cavities.

MY DEVIL

ASSEMBLY

3 to 4 finely minced shallots or small onions; 1 large crushed garlic clove; 1 faggot of herbs; 18 fluid oz good stock; salt; 1 level teaspoon freshly milled black peppercorns; a few drops of Worcestershire Sauce; 1 flat

teaspoon curry paste; 1 flat dessertspoon concentrated tomato purée; 1½ oz butter; 1½ oz flour.

PROCEDURE

Place herbs, garlic, shallots, pepper and stock in a thick pan and bring to the boil. Level off at a gentle simmer and maintain for twenty minutes. Remove herbs, measure pan contents. Make up with more strongly reduced stock to original quantity. Dissolve butter in separate pan, stir in flour and stir to a smooth, thick paste. Then begin adding liquid mixture gradually, beating well with a wooden spoon after each addition. After first addition work in the curry paste, tomato purée and Worcestershire sauce. When all liquor is absorbed, taste, correct seasoning with salt, pass through a tammy (*sieve, F.C.*) and use.

DEVILLED CHICKENS' LEGS

Place six to eight drumsticks and six to eight 'oysters' in a chafing dish, pour the sauce over and allow to simmer, turning frequently, for five minutes. Dish up and send to table with a light sprinkling of parsley.

BAKED GAMMON WITH RASPBERRY LEAVES

This was a piece of meat which Mr Holmes much liked to have upon the sideboard at breakfast time to appease small corners of his appetite. He never failed to remark upon the excellence of this treatment although Dr Watson, who poor thing, had had his palate totally spoiled while in that India, spread one of his Chutnees all over each slice and thus totally destroyed the delicate flavour!

ASSEMBLY

1 large piece of Corner Gammon; cold water; a wisp of clean hay; a faggot of herbs in a scrap of muslin; 1½ lb sifted flour; dried raspberry leaves.

PROCEDURE

First soak your gammon in clean water – country-dwellers will always use clean rain-water for this – for a minimum of twenty-four hours. Nothing be more distasteful than a salty gammon! Remove, wash well under a running tap and immerse in cold water with a twist or wisp of clean hay. Bring to the boil as fast as possible under a well-fitting lid, then draw to the side of the stove and allow to simmer steadily until just slightly resistant to a skewer when tested. Remove from the water and pull off the skin while the piece be still very hot. Then allow to become perfectly cold.

Make a paste with the flour and sufficient cold water to bind to a pastry-like consistency. Roll out upon a floured surface – without stretching or tearing – until large enough to enclose the gammon completely. Lay down overlapping raspberry leaves (see How to Dry Raspberry Leaves, p. 19) in the centre to the size of the gammon's fatty side. Set the piece over. Cover the rest with raspberry leaves, pull up the paste gently up and over, wetting all edges thoroughly and laying them one above the other. Turn all right over (fatty side uppermost), set on a floured baking tin and bake for forty-five minutes in a hot oven (*Gas Mark 6, mid-shelf, F.C.*). You will then be able to break away the hard, inedible crust easily and the leaves will come away with it. Set upon a ham stand that it may be carved easily when set upon the sideboard.

SOUPS

Soups

My Oyster Soup
My Remedial Broth
My Aunt's Hop-Top Soup
Rabbit Soup with Sorrel
My Jerusalem Artichoke Soup
My Giblet Soup
Mulligatawny Soup
Strong Fish Stock
An Appetising Soup from York Ham Liquor
Beer Soup
Eel Soup
My Gravy Soup
Beef Jelly for Invalids

MY OYSTER SOUP

THERE was never any problem about this soup. It was my gentlemen's favourite. Whenever I placed the steaming tureen before my master he would rub his long fingers together and quote Mr Sam Weller, the character in that Mr Dickens book which I personally never took to; saying 'It's a very remarkable circumstance sir that poverty and oysters always seems to go together.'

When no more of my soup remained in the tureen and I came into the room again to remove it my master would then say, 'capital, capital, thank you Mrs Hudson', then he would pause and after this pause append another quotation from the same source: 'It's over and can't be helped, and that's one consolation, as they always say in Turkey ven they cuts the wrong man's head off,' and I would carry the tureen away to the sound of Dr Watson's hearty laughter.

ASSEMBLY

3 dozen sauce oysters; 2 separated egg yolks; 2 quarts strong fish stock (please see p. 50); 3 oz flour; 3 oz butter; ½ pint thick cream; the strained juice of 1 lemon; white pepper; a little salt; 14 rough-crumbled Thin Captain biscuits.

PROCEDURE

Beard all the fresh-opened oysters and drain the liquor into a small bowl. Dissolve the butter in a thick pan, blend in the flour and dilute gradually with the fish stock, being sure to beat well between each addition. When all is absorbed, beat well and allow to come to boiling point, then draw to the side of your stove and let all simmer gently for thirty minutes (*lowest gas and asbestos mat over flame, F.C.*). Work in 8 fluid oz of the cream and allow to boil again. Correct seasoning with salt, white pepper and if liked a pinch of nutmeg. Gently mix in the egg yolks with the remaining cream, stir into the soup but *do not boil again*. Slide in the oysters, stir in the lemon juice and oyster liquor, allow five minutes, then pour into a heated tureen and scatter the crumbled biscuits upon the surface immediately prior to taking to table.

MY REMEDIAL BROTH

ASSEMBLY

2 lb good quality stewing beef; 3 pints carefully cleared, strained, beef-bone stock; salt; pepper; a herb faggot.

PROCEDURE

Cut up the beef into convenient pieces, removing all skin and fat. Place in a roomy stone jar. Stand the jar upon a piece of wood in a large saucepan and pour in boiling water until it comes a little over half way up the jar's sides. Sink in the herb bag, pour over the boiling hot, cleared stock. Cover with a piece of parchment (*double fold of kitchen foil, F.C.*) and set to simmer gently on the side of your stove. Leave so, replenishing water as this diminishes, simmering for a total of seven hours. Remove to a cool place. Allow to become chilled and then remove all small particles of grease which have accumulated on the surface. Reheat, strain, simmer down in a clean pan to 1 pint of broth. Correct seasoning with salt and pepper. Serve hot in heated bowls.

MY AUNT'S HOP-TOP SOUP

This is a soup to which I have ever been addicted. Mr Holmes and Dr Watson have also drunk it without complaint.

ASSEMBLY

1 lb shelled peas; their well-washed pods; 1 ham bone; 1 Spanish onion; 4 quarts water; 2 fat handfuls of fresh-picked hop-tops chopped fine; 1 pint milk; pepper to season; 1 teaspoon salt; 1 teaspoon sugar; butter.

PROCEDURE

Cover the ham bone with the water, sink in the pea pods, bring to the boil, then set to simmer on the side of your stove for at least four hours. Liquor should cover all and come a good $1\frac{1}{2}$-inches above the pods at the commencement and be reduced so as to be just showing between the pods when cooking time is completed. Drain off all liquor, turn in the peas and let them simmer gently with a flat teaspoon of salt and of sugar until tender. Rub all through a sieve. Add the milk and re-raise all to boiling point. Stir in the chopped hop-tops with the strained juice of one coarse-grated Spanish onion and cook ten minutes only. Correct seasoning with salt and pepper and stir in a fat walnut of butter just before service. Pulled bread should always be served with this soup.

PULLED BREAD

Tear up the crusts from the top and sides of a cottage loaf. Strew them upon a flat baking sheet and allow them to become dry and crisp in a very slow oven (*floor when baking, F.C.*). Serve wrapped in a napkin.

RABBIT SOUP WITH SORREL

Consider this as a country soup. My dear aunt taught me to make it for my father and this I did whenever he happened to snare enough rabbits for me to use for puddings and pies, yet be able to set aside the heads, livers, hearts and rib cages for my soup. The sorrel we always grew in the garden, but as this is a very powerfully flavoured leaf it is advisable to treat it to one quarter of its own weight in common spinach leaves, well-washed and denuded of base stems. Take off to where the leaf commences.

ASSEMBLY

The rib cages, heads, livers and hearts of 3 wild rabbits; ½ lb shin of beef; 1 lb knuckle of veal; ½ lb of bacon trimmings, which are obtainable for one penny per pound; 1 medium trimmed carrot; 1 medium peeled onion stuck with 4 cloves; one well-washed, trimmed leek of 1-inch diameter at root end; 1 blade of mace; 6 quarts water; 3 egg yolks; 1 gill cream; ½ a lemon; 2 oz butter or carefully cleaned dripping; salt; pepper; some fresh, fine-chopped parsley heads; 1 large handful picked, washed sorrel; 6 spinach leaves; flour.

PROCEDURE

Cut the rabbit pieces up small with a chopper and a knife, also beef shin and veal knuckle, split the heads, then chop into four pieces per head. Dice the bacon trimmings, dissolve the chosen fat in a meat tin over a modest fire, toss in the bacon and fry three minutes. Place in all the pieces and put into the oven under another upturned meat baking tin and thus cook slowly for thirty minutes. (*Gas Mark 4, mid shelf, F.C.*) Remove from the oven. Sprinkle over flour, turn well, until the fat is well taken up, then scrape into a large saucepan. Pour on the water, add the mace and prepared, sliced vegetables, excepting spinach and sorrel, bring to the boil, skim carefully and allow to simmer on the side of your stove and under a lid for three hours. Take off the fat with tissue paper as explained in Mulligatawny Soup, p. 50, strain. Pick off all meat from rib cages, brain, tongue and cheeks from heads, and dice all with livers and hearts. Simmer on for thirty minutes, and then rub through a sieve, remembering to remove the cloves from the onion first. Return to your stewpan, taste and correct seasoning with salt. Add lemon juice. Take up both sorrel and spinach leaves after removing stems and tear small. Throw into the pot. While all this simmers gently mix the egg yolks with the cream and stir into your soup. Now comes the part which must be regarded as of the utmost importance. *Never allow your soup to boil again or the eggs will surely curdle.* Once the eggs and cream have bound the mixture, and the spinach and sorrel have dwindled into mere threads as they surely will, just pour into a heated soup tureen, scatter parsley upon the surface and send to table.

MY JERUSALEM ARTICHOKE SOUP

Mr Holmes had many grateful clients whom he had aided at one time or another in their Hour of Need. One such old gentleman who lived with his daughter in Norfolk was wont to journey into London twice every year, once for the Eton and Harrow Match at Lords and once for a Rugby International at Twickenham. He never failed to stop his carriage outside our door upon his arrival for each of these visits. Then his coachman would come in with a basket laden with good things from his estate and garden. It was from this source that I obtained my winter supply of Jerusalem artichokes.

ASSEMBLY

$1\frac{1}{2}$ pints thick white sauce; 3 oz grated Parmesan cheese; 1 oz butter; 2 lb Jerusalem artichokes; the strained juice of 1 lemon; an equal amount of water; salt and pepper to season; $\frac{1}{4}$ pint thin cream.

PROCEDURE

Make your thick sauce in the proportions $1\frac{3}{4}$ oz flour and the same of butter to $1\frac{1}{2}$ pints milk. Then peel very thinly all the given artichokes and slice them thickly into a shallow container. Strew them about. Mix the lemon juice and water and pour over them. Leave thirty minutes. When time is up turn them into a sieve, set the sieve over gently bubbling water in a base pan and cover the sieve with a lid. So cook the artichokes without any water until they are just tender, remembering that there are only a few seconds between their becoming so and collapsing into a nasty pap! Rub them while hot through a clean sieve and into the thick white sauce. Stir in the cheese and stir over a low fire until all is smooth and the cheese has completely melted. Taste, correct seasoning, stir in butter, then when dissolved, the cream and all is done.

MY GIBLET SOUP

This inexpensive, nourishing soup is a very fine one. Regrettably it constituted an area of dispute between Mr Holmes and Dr Watson. He, being a doctor, expressed himself somewhat coarsely, and at the dinner table, concerning the contents which had formed the basis for my soup. He said, though delicacy restrains me from quoting his remarks in their entirety, 'after a day in hospital, dealing with "human intestines" in progressive stages of disease and decay etcetera... etcetera... etcetera'. (The substitutions in quotes are mine.)

ASSEMBLY

4 sets of giblets; 4 slices 'streaked' bacon (de-rinded); 2 oz butter; 1 large carrot; 2 very small turnips shaped like small flattened tennis balls; 1 large Spanish onion; 2 oz flour; the strained juice of 1 lemon; 2 quarts of very strong stock; 1 sherry taster of dry sherry; $\frac{1}{2}$ a sherry taster of old brown sherry; salt and pepper to season; 1 faggot of herbs; 1 torn bay leaf; 1 blade of mace; 1 fluid oz olive oil.

PROCEDURE

Dissolve 1 oz butter in a thick pan with the oil. When both are 'singing' turn in the giblets and sizzle fast until well sealed. Remove and fry diced bacon, remove and fry chopped vegetables adding a dessertspoon melted butter and a dessertspoon extra oil if needful. Let them lie. Shake over them the flour, work up with a wooden spoon and cook on, stirring for three minutes to expel all taste of flour which will otherwise linger no matter how long the item is cooked thereafter. Return the bacon dice and giblets to the pan, work in the stock gradually, add herbs and spice, then raise to a slow rolling boil. Maintain this for one and a half hours or until giblets are tender. Dredge out the giblets. Remove all neck bones and chop all giblets into small dice. Place these in a heated tureen. Correct soup-seasoning with salt and pepper, add the lemon juice, stir in sherries, remove bay leaf, mace and herb bag. Pour over tureen contents, stir well and send to table.

MULLIGATAWNY SOUP

Here again I was in trouble, for while Mr Holmes dismissed this Famous Anglo-Indian soup with some scorn Dr Watson positively doted upon it, so I reserved its service for those occasions when the good Doctor was certain to be dining and served another soup to my fastidious employer.

ASSEMBLY

1 lb scrag end of neck of mutton; 1 small sharp apple; 1 large Spanish onion; 1 tennis-ball sized turnip, all peeled; 1 trimmed, very carefully washed leek not more than 1 inch in diameter across the root end; 1 oz butter; 1 fluid oz olive oil; 1 oz flour; 2 level dessertspoons Venticachellum's Curry Powder; ½ teaspoon 'Punjab Brand' Indian curry paste; a squeeze of lemon juice; 2 oz boiled rice, (please turn to p. 37); 3 pints mutton stock; salt.

PROCEDURE

Trim as much fat away as possible from the scrag end. Chop up into small neat pieces. Prepare and slice the vegetables and apple thinly. Dissolve the butter with the oil and when 'singing' turn in the vegetables and apple. Fry, still turning, over a brisk fire. Work in the curry powder and paste after four minutes, then the flour and finally the stock and the pieces of neck. Bring to a slow rolling boil, skim carefully and thoroughly. Simmer gently for one and a half hours. Remove pan from heat. Take up some scrumpled pieces of tissue paper. Smooth these out, then tow them over the surface of the stilled soup, thus removing, with patience, every particle of grease. Excavate all bones. Rub away into the liquor all clinging particles of flesh. Then rub all through a medium sieve. Taste, correct seasoning with salt and place the plain boiled rice in a small side dish for passing at table that each person may shake in a spoonful and stir it round.

STRONG FISH STOCK

ASSEMBLY

2 soles' heads, spine bones, skins and other trimmings; 1 whiting cut into 1-inch pieces across the body; 2 leaves of lemon peel pared thinly; the strained juice of half a lemon; 1 torn bay leaf; 6 peppercorns; 1 blade of mace; 1 tiny sprig of fennel; 8 stout parsley stalks; 2 quarts water.

PROCEDURE

Bring all slowly to boiling point. Draw to the side of the stove. Skim off all scum which has risen to the surface. When liquor is clear again toss in 1 small teacup of cold water, allow to regain boiling point over a fairly brisk fire and maintain at a strong simmer for exactly twenty minutes. Strain carefully through a tammy cloth (*tamis, metal, F.C.*) into a clean pan. Raise once more to boiling point, simmer down to 3 pints. Add 1 pint of dry white wine and use as instructed.

AN APPETISING SOUP FROM YORK HAM LIQUOR

When Mr Holmes was at his most difficult, after a protracted indulgence in his Sad Vice, I have never failed to persuade him to put down his violin and sup a bowlful of this particular soup, which has exerted such an influence upon him as to restore him to his usual state again – for a while.

ASSEMBLY

1 lb onions; 1 lb carrots; 1 lb green and white of leeks; ½ lb young turnip tops; 2 quarts liquor from a York ham; ½ pint sherry or dry Madeira; salt; 2 crushed cloves of peeled garlic; ¼ pint thick cream; 1 thick slice of York ham; black pepper.

PROCEDURE

Slice and then chop peeled onions fine. Trim, wash and slice leeks into very thin rounds. Scrape, wash and dice the carrots and turnip tops, then place all the vegetables, liquor and seasoning in a stock pot or jam kettle. Bring fast to the boil, steady off at simmering, skim to remove any impurities risen in scum to the top surface then refresh with a further tumblerful of cold ham stock. Maintain at a steady simmer for two hours. Rub through a sieve, return to the pan, season with pepper to taste, stir in the sherry, then the cream, then stir carefully until mixture reaches boiling point. Toss in the finely-chopped ham, stir well, pour into thoroughly heated soup bowls and hand a side dish of Pulled Bread (see p. 47).

BEER SOUP

This was ever a favourite with my gentlemen who always desired that I serve anchovy toast to accompany it. (Please turn to p. 221 for the toast.)

ASSEMBLY

2 oz butter; 2 oz flour; 3 pints old ale; 1½ fluid oz white rum; 1½ fluid oz medium sherry; a small piece of root ginger, slightly bruised; a 1-inch stick of cinnamon; 1½ oz of soft brown pieces sugar; the thin rind of half a lemon; 6 egg yolks well-whipped; 5 egg whites stiff-whipped.

PROCEDURE

Place the butter in a stew pan and melt it slowly. Stir in the flour and cook, ever stirring, for five minutes over a moderate fire. Add the beer gradually, stirring well between each addition. Draw to the side of the stove and leave it be for thirty minutes. Meanwhile, place in a small pan the rum, sherry, sugar, cinnamon, ginger and lemon rind. Cover and set on the side of the stove to infuse. Take the well-whipped egg yolks and whisking the while, pour upon it the soup and whisk on over the fire being quite sure this be mild enough to ensure the mixture does not boil for thus will it curdle and all be wasted. Strain in the infusion from the small pan, and finally whip in the stiff egg whites. Thus into a heated tureen and hand the anchovy toast separately.

EEL SOUP

Many is the time that I have heard Mr Holmes quote, and the good Doctor laughed heartily thereafter, a somewhat coarse excerpt by someone called Calverley. It concerned a certain Lady Jane – who should with her upbringing have known better – and her foot page whom she was so tasteless as to take unto herself in a most intimate and unseemly manner, Sir John her husband being a great many years older than she. The time comes when Sir John disappears. He is sought high and low and eventually discovered face down in the eel pond. The footman who bears these sad tidings to her ladyship in her boudoir finds her with the aforementioned youth! While I misremember the words of it, her ladyship then cried out to the man to replace her dead husband, denuded of eels, 'that he may catch *us* (!) some more'. It quite turned me against eel soup but my gentlemen joked about it and much liked the dish.

Soups

ASSEMBLY

The head cut with 2½ inches of the eel's body and the tail likewise; 3 quarts of My Special Fish Stock (p. 50); 4 oz sweet butter; one 1-inch diameter leek, trimmed and cleaned; the blossoms and leaves of 5 dwarf marigolds; ½ pint shelled young peas; 6 parsley stalks and one half teacup of fine-chopped parsley heads; 1 small faggot of thyme; 2 rounded tablespoons sifted flour; 1 pint milk; salt and pepper.

PROCEDURE

Place head and tail in given stock and simmer on the side of your stove with the parsley stalks therein for two hours or until the flesh falls all away very softly. Strain. For this I ever use a china colander. Return liquor to carefully wiped pan. Add the butter, the sliced leek, the thyme tied into a scrap of muslin, the peas and marigold leaves all chopped small. Cover and simmer until the leeks are quite tender. Remove the thyme, work flour to paste with a little cold milk, boil the remainder with the marigold petals, then strain. Stir strained milk on to flour paste. Scrape back into pan. Stir until very thick, then add a little of the pot liquor and beat until very smooth and so use up all the milk by easy stages. Stir in the half cup of parsley, correct seasoning with salt and pepper. Set 4 slices of toasted bread in the base of a heated tureen. Pour the soup over and so send to table.

MY GRAVY SOUP

'It may be simple,' observed our good Dr Watson, on the first occasion that he supped this, 'but 'pon my word Holmes it is remarkably good!' For once I approved his judgement.

ASSEMBLY

6 lb of cheap Shin of Beef; 2 large carrots; 1 celery head; 3 large Spanish onions; 1 fat leek; a bunch of sweet herbs, (*1 bay leaf, rosemary sprig, thyme sprig, 8 fat parsley stalks, 6 peppercorns, and a piece of both dried lemon and dried orange peel pared very thinly from these fruits and tied in a piece of muslin, F.C.*); 2 oz butter; 2 firm, white turnips; stock to cover.

PROCEDURE

Cut all the meat from the bones. Put the butter upon the base of a sturdy iron stew pan. Slice two peeled onions thinly, then chop them and strew them about in the melted butter. Let the pot stand on the stove with the hod closed down (*medium gas, F.C.*) that the onions may brown by your turning them with a wooden spoon. Then add the meat cut into small pieces. Let this brown in the butter and the juices which escape from the meat pieces until it is almost a glaze in the pan. Then add the stock and all the residual bones chopped fairly small, likewise the trimmed white and green of the leek, the remaining onion, quartered, the herb faggot, the trimmed, carefully washed, fine chopped celery head and the quartered, peeled turnips. Let the mixture come fast to boiling point over a brisk heat. Skim very thoroughly, tip in one tumbler filled with very cold water, stir about, and then adjust your top-of-stove heat that all may simmer very steady for six hours. Line out a large colander with a clean cloth, having first wrung out the cloth in warm water. Pour the liquor through. Remove colander and cloth and let the liquor lie until morning. Skim off every particle of fat, reheat, taste, correct the seasoning to your taste and send to table with a dish of pulled bread (see p. 47).

BEEF JELLY FOR INVALIDS

Take a glass bottle such as you keep pickles in, or a jar. Shred lean beef very thin indeed to fill the bottle full which takes about two pounds of beef or thereabouts. Put in a teaspoonful of salt – no more – and straightway cover with a thick fold of butter muslin and tie this very close indeed about the neck. Place the bottle upon a small piece of wood in a large pan half-filled with cold water. Gently bring up the water to boiling point and then draw to your stove rim and leave it be for eight hours. Now line a superfine hair sieve out with a fold of butter muslin and set over a basin. Turn the jar's contents over the muslin and leave to drip until the very last drop has been expelled into the basin below. Set the basin upon a cold slab and leave until it becomes a jelly. Feed very sparingly in teaspoonfuls. NEVER ADD A SINGLE DROP OF WATER PLEASE.

FISH

Fish

Court-Bouillon
Mr Holmes' Truite au bleu
Baked Soles
My Fish Chowder
My Fish Stock for Fish Chowder
My Potted Shrimps
My Easy Shrimp Sauce
On Sprats
My Fish Pie
A Fish Faggot
Mackerel with Gooseberry Sauce
Oysters in their Own Liquor
Turbot with Lobster Sauce
Calcutta Jumble
My Lobster Dumplings
How to Fry White-Bait Properly

FISH

I have put together a few observations concerning fish in general for the benefit of those less experienced than myself.

Thus, first and foremost, in the considerations which a good cook must direct towards both freshwater and sea water fish and crustaceans is FRESHNESS.

It must be clearly comprehended by the purchaser that fish of dull appearance, with dull scales, limp gills and bleary eyes must never be considered for an instant. Fresh fish will invariably present a shiny, gleaming appearance upon the fishmonger's marble slab. The scales must gleam, the eyes be bright and clear, the fins brisk and crisp. Then and then only is any purchase made of such articles.

Among this assembly there are certain fish which must be purchased alive. In this category we find eels, to which Mr Holmes was Very Partial – either in the jellied way or cooked in the French manner – also crabs, lobsters, mussels, winkles and whelks.

In the matter of selection among these live purchases I would make certain observations which may be regarded as both constant and infallible.

CONCERNING CRABS

The wise purchaser will always choose cock crabs. These may be detected readily by the absence of eggs clustered about a certain part. When plunged into their cooking liquid, the hen crabs throw off their legs thus admitting, through the spongy parts beyond, a seepage of fluids which wholly spoils the flavour while cock crabs retain their legs during cooking.

CONCERNING LOBSTERS

The dictum here goes absolutely in reverse. Always choose *hen* lobsters and disregard the cock lobsters. It is as simple as anything can be to request the fishmonger to line up for you on his slab a range of lobsters of the required weights in such a manner that their tails are tucked in

The Sherlock Holmes Cookbook

and their backs disposed towards you. Thus you may observe immediately that the females have wide rounded backs while those of the males are much narrower and distinctly pointed. Thus may you obtain the very best. Hen lobsters contain the precious coral as the so-coloured egg mass in each one is called. These are indispensable in fine saucings for this crustacean.

Should you for any reason wish to make a purchase of lobsters twenty-four hours before you desire to cook them, then be sure to sink a complete newspaper into cold water until thoroughly impregnated to wrap around each lobster so as to enclose her – save at both ends! Secure these wrappings with a rubber band or a piece of twine and *put into your charge cave** until required. Thus do you enable the lobsters to remain alive and by the moisture which each one absorbs through the *joints* in their shells to abstain from so feeding upon their own 'milk' that they dry themselves out; for a dry lobster is a dreadful culinary object.

CONCERNING MUSSELS

These can be made to enlarge themselves and self-clean also in the most elementary but highly rewarding manner. Make a firm rule always to place your order for purchase *twenty-four hours in advance*. Tumble the soiled mussels into a bucket, loosely. Then hand-scatter 1 lb coarse oatmeal over every 10 pints of mussels. Take up the bucket, give it a good shake and put into some conveniently dark place, like, for example the back of a broom cupboard. Just as soon as they be enclosed in darkness the mussels will open up and gorge themselves upon the oatmeal. When they are turned into a tub of cold water, the 'beards' tugged off and the shells well-scrubbed, it will be found – after cooking – that they are perfectly clean and consequently very light in colour, and considerably increased in size owing to this period of intensive feeding!

CONCERNING WINKLES

This may be thought to be an inconsiderable matter. It must be remembered therefore that from time to time Mr Holmes was in the habit of bringing many Inferior Persons into my kitchen during the course of his Remarkable Investigations. A great white enamel mug containing very strong, sweet Indian tea, a platter of crusty bread and butter and a bowl apiece of winkles was far more to such persons' taste than a Dainty Afternoon Tea Assembly. Thus for persons not forced to

---

* Zinc container for ice – a substitute for refrigeration, *F.C.*

Fish

particularise in this manner; but say moving in to a new establishment, labourers, removal men and the like will work the better and the more cheerfully for the giving of such a repast.

The only requirement, (save for some long, coloured-headed pins, for these are the more readily discernible and not likely to become intermingled with the food!) is some sea water or some salty water. In the absence of the former, the latter may be made by mixing enough rock salt to make an egg float in 1 pint of cold water and thereafter adding 1 further pint of water to dilute. Bring to the boil, immerse the winkles, cook for ten minutes over a fast fire, drain, cool and serve. So much then for *freshness* and for *living purchases*.

Thus do we come to the varying manners of cooking.

I once heard Mrs Agnes Bertha Marshall remark that 'fine fish should never be boiled'. She gave to her pupils a receipt which my Cook gave to me when she was a very young girl. Cook called it a Curt-Bullion; but when I wrote the way of it down to her dictating she spelled it this way: *Court-Bouillon*. The preparing of it is very simple and I do give it herewith.

COURT-BOUILLON

ASSEMBLY

1 quart dry white wine; 1 quart water; 3 oz minced onions; 1 large faggot containing parsley stalks and if possible a bit of cleaned root, 1 small piece of fennel or dill, a sprig of thyme, a bay leaf, 6 peppercorns and a curl of dried orange or lemon peel, all tied together in a small square of muslin, ½ oz coarse salt, preferably grey.

PROCEDURE

Bring all together in a pan to boiling point, skim carefully and simmer for thirty minutes. It is a curious fact that if simmered for longer – unlike other stocks – the liquor does not improve, but rather diminishes in flavour and quality.

MR HOLMES' TRUITE AU BLEU

One day I had a cookery lesson from Mr Holmes. He had but recently descended from the night train from Scotland and was washing his hands prior to taking his place at table for breakfast. He called to That Boy, 'Take this bundle down to Mrs Hudson and inform her that I will follow it.'

The 'parcel' was tied with bass (the inner bark of the lime tree). The wrappings were grasses and inside were a number of fine trout, caught no doubt in Scottish waters.

True to his word, Mr Holmes descended to my kitchen and proceeded to instruct me in the manner of cooking trout 'O Blurr' as he called it! But again I was confounded by the foreign tongue for when, as was always my custom, I made my notes and inquired as to the spelling of 'O Blurr' I discovered to my chagrin it was *au bleu*. ' "*Truites au bleu*",' lectured Mr Holmes, 'are among the really great delicacies of the French table, being served naturally, with no fine sauces to dress them but just the very best and purest of butter, preferably from the *Gironde* which in my opinion ever takes precedence over " *Beurre Normand*".'

Well it was simple, and my Master, having ascertained that I had not as yet breakfasted, insisted I eat one myself. It was delicious, so thus I added a new receipt to my collection, a foreign one.

ASSEMBLY

2 quarts water; a mean ¼ pint white wine vinegar; ¼ oz peppercorns; 5 oz minced, raw carrots; 7 oz minced, raw onions; 1 oz parsley stems; ¾ oz coarse, preferably grey salt; 1 bay leaf; 1 sprig of thyme.

PROCEDURE

Place water, salt, vinegar, carrots and onions together in a pan with the parsley, bay and thyme bunched together. Raise to boiling, skim carefully, simmer for fifty minutes, add peppercorns tied in a scrap of muslin and simmer on for a final twelve minutes. Strain carefully and set aside for use in the cooking of freshwater trout. These may be gutted, but never must the heads be removed, for behind the gills lie the 'pearls' or little oyster-shaped pieces of white flesh which are regarded by *gourmets* as major delicacies! Mr Holmes, in more fanciful mood would exclaim, while dissecting a trout with those long tapering fingers of his, 'One of these days my dear Watson we will obtain a sufficiency of trout to eat only the 'pearls' as did the Romans in the, er, heyday of the Roman Empire.' Looking up from his fish Dr Watson inquired with his usual practicality, 'What became of the fish?' Mr Holmes then informed him that this was thrown to the slaves, and the Doctor grunted, helping himself to a fourth trout, 'Never did care for

Fish

the Romans,' which quite ended the conversation. But Mr Holmes further instructed me that morning saying, 'The perfect way to do this is to catch the trout, stun them with a stone, gut, wash and slide into the *court-bouillon,* all in the space of a few moments. The liquid in which they are immersed must be absolutely boiling* and this 5-inch deep chafing dish of yours Mrs Hudson is admirable for the job. I daresay that these trout, caught at sundown last evening, will do very well indeed for us.'

Saying which, my Master slipped the trout into the liquor and stood looking down at the potful. 'Remark,' he invited 'how the skin has shrivelled instantly and is now breaking in all directions! Dish your trout upon a napkin and accompany them with a sauceboat of melted butter, a pot of steamed, new potatoes and a few fat pieces of cut lemon. In the absence at this moment of new potatoes give us some very thin brown bread and butter.' So saying he marched from the kitchen calling to Dr Watson that they must not linger over breakfast since both were late for an urgent appointment. Thus may you glimpse something of my Master's character. *Everything* was of great interest and over the years it seemed as if he knew a very great deal about everything too.

Whenever I went down to see my friend in Billingsgate, whose circle of acquaintance included several workers in the Fish Market, I made a particular point of obtaining fish for Mr Holmes and, more often than not, for Dr Watson as well. They were particularly partial to a dish of Baked Soles and for this I always purchased medium-sized lemon soles, while for Fish Chowder, a positive obsession with the good Doctor, I always sought out hake. Here then are the two receipts, simple enough for any young, inexpcrienced housewife to follow as I later explained to Dr Watson's bride when she came to me for her learning.

BAKED SOLES

ASSEMBLY

2 medium-sized lemon soles; one 5 oz (peeled weight) Spanish onion; 2 firm but ripe tomatoes; 2 oz butter; 2 teaspoons anchovy purée (this may be purchased); 3 tablespoons thin cream; a little flour; 1 oz grated Parmesan cheese; 2 tablespoons medium sherry; freshly-ground black peppercorns.

* An 8 oz trout requires between four and a half and five minutes' immersion in boiling court-bouillon. *F.C.*

PROCEDURE

Use half an ounce of the butter to rub over the base and sides of a pie dish just large enough to contain the fish. Turn these in flour, and tap off any surplus. Make three fairly deep, slanting cuts in the upper part of each fish and rub into these one teaspoon apiece of the anchovy purée. Slice peeled onions with really *extreme* thinness, otherwise these will not be sufficiently cooked when the fish is done. Lay the fine, separated rings on the buttered pie-dish's base. Lay on the soles, cover these with the thinly sliced tomatoes, moisten with the sherry, season moderately with the pepper and sprinkle the Parmesan evenly over the surface. Finally, drip on the cream as evenly as possible, dot with the remaining flakes of butter and bake in a fairly hot oven for twenty-five minutes. (*Gas Mark 4, one shelf below centre, thirty to thirty-five minutes, F.C.*).

MY FISH CHOWDER

This is a truly delicious dish to which I admit being Distinctly Partial myself, though as yet I have not found a correct quantity for sending into the dining room which permits of there being an ample serving left over.

ASSEMBLY

1 lb pickled pork, diced small; one 6 oz Spanish onion minced fine; very clean dripping for the frying of these items; 2 lb of potatoes well-mashed with a knob of butter after cooking; 3 lb hake or turbot; 1 rounded teaspoon each of marjoram, thyme and parsley heads, the same of powdered mace; 6 black peppercorns; 1 flat teaspoon grated nutmeg; salt to taste; ½ bottle modest claret; ½ bottle fish stock (see following receipt).

PROCEDURE

Dissolve about 2 oz dripping in a thick iron frypan and when sizzling briskly over the fire, fry the onions over closed heat so that they may become tender but not browned. After five minutes, put in pickled pork and continue, turning occasionally for a total of fifteen minutes. Put half this mixture into the base of a generous pie dish, cover with half the mashed potatoes, cover with half the fish sliced neatly. Repeat, then scatter over all the seasonings, and pour on both claret and fish stock. Cover lightly with butter papers and bake in a slow oven (*Gas Mark 3, F.C.*) on a low shelf (*one above oven base*) for one hour.

MY FISH STOCK FOR FISH CHOWDER

Obtain from the fishmonger all the trimmings from 1 lb of sole and with it a hake's head split and the trimmings from your own chosen fish. Set these in a pan with 1 quart of water, 1 large piece of thinly-cut lemon peel and 2 fat, crushed fennel seeds. Let it come to the boil very slowly. Skim off all foam and impurities. Simmer steadily for twenty minutes. Strain through a tammy cloth (*a sieve, F.C.*) and use.

MY POTTED SHRIMPS

The great advantage of putting up this mixture, always to be considered in *my* household, was that sudden and unexpected visitors could always be assured of a tasty side dish, served with hot snippets of toast; even as Cook herself could thus have the wherewithal for a Good Fish Sauce always to hand whether the available fish be Salmon, Salmon Trout, Turbot Fillets, Sea Trout, Mackerel, Halibut Steaks, Cod or Hake. All respond equally well to a good shrimp sauce or stuffing.

ASSEMBLY

4 lb picked (*shelled, F.C.*) shrimps either pink or brown may be done this way; 1¾ lb sweet butter; 1 flat teaspoon of freshly-milled black peppercorns; 4 small bladelets of dried mace; 2 dried bay leaves, torn into small pieces.

PROCEDURE

Take up two 2 lb stone jars of the kind in which Mr Cooper's famous Oxford Marmalade be sold. Then place 1 lb butter in an enamel pan (*vitreous enamel IF you please, F.C.*) and set against the very rim of your stove that the butter may liquefy with infinite slowness. As the procedure gets under way add the pepper, mace and bay, and allow to infuse for a total of fifteen minutes. At the end of this time stir in all the prepared shrimps and turn over thoroughly, that seasonings may be evenly distributed. Turn into the jars and if, when all are in and you press down the shrimps gently in each one with a wooden spoon the butter does not clear the shrimps by a quarter of an inch, add more until it so does. Place in the coldest corner of your larder under a firm-tied parchment covering, where it may be kept for at least five days in winter and four days in summer, or in a charge cave well lined with ice where it may stay sweet for many more days.

Note In a modern freezer the flavour begins to diminish after six months! – that's all. (*F.C.*)

MY EASY SHRIMP SAUCE

ASSEMBLY

4 oz of shrimps-in-their-butter, see previous receipt; ¼ pint dry white wine; ¾ pint thin cream or half and half cream–milk; 1 heaped tablespoon of fresh finely chopped parsley heads; 1 tiny sprig of very finely chopped fennel (*leaf of Florentine Fennel, F.C.*); freshly milled black peppercorns to season; 2 oz sifted flour; extra milk if needed.

PROCEDURE

Place the potted shrimps in a thick pan and allow the butter to dissolve from them over a slowish heat. Stir in the given flour with a wooden sauce spoon and continue stirring, slowly first and gradually accelerating speed until you are beating vigorously. Thus should the mixture form a soft ball leaving base and sides of pan clear in many places. Stir on, slowly again, for a minimum of three and a half minutes to ensure that no trace of flour taste remains. It is a curious and interesting fact that if the flour be not cooked out of taste altogether before the first induction of fluid, it will never be eliminated thereafter with such complete thoroughness. Add wine, allow this to bubble in pan without stirring, then stir again, slowly at first and gradually increasing speed to vigorous beating until mixture is absolutely smooth and quite thick. Add one third of milk and cream, or just cream, repeat explained procedure until all given fluids are absorbed. Stir in the herbs and seasonings to taste, correct any unbalance in flavours and decide whether or not your sauce is too thick for its intended purpose. If so, add more milk or cream as desired. Note—By this method may all the thick sauces for everyday use be made.

There is another method which is considerably more extravagant but exemplifies a Much Higher Form of the Art of Cookery. This is to make a great deal of lightly flavoured fluid, tasting more of soup's character than the more concentrated one of any sauce, and obtain the latter without thickening the former. This is done by simmering very slowly at the side of the stove (*over an asbestos mat with Gas at Low, F.C.*) until the large lightly flavoured quantity becomes a small highly-condensed-in-flavour quantity. Thereafter, having obtained the *texture* required, you may have transgressed the limits of *subtle* saucing, by overstrength, which can be rectified in moments by the smoothing off of flavour which comes from adding thick cream, a little at a time, and allowing this to boil up after each respective addition. I have found this method to yield me the most unctuous of sauces with the absolute

Fish

minimum of effort, for, save to ensure your fire burns properly and thus gives you the bottom heat needed for your simmering pan – and everything else which may be situate about the hob – the sauce takes care of itself right to the very end. Then Cook must taste, adjust flavouring here or there that all may be borne proudly to table.

ON SPRATS

These I am in the habit of serving as the fish course at breakfast for my gentlemen. There are so many silly things said, and indeed written, about what must be done to sprats to make them properly edible, that in protest I give the only method ever necessary for this end! Place the sprats in close rows, one tail first, then one head first, and so on down an ordinary baking sheet until this be filled. Place in a moderate oven for fifteen minutes. Lift on to a d'oyley covered dish and dress with a few parsley heads and pieces of cut lemon. Hand thin brown bread and butter or hot brown rolls in a napkin with the contents of a butter dish near by.

My Master was proper finnicking over the matter of railway train 'Tiffin baskets' as he was wont to call them. Having proclaimed that cold roast chicken eaten in the fingers was a grossly overrated article, dismissed sliced ham as 'depressing', he fair taxed my repertoire until I remembered what my mother called her Pasty to separate it wholly from Cornish Pasty which was something to be avoided by those who like my family *disliked turnips!*

Anyway, recalling this article and wishing to try my luck, I put into the 'Tiffin Basket' the following items which I will transcribe in the hope that they may be of service to others who find the prices exhorbitant for picnic baskets sold by the Railways of the British Isles.

MY FISH PIE

For the assembly of this speciality you will require proper puff pastry (p. 156), a good white sauce base, correctly boiled hard, shelled eggs for which there are certain constant instructions and a 'fish faggot'. Therefore I first conduct you straight through my receipt and its procedure and thereafter append the vital supplements.

ASSEMBLY FOR A PIE SUITED TO TWO HUNGRY TRAVELLING GENTLEMEN

2 hard, shelled eggs; 2 oz thin-sliced, unskinned mushrooms; two 1-inch thick slices from a middle cut of salmon; ¼ pint thick cream; 1 rounded tablespoon of fresh, fine-chopped parsley; 2 scallops, scraped off their shells and rough chopped, coral with white flesh; 2 small cod 'steaks' from a middle cut; 20 prawns shelled, but the eggs included if so be they are spawning; freshly milled black peppercorns; finely ground salt; some white sauce; 1 oz fine-grated Parmesan cheese.

PROCEDURE

Line your pie dish with thinly rolled puff paste. Take up the salmon and remove the skin all round each piece being careful to scrape the skin thereafter that the best part – the brown which clings to the skin – be removed and spread over the fish. Perform the same office for the two cod steaks, and then rub sweet butter liberally over your puff paste and lay in one layer of alternate, cod and salmon pieces with the bones removed. Having so done make up your sauce according to the procedure below. Incorporate into it cheese, season with pepper and salt and pour half over the fish in your pie dish. Lay a half-mixture of shelled prawns and chopped scallops over. Spread with half the thick cream and scatter thereon half the chopped, hard-boiled egg, a very light seasoning of salt. Return to stage one and repeat from beginning to end. This is your pie filled.

Roll out more puff paste one eighth of an inch in thickness. Insert a good-sized pie funnel centrally and then lay on the paste, cutting it one inch below the rim all round with a pair of sharp kitchen scissors. Tuck all but one quarter inch of the paste edges under and pinch them along between thumb and first finger – quite forcefully. Thus you will obtain a fitting lid, so eased as to obviate the possibility of shrinkage during baking. Brush all over with beaten, strained, raw egg. Bake in a strong oven for twenty minutes, place in a cool one and allow to cook the pastry through, which by now should be lightly browned and fully risen.

THE SAUCE

Dissolve one ½ oz butter in a very small pan. Stir in one ½ oz sifted flour and stir on with a wooden spoon over a moderate heat until three minutes have passed in so doing. In the meantime place 4 fluid oz sweet milk in another small pan and set beside your stove that a 'fish faggot' (see page 67) may infuse therein. When the three minutes have expired pour 2 fluid oz of dry white wine into your mixture, allow to bubble before stirring, then stir with increasing celerity until a smooth, far-too-thick mixture be obtained. By this time you may remove your herb infusion from the milk. Add this in two parts to the sauce, treating each in the manner described for the wine. Taste, correct the seasoning with salt and pepper. Stir in 1 oz of Parmesan cheese grated very fine, stir in 1 rounded dessertspoon of fresh finely-chopped parsley and use as explained above.

Hard Boiled Eggs Must always be lowered gently into boiling water. When bubbling is resumed, maintain for eight minutes. Lift out eggs and plunge immediately into cold water. After a brief lapse of time tap the eggs all over against the side of the sink that the shell may be completely broken, remove a minute scrap of shell carefully, then allow a very thin stream of cold water to run down upon the hole thus forcing both inner skin and shell away and enabling you to obtain an unblemished egg each time! For this dish chop eggs finely.

A FISH FAGGOT

Tie together into a square of butter muslin, a sprig of fennel, a sprig of dill, a sprig of thyme, 3 bruised peppercorns, two parsley stalks and a piece of oven dried lemon peel cut extremely thin.

MACKEREL WITH GOOSEBERRY SAUCE

When we were not entertaining, (mackerel is not a formal fish), I frequently served this dish to my gentlemen. Mr Holmes was wont to remark upon it, 'A dirty feeder but a most excellent flavour,' to which Dr Watson invariably replied, 'Let us not question the habits of God's creatures but merely be thankful for them, is what I say.'

ASSEMBLY

My Gooseberry Sauce; 12/14 oz mackerel; 1 oz coarse oatmeal; 2 oz lard; salt and pepper to season.

PROCEDURE

Top and tail and clean the mackerel without splitting them. Heat the lard in a good iron frypan over a moderate heat and meanwhile turn the wet fish thoroughly in the oatmeal. Slide them into the sizzling fat and fry them, damping down the heat a little to ensure they are cooked right through before being darkened too much upon their outsides. Dish on a d'oyley covered platter and hand my gooseberry sauce separately.

MY GOOSEBERRY SAUCE

ASSEMBLY

1 lb green gooseberries which have been neatly topped and tailed with a small pair of scissors; a little cold water; a generous grating of nutmeg; $1\frac{1}{2}$ oz sweet butter; Barbados sugar to taste.

PROCEDURE

Place prepared gooseberries in a medium sized pan. Cover very meanly with cold water, raise to boiling point and steady off at a steady simmer. Maintain until fruit is perfectly collapsed. Rub through a tammy (*sieve, F.C.*), return pulp to well-wiped pan. Add nutmeg, butter and a little sugar but not sufficient to nullify the essential tartness which gives this sauce its distinctive character. Turn the sauce into a sauceboat and serve with the fried mackerel.

OYSTERS IN THEIR OWN LIQUOR

It is to be taken for granted by cook/housekeepers of any standing that they are fully conversant with the use of an oyster knife (*obtainable from Jaeggi Leon & Sons Ltd, 232 Tottenham Court Road, London W.1. F.C.*), for my receipt begins with the instructions to open the oysters immediately before serving and to have a basin ready in which to capture every drop of liquor which falls from each opened shell.

ASSEMBLY

24 Whitstable Natives; the strained juice of one half a medium lemon; the conserved oyster liquor; $\frac{1}{2}$ a blade of mace; 6 fine pounded peppercorns; 1 flat afternoon-teaspoon of fine-grated lemon zest; one fat pinch cayenne pepper; 1 oz good, sweet butter; one quarter pint of Jersey cream; two slices of white bread with the crusts remaining, these are then cubed small and frizzled in dissolved bacon fat.

PROCEDURE

Open the bivalves. Beard them and remove into a basin, add the lemon juice and let them be for a while. Place the beards, liquor, mace, pre-

Fish

pared peppercorns, cayenne pepper and lemon zest into a very small copper pan making sure that this is in perfect trim internally by having been retinned recently. Nothing is more deleterious to health than cooking in a copper pan which is in need of re-tinning! Simmer the juices at the side of the stove very gently for fifteen minutes. Strain into another pan, stir in the cream and continue stirring until very smooth and quite thick. Tumble in the oysters and count forty fairly slowly. Transfer the pan contents to a small (previously heated) tureen and at the moment of carrying to table also tumble in the little frizzled bread cubes.

TURBOT WITH LOBSTER SAUCE

Not only fit for a King but actually served to one – and of course, made by me. (Please turn to p. 214 if your curiosity is aroused.)

ASSEMBLY

One whole, cleaned, but otherwise untampered-with turbot of 4 lb in weight; 1 quarter bottle of champagne; $\frac{1}{2}$ pint of My Fish Stock (to be found on p. 50); 1 lb hen lobster; $\frac{1}{2}$ pint Holland Sauce (p. 219); 12 crescents stamped from puff pastry and baked; 1 pint thick cream.

PROCEDURE

Butter a large shallow dish, skin your turbot carefully and remove all four fillets. Divide up the fish trimmings, making them small and employ these for My Fish Stock in place of sole trimmings. After their twenty minutes of cookery, place the strained liquor in a clean pan and simmer down to precisely $\frac{1}{2}$ pint. Lay your fillets, divided into neat portions, over the buttered surface of your chosen oven dish, then swill with both fish stock and champagne. Cover with a piece of protective parchment (*aluminium kitchen foil*, F.C.) and place in a moderate oven to cook for twenty-five minutes (*Gas Mark 4, mid-shelf*, F.C.). Keep warm without enough heat to cook on. Place the cream in a thick pan and simmer extremely gently until pale yellow and considerably thickened. At this point permit an Old Hand a word of warning – this is a dish which must be encompassed within certain strictures, for once the Holland mixture be upon it, it must go forthwith to table or dissolve, separate and be a Total Ruin. Pour off the liquor from your turbot fillets but still keep *them* warm. Place liquor in yet another small thick pan and simmer it down to a mere 5 fluid oz. Have your made Holland Sauce beside you. Lift up your hot fish portions and arrange them daintily upon a heated dish, cover immediately and go on keeping warm. Also have ready your golden brown puff-pastry crescents and the lobster. First remove the coral, break it up fine and stir it into your simmering cream. Then slice your lobster down the centre with the tail tucked under so that the ridges of shell may not be torn or broken. Then remove the main body flesh entire and slice into small slices or 'medallions' of one quarter inch thickness. Keep these warm along with the turbot but in a separate small container. Now crack all the shell of the claw flesh and add the claws which will be used to surmount all centrally at the moment of service. Remember too that Holland Sauce may always be kept after making *at room temperature*. When your cream be yellow and very thick, your champagne liquor fully reduced and your lobster ready, proceed with controlled haste and complete concentration. Stir the fish stock into the coral cream. Let it bubble on again until very thick, then quickly put in four gravy ladles of Holland Sauce and snatch from the fire. Cover for warmth. Bring out the fish. Arrange the lobster medallions upon each portion. Throw over all the completed sauce, arrange the crescents around the outer edge, place the claws in the centre and send speedily to table.

CALCUTTA JUMBLE

This, as you may conjecture from the name, is an Indian dish. Dr Watson brought it to me in my kitchen. After asking if he might enter, and obtaining my reply in the affirmative, he advanced holding his writ Calcutta Jumble out to me saying, 'When next you have the opportunity Mrs Hudson may we have this for *tiffin*. It has long been my desire to eat it again.'

ASSEMBLY

Four 10 oz sole fillets; 2 large, raw egg yolks; 1 tablespoon anchovy purée from a bottle; one slightly rounded teaspoon curry powder and one tiny tip of an eggspoon of real curry paste; a shake of cayenne pepper; a little salt; 1 raw green chilli chopped very fine; ½ lb of the very best Patna rice (for the cookery of it please turn to p. 37).

PROCEDURE

When the rice be cooked and strained, work into it all the other ingredients one by one, stirring each in fast and thoroughly and omitting only the sole fillets. When all are incorporated, mound high upon an entrée dish and keep warm in a gentle oven while you fry the sole

Fish

fillets in a little butter. Please bear in mind when so doing that when the fillets be stiffened right through they are cooked and continued cooking only serves to make them *hard*. Divide each of the cooked fillets into two pieces, press against the side of the mound and serve. Mr Holmes' comment upon first tasting was, 'Barbaric, my dear fellow, absolute ruination to the palate.'

MY LOBSTER DUMPLINGS

These are rather fancy. They are therefore suitable for entertaining and are generally Much Appreciated.

ASSEMBLY

One 1½ lb hen lobster; 2 large eggs; a shallow dish of very fine, white breadcrumbs; 2–3 oz sweet butter; white pepper; salt; cayenne pepper; a little lemon juice; many neat sprigs of well-washed, carefully dried parsley; a little cream. Also a small pan containing deep olive oil for frying.

PROCEDURE

Divide your lobster. Remove the pocket which is tucked in at the head end. Take out the coral with great care. Detach all claws. Excavate from these every tiny piece of flesh. Chop the body meat. Turn all into a mortar. Pound with a pestle with the 'coral' (eggs) and a squeeze or two of lemon juice to enhance the flavour and lessen the labour of this task. When all be pap, weigh it, and add until it is its own weight in the crumbs and add salt, pepper and cayenne to taste. Add one egg yolk, a little thick cream and so adjust the content of crumbs that you can roll the mixture into small, very neat balls. Roll these in sifted flour, pass through the remaining beaten egg, drain and finally bury in crumbs and pat all thick and tight. Heat the oil, lower each ball upon a perforated spoon into the slightly-smoking hot oil and let them all bounce about, giving an occasional flick to turn them over. When they be richly golden browned all over, use the same perforated spoon to lift them out, then lay them upon scrumpled old tissue paper to absorb any particle of oil. Set them in a neat pyramid upon a d'oyley-covered entrée dish. Keep them warm while you toss, one by one, the washed, wiped parsley sprigs in the hot oil. Lift each out fast for they fry extremely quickly. Lay them with great caution upon the tissue which you have by this time turned about, for they are very brittle. Arrange them in a circle of dark green about the lobster dumpling pyramid and so send to table with more cayenne pepper set thereon, thin brown bread and butter for each person and a segment of cut lemon to set upon each plate.

HOW TO FRY WHITE-BAIT PROPERLY

I well remember the occasion on which Mr Holmes came in with a box tucked under his arm, beneath that famous ulster of his. He had journeyed to Hastings upon a case and there, on the successful conclusion of the matter had been made a gift, of a box of white-bait come fresh from the sea. All forgetting that wooden boxes containing fish have a Very Strong Smell, and deep in his ponderings upon some problem, he carried these upon the rack in the train, but on leaving the cab, placed the box under his arm. I will say nothing of the state of that ulster, nor of his coat and shirt, all of which had to be hung out to make them fit to wear again; but such was ever the way with my master, genius scarcely concerning itself with such mundane matters! Be that as it may, Mr Holmes gave me the most explicit instructions upon the cookery of these little silver objects which revealed themselves when I prised open the box.

ASSEMBLY

1 lb fresh white-bait; 1 quart pure olive oil set in a deep pan with a frying basket immersed therein; salt; pepper; sifted flour; cayenne pepper; parsley sprigs; thin bread and butter; lemons.

PROCEDURE

Set the pan over a strong fire that the oil may become so hot that it throws a faint haze from its surface. Take up a small handful of the fish, turn them in flour, place them in an ordinary sieve and shake off the surplus flour so that none have time to be soggy! It is vital to remember that this process must be done each time one handful is immersed in the hot oil and not altogether, which will spoil everything. Shake the little floured fish lightly over the hot oil and then turn them quickly and briskly until they are well browned. This is a matter of seconds only if the oil be right! So continue, flouring the fish, shaking them in the sieve, scattering them over the oil, lifting them out, draining them upon cheese cloth (*absorbent paper*, *F.C.*) and turning them thence on to a d'oyley covered salver and keeping warm. When all the fish are so

Fish

fried and keeping warm in a pyramid, then wash your parsley sprigs, dry them very carefully, toss them into the hot oil, leave an instant only and take up. They will be crisp and most delightfully edible. Set them around the white-bait as a ring or border, intersperse them with cut lemons, and scatter salt and pepper. Hand brown bread and butter, cut extremely thin, on a separate salver and should you chance (what a remote possibility) to have such an employer as mine, pour well-chilled Chablis into wine glasses until they be two thirds filled only, for this is the golden rule my master taught me for the service of ALL WINES ON ALL OCCASIONS. Below stairs, particularly when my two favourites from Scotland Yard were present, they always asked for Guinness to accompany subsequent dishes of this fish; but then they had every right so to do, they knew no better!

POULTRY
AND GAME

Poultry and Game

To Roast a Goose Digestibly
Goose Pudding for Serving with a Roast Goose
Apple Stuffing for a Roast Goose – Sage and Onion Stuffing
Devilled Goose
How to Preserve a Goose
Pheasant Cutlets Pandora
French Pheasant for a Dinner
Starling Pie
Woodcock Pie
Roast Partridges
How to Roast Snipe
Roasted Grouse
Roast Capercailzie
Venison
How to Roast a Haunch of Venison
To Boil a Capon As I Did for His Grace the Duke of Holdernesse
My Way with Jugged Hare

TO ROAST A GOOSE DIGESTIBLY

As Mr Holmes was wont to be distinctly Vulgar about the propensities of fatty goose upon the digestion I shall refrain from quoting him upon this matter.

ASSEMBLY
1 fat goose and nothing else!

PROCEDURE
Place the goose upon a wire rack (*from a modern grill-pan, F.C.*). Take a table fork in each hand and stab the bird all over with prongs until it is evenly and completely pitted with small holes. Place rack and treated bird in a baking tin and roast in a fair oven (*Gas Mark 4/5, mid shelf, F.C.*). After one hour and a half withdraw all from your oven. Lift bird and rack upon the table. It will be seen that surplus fat has oozed out through the fork holes to run down the sides and flanks in little trickles and thus fall into the pan below. By the time roasting is completed, so much fat will have run out in this fashion that there might be danger in not draining off the fat as it accumulates. Allow as a general rule, and if your fire is drawing well, twenty minutes for the first pound and fifteen minutes for every pound thereafter.

You will then observe how the fat conveys with it some particles of escaping juice – not enough to diminish flavour; but unquestionably, as you will see, sufficient to darken the path of the rivulets, until by the time the bird is completely roasted the whole skin will have crisped up and become deliciously edible while turning a rich mahogany brown. Thus is it rendered altogether delectable and at the same time the more delicate stomachs, which otherwise suffer from eating this bird, may partake without the slightest qualms for their digestions.

GOOSE PUDDING FOR SERVICE WITH A ROAST GOOSE

My gentlemen always ate Goose Pudding with Roast Goose and I have heard Mr Holmes expounding upon this pudding to Dr Watson. He informed his friend that it originated in the county of Yorkshire, the county which claims Yorkshire pudding for its own, though I have learned from Mrs A. B. Marshall that this claim is in fact false.

ASSEMBLY

4 thick slices from a Coburg loaf; 3 oz finely chopped, skinless beef suet (*use packet suet! F.C.*); 3 tablespoons skinned, chopped Spanish onion fried softly in a little butter (*and then carefully drained, F.C.*); a little sweet, new milk (*sic, F.C.*); salt and pepper to season; 1 neatly rounded teaspoon crumbled, dried sage.

PROCEDURE

Soak the bread in water until pappy. Wring out in a piece of clean linen and then turn into a mixing bowl. Add the suet, onion, sage, a flat teaspoon of salt, a flat eggspoon of black pepper and bind to a loose dough with milk. Turn into a medium pie dish, which you have brushed with some of the fat from the roasting goose and put into a steady oven (*Gas Mark 6, F.C.*) for thirty to thirty-five minutes. Serve fat slices with each portion of goose.

APPLE STUFFING FOR A ROAST GOOSE

ASSEMBLY

12 good pippins, peeled, cored and sliced thinly; 2 oz goosefat from a previous roasting; 1 flat teaspoon each of powdered cinnamon, powdered ginger and powdered cloves; a generous pinch of pepper; 1 oz Barbados sugar; 2 oz coarsely mashed, fresh, white Stilton cheese.

PROCEDURE

Dissolve the fat in a frypan, add the prepared apples and turn fry over a gentle fire until pappy. Work in all remaining ingredients being careful to blend them very thoroughly. Place in a linen piping bag (*nylon icing bag, F.C.*) without any piping tube affixed. Place the narrow, filled end of the bag into the vent end of the goose and thus easily squeeze out the contents into the goose's interior.

SAGE AND ONION STUFFING

ASSEMBLY

3 lightly rounded teaspoons crumbled, dried sage; 3 generously rounded teaspoons finely chopped parsley heads; 3 oz suet; 6 oz fine, soft breadcrumbs; 1 flat teaspoon salt; 1 flat eggspoon pepper; 10 oz finely minced, peeled Spanish onions; 2 large eggs.

PROCEDURE

Break eggs into a bowl and whip them very thoroughly. Turn all remaining ingredients into a mixing bowl and sift them together until well-blended. Work in the beaten eggs with a table knife and if needed to obtain a piping consistency of mixture, add a few tablespoons of good poultry stock. Follow the insertion procedure outlined in my preceding receipt for Apple Stuffing.

DEVILLED GOOSE

Please be so obliging as to turn to my receipt for Devilled Chickens' Legs which you will find on p. 40. The procedure is identical, replacing the fowl drumsticks and 'oysters' with the drumsticks and divided thigh pieces of a goose, plus, of course, the all important 'oysters'. This was a much favoured supper dish, when my gentlemen returned together after one of their frequent nocturnal adventures. It was also a great favourite of That Policeman whom I did not take to *ever*, if only for his constant belittling of my master's unique efforts – at the onset of a case – though he was quick enough to climb down at the end and take all the credit to himself; and also for his unsuitable habit of sitting to table with his knees spread wide and his hands clasped upon them in vulgar anticipation.

HOW TO PRESERVE A GOOSE

It is no mortal use *minding*, or trying to refute the fact that those Frenchies know a Very Great Deal when it comes to culinary matters, though many of their customs leave much to be desired! It was they who discovered that goose may be quite remarkably preserved, for use upon special occasions, by a method which is simplicity itself. They give to it some outlandish name which quite escapes me (*Confits D'Oies, F.C.*); but the flavour leaves nothing to be desired.

PROCEDURE

First skin a large, fatty goose, and take from the bird every particle of fat. This is most important. Place both fat and skins into a very large iron or earthenware pot. Divide the entire bird into neat pieces cutting through the bones, dividing each leg into two, also each thigh, but discarding the wing-tips altogether. (These may be placed in the stock pot that nothing be wasted.) Pack the goose portions neatly and firmly down upon the fat and skin. Lay small sprigs of fresh rosemary between, each one measuring 4 inches and using six altogether. When this be done, pour 1 pint of boiling water on to the portions. Cover close, seal the joins between lid and container with a fat sausage of flour and water paste rolled out to the thickness of a large pork sausage. Press this down securely all round and put your pot into a gentle oven (*Gas Mark 2, low shelf, F.C.*), and there leave for four hours. By which time all the water will have evaporated; but such is the nature of this fatty bird that all the portions will be completely covered with goose fat. Do no more, save carry the covered pot into a *cold, absolutely dry place*. When two or more portions are desired, then cut away the paste, remove the lid, excavate from the soft goose fat the number of pieces required, being careful to scrape the goose fat back which adheres to these pieces. Then cover and leave once more until the next time.

TO SERVE

Put a thick frypan over a fierce heat and when almost white with heat, place in the goose pieces. Immediately pour 2 fluid oz of cooking brandy over and shake the pan vigorously to maintain the flames for as long as possible. When they die down pour on one quarter pint of thick cream and remove pan to the side of the stove. Stir about with a wooden spoon, season with salt and pepper and when the cream be bubbled and somewhat darkened by the goose juices, and the pieces themselves be hot right through, set them upon pieces of crustless bread, passed through a mixture of 1 egg to 4 gills milk and both well beaten together. Then fry in hot oil briskly until puffed and golden brown. Pour the sauce over the goose pieces, scatter with fresh-chopped parsley heads and so send to table.

MR MYCROFT HOLMES' FAVOURITE DISH

Though I was not exactly partial to this brother of Mr Holmes' I am bound to say he did appreciate good cooking.

I must even so explain how such a Special Dinner Party Dish was put before Mr Mycroft. It has ever been my custom to cook any new dish before giving it to any employer's guest. This rule was made for me by my Lady who said, 'There is ample to concern a good hostess when giving a dinner party, without the added anxiety as to whether some new dish will come up to expectations.' She therefore decreed, 'Any new dish must be "rehearsed" before incorporating it in any of my menus.'

Thus it was at the time of my 'rehearsal' Mr Mycroft paid us a visit.

PHEASANT CUTLETS PANDORA

ASSEMBLY

$\frac{1}{2}$ lb pheasant breasts which have been cooked in butter in a slow oven until just tender; 2 tablespoons Spanish Sauce (for this please turn to p. 220); 1 small sherry glassful of sherry; 2 oz pâté de foie gras (*or substitute foie gras pâté, F.C.*); $\frac{1}{2}$ pint well-reduced stock obtained by simmering down the smashed bones and carcase of the pheasants until a very strong concentrate is obtained; $\frac{1}{4}$ oz leaf gelatine (*powder please, F.C.*); 1 large truffle chopped very fine (*optional, F.C.*); paprika; few sprigs watercress.

PROCEDURE

Ensure that the cooked pheasant flesh is free of all bones, skin and gristle. Pound in a mortar with a pestle and then mix in the Spanish sauce, sherry and foie gras. Add the strong game liquor into which you have stirred and dissolved the gelatine. Stir in the truffles. Stir over broken ice until on the point of setting. Pour on to an oiled marble slab (*bit of an old marble washstand does admirably! F.C.*) and leave until set, ensuring mixture is a good five eighths of an inch in thickness. Then with the tip of a very sharp pointed-end knife cut out in simulation of shortened, trimmed cutlets. Gather up the remainder, dissolve over hot water, stirring carefully and thus make more cutlets down to the last possible scrap. Take a nice round metal platter or silver dish and arrange in a slightly overlapping circle with finely forked or chopped aspic in the centre and as an outside border. Melt any remainders of aspic and pour carefully over the cutlets. Conceal any tiny imperfections which may result by piping the top of each over-lapping cutlet with tiny rosettes of whipped cream. Dust with powdered paprika and make an outer border at the last moment with sprigs of well-picked, washed and dried watercress.

FRENCH PHEASANT FOR A DINNER
(Faisan Souvaroff, F.C.)

PROCEDURE

Take a plump pheasant which has been hung until high. Pluck and draw, but do not truss at this juncture. Poach 6 medium-sized truffles for five minutes in $6\frac{1}{2}$ fluid oz of Madeira – a Verdhelo will be admirable for this purpose, also 6 fluid oz of a light meat glaze obtained by simmering down a pint and a quarter of game consommé until it is slightly syrupy. Then withdraw the truffles, and place them in a roomy, lidded terrine or earthenware casserole pot. Cut half a pound of foie gras into large dice, toss them into the truffle liquor and stiffen them by a brisk, three minutes poaching. Drain, stuff into the bird and truss it. Wrap it in de-rinded slices of No. 3 cut back bacon and lower it into the chosen cooking pot. Add the truffle liquor, another small port glass of the Madeira, the same of game gravy and place the lid in position. Make a flour and water dough to the consistency of rather moist bread dough. Shape into a long sausage and affix thus all around the lid to seal the contents in hermetically. Cook for forty minutes very briskly. (*Gas Mark $7\frac{1}{2}$, one shelf above centre, F.C.*) Carry to table. Run a sharp knife through the sealing-crust so that the diners may take the remarkable odour which escapes. Carve and serve with a truffle to each person and some of the pan liquor.

Note: Some cooks prefer to turn the stuffed bird in the truffle liquor over a brisk fire and under a lid (when not turning) for twenty-five to thirty minutes, then seal it and cook in the oven for only fifteen minutes, but this has never been my way. *Mrs Hudson.*

STARLING PIE

My dear father had a sister, some years older than himself, who lived in Essex. When I was a little girl my father would take me there on a

Poultry and game

tram. We walked, I remember, along the Hainault Road in the pretty village of Leytonstone and from there father would set out with two of his Hoxton cronies to shoot Starlings for a Pie. He it was who taught me that for a good pie there must always be one or two small, sweet young turnips and a tumblerful of porter in the gravy. As the little birds were shot so my father and his two friends pulled off their heads right at the body line. Then they were given to me to pluck. I shall never forget the first time he saw me laboriously picking out the little feathers – 'That's not the way of it my girl,' he cried, 'here give that to me,' and so saying took the bird from me, ran a horny thumb between skin and flesh where the neck had come away and with a quick jerk split feathers and skin to the vent. Then he took both sides of the skin and ripped them off in a trice, feathers and skin too! It then was but the work of a moment to remove the odd feather, gut and clean the little things and then wipe and season them for the pot.

Many years later when I was beginning to learn cookery with Cook at my Lady's house she, going to work on three brace of partridges, did exactly the same thing. When I timidly asked her why she did not use the skin she said sharply, 'skin on birds is for spit roasting, not for cooking in fine sauces. It would not be at all the thing to leave the skins on for this my girl', and of course ever since then I have always pluck/skinned my poultry and game the quick, easy way, except, as Cook ruled, when roasting by spit and basting before the fire.

ASSEMBLY

40 starlings, well salted and peppered inside; 4 smallest young turnips; 2 dozen shallots; a pint of Brown Sauce; 1 tumblerful of porter;* 6 spring carrots, scraped, washed and then cut into rounds very thinly; 4 hard-boiled eggs (eight minutes is the time for these); 1 dozen small forcemeat balls (see p. 86) the size of a dessert gooseberry; about 1 lb of puff paste, made Francatelli's way (see p. 156).

PROCEDURE

Take a generous-sized deep pie dish and a pie funnel for the centre. Put this into the dish and put twenty starlings around. Scatter half the peeled shallots and sliced carrots in between, and half the peeled, quartered turnips. Do the same all over again. Mix the porter with the Brown Sauce. Stir well together, pour over the pie dish contents, cover with a piece of parchment (*foil, F.C.*) and put into a slow oven (*Gas*

* A dark brown, malt liquid thus called because it became a great favourite with Smithfield Market Meat Porters.

83

Mark 3, F.C.) to cook until tender but not quite come to the falling-off-the-bone stage. Take from the oven, uncover and leave in the larder (*refrigerator, F.C.*) overnight. In the morning, sink in the hard eggs, quartered lengthwise and the forcemeat balls. Wet the pie dish edges and roll out the puff paste with little jerky movements which makes air bubbles form very quickly. Roll out to a mean ¼-inch thickness. Put over the pie and scissor through the edges with 1 inch overhanging. Tuck in the overhang and pinch strongly between finger and thumb to make the edge fluted. Make an X in the paste where it rests upon the tip of the pie funnel. Fold back the four little points and brush all over the top of the paste with 1 small egg first beaten and then strained, and mixed with 1 tablespoon of pure olive oil and a flat-teaspoon of salt. This is the mixture which imparts a high, fine, brown glaze when baking is completed. Put immediately into a strong oven fairly high up, about 5-inches from the roof and let bake until pale brown and highly risen (*Gas Mark 7, F.C.*). Take quickly out and re-install in your cool oven to cook on. I recommend twenty-five minutes for the first baking and a further twenty minutes in the slow oven. The treatment ensures layers of melting, paper-thin pastry leaves as if laid one upon the other which of course it is not. Please remember that the same may be done for a Pigeon Pie; when you must use only the breasts of these pestiferous birds.

BROWN SAUCE (*Sauce Espagnole*)

ASSEMBLY

1 medium, coarsely-grated onion and carrot; 1 sprig thyme; 1 crushed bay leaf; 4 oz finely-chopped celery; 1 oz each butter and oil; 1 tablespoon Madeira, or cooking sherry.

PROCEDURE

Put both butter and oil in a small thick pan. When 'singing', add all remaining ingredients and simmer with great gentleness until all are tender. Use in the Sauce.

MIREPOIX

ASSEMBLY

1 oz each of butter and flour; 2 pints strong, brown stock; 4 oz skinned rough-cut tomatoes.

PROCEDURE

Dissolve butter in small thick pan. Stir in flour and continue stirring until this mixture is brown. Add stock gradually. Beat it well before each further addition. Add tomatoes. Now poach for three minutes precisely and stir in *mirepoix*. Strain and press down in strainer to extract every drop of moisture/flavouring.

WOODCOCK PIE

In Yorkshire, Mr Holmes had some friends whom I believe became so after being clients. In gratitude to Mr Holmes they were in the habit o sending him two brace of woodcock at regular intervals during the season. These I was always instructed to 'make up into the Woodcock Pie which Her Most Gracious Majesty enjoyed having made in the Royal Kitchens when she was at Osborne'. Here is the receipt for same.

ASSEMBLY

4 woodcock; 4 shallots; 1 faggot of herbs; 1 lb minced, lean veal; ¼ lb minced, raw unsalted pork fat; 2 large truffles sliced thin; salt; pepper; 2 quarts water; ¾ lb puff paste; 1 egg and 2 hard-boiled eggs; 1 port glass brimming with port; 2 tablespoons brandy.

PROCEDURE

Bone out the woodcocks, after plucking and drawing. Put the bones in a stewpan with the gizzard, heart and liver of all four birds. Add the cold water, faggot of herbs and shallots, plus the drained fluid in which the truffles were tinned. Bring to the boil over a strong fire. Withdraw to the edge of the stove and skim, then simmer gently for two hours. Strain and reduce by further simmering to half a pint. Add to it the port, stir in the brandy and set aside.

Lay out the woodcock skin-side downwards. Mix the veal, pork fat, some salt and black pepper, divide equally between the four birds and spread over. Place in a pie dish one woodcock, forcemeat uppermost, and strew a quarter of the truffles in between. Repeat three times more which absorbs all the birds, forcemeat and truffles. Slice the hard-boiled eggs and spread them overall. Cover the pie with about ¼-inch thick puff paste and wash over the raw, beaten, strained egg. Put into a strong oven and bake for thirty minutes until golden brown. Remove to a very gentle oven (*Gas Mark 7 and then 3, F.C.*) and let the pie be for at least a further forty-five minutes. Pour your sauce through the hole left at centre and either send to table or put into your larder to become cold.

ROAST PARTRIDGES

According to my Master's tastes these birds must always be filled with a certain forcemeat about which he was Very Particular. 'Good wine needs no bush, as we all know,' he would acknowledge and then go on to say, 'but there is an exception to every rule and in my opinion a forcemeat is essential, whether this "bushes" it or not!' at which Mr Watson would always laugh heartily.

Note: These birds (two for this receipt) must be hung for at least five days. Then pluck, draw and truss them.

ASSEMBLY FOR THE FORCEMEAT (FOR EACH BIRD)

2 oz fine crumbs; as much salt and also pepper as will stand upon a threepenny piece; 6 grates of a nutmeg; 1 oz sweet butter; a flat teaspoon finely chopped, fresh parsley; 1 teaspoon strained lemon juice.

PROCEDURE

Dip two sheets of notepaper (*thick foolscap does very well, F.C.*) into pure olive oil. Peel, then mince finely 3 fat mushrooms and their stalks, and also mince 1 moderate-sized carrot, 1 small onion, 2 tablespoons parsley leaves and 6 leaves of thyme. Divide all these, well-mixed, into two equal portions, then spread them evenly over the oil-impregnated notepaper. Mix all forcemeat ingredients together and blend well. Stuff into the interior of each bird set upon its vegetable-spread paper in a baking tin. Cover the breast of each with very fatty bacon tied securely into position with fine twine, and bake in a good oven for thirty-five minutes basting twice during this period. Pray now turn your attention to the accompanying Sauce. For it, you must put ½ pint of very good, cleared stock into a sauce saucepan with 1 shallot or very small onion and let it simmer thirty minutes. Strain, thicken with 1 dessertspoon flour, 2 tablespoons claret and the minced vegetables from the papers. Allow to boil up, maintain four minutes and serve.

HOW TO ROAST SNIPE

Mr Holmes was wont to observe when I removed the silver meat-cover from a dish of snipe that, 'if there were no grouse to be obtained I dare swear Snipe would be regarded as the greatest delicacy'.

Poultry and game

PROCEDURE

To roast snipe you must first pluck the birds very carefully. The skin is extremely tender and must not be torn. Singe well and truss *without drawing*. This is extremely important. Hang the birds from a jack-spit and before a strong fire and allow them to become well-heated. Then baste them frequently with good, sweet butter. After five minutes place 1 slice of buttered toast in a shallow container below and be sure, thereafter, to hold a dish under the birds when re-basting. The droppings of the trail will fall upon the toast, providing what gentlemen like mine consider to be an even greater delicacy than the birds themselves! I cannot abide them, but that is of no consequence! When roasting has completed for eleven minutes precisely, take down, remove all trussings, place a bird upon each toast, set a fat slice of lemon beside and hand a gravy boat of melted butter.

Note: As Dr Watson has always maintained snipe are not fit to eat unless served piping hot. It is advisable for gentlemen who are dining alone and are devoted to snipe, to lay finger bowls and provide extra table-napkins. They get themselves in a sorry mess with nibbling the bones!
Having supplied you with the perfect method, it is only fair to say that, if well basted, with the birds set upon their toasts in the oven – and given twelve minutes in a fierce one – they do very well if not perfectly.

ROASTED GROUSE

This is the King of game birds. My Master, whose contacts included some of the Noblest in the Land, was habitually in receipt of game-bags throughout the shooting season. I have even known him to break off a very serious investigation in order to return home for a feast of grouse! Very partial to them he was, always.

PROCEDURE

Pluck and draw the birds. Place 3 oz butter inside each. Place them in a baking pan and bake them briskly in a good oven for five minutes, basting when half this period of time has elapsed. Lift them on to prepared Toasts. The slices of bread must be $\frac{3}{4}$-inch in thickness and with all crusts removed. You then place the birds' livers in a very small pan with a few spoonsful of consommé and allow them to simmer gently under a lid for four minutes. Drain them, pound them to a paste with 4 oz butter, 2 very generous pinches of cayenne pepper and 2 small pinches of salt. Spread this mixture thickly upon the toasts. Roast birds thus for thirty minutes in a brisk oven (*Gas Mark 6, mid-shelf, F.C.*) for very plump birds, twenty-five minutes for slightly smaller ones. During roasting, cover the breasts with slices of the very best, de-rinded back Bacon No. 4 cut, and remove just before the bacon becomes crisp. Keep warm, serve with the grouse on toast. Also hand fine crumbs of bread fried in butter until lightly browned and rather crisp and a very clear thin gravy made by stirring a teaspoon of flour – no more – into the pans' residue and then incorporating ½ pint of consommé including that in which the livers have been poached. Some people insist upon red currant jelly as well but Mr Holmes would not hear of it. I once made the mistake of sending it to table. His cry of, 'Oh Mrs Hudson not *jam* with *game*! this is a most noxious mixture and positive ruination to a discerning palate,' ensured, I never served it again.

ROAST CAPARCAILZIE

PROCEDURE

When plucked, drawn and trussed, place the grouse in a well-buttered baking tin and cover each breast with very fatty bacon, this will remain upon it or them until roasting is completed. Baste frequently and bake in a moderate oven for one and a half hours (*Gas Mark 4, mid-shelf, F.C.*). Send to table with bread sauce, brown gravy and segments of skinless orange.

VENISON

I never ceased to be astonished at the extensive and detailed knowledge which my Master displayed upon every subject. He was a walking encyclopaedia, which no doubt accounted in some part for his detection talents when one considers it in relation to a Most Sharp Perception At All Times. Never was this more in evidence to me than when Mr Holmes inquired of me, 'What can you tell me about your capabilities for cooking venison?' (as the Gentry called this meat). Even at this time, so early in my association with him, I could perceive that he had not yet finished so I made no reply. Sure enough he went on, 'It is my considered opinion that a woman may not be called a good cook for single men unless she has a proper knowledge of the selection and preparation of a good piece of venison, so pray tell me what experience you have in this matter?' Saying which he tilted his long head somewhat to one side and placing his long fingers tip to tip dwelt upon my words with great thought as I uttered them.

I replied, 'I was taught sir, in my last place, that there are three kinds which are most known to us in the British Isles, the red deer which comes principally from Scotland and Ireland, the roe deer which is obtained in the North of England and the fallow deer which is the most readily obtainable in England, a great deal of which comes from Hampshire in the New Forest. I also reckon sir,' I continued, 'that the buck deer is the best of these three and I do not care to purchase it for your consumption save in the months of October, November and December.'

'For how long do you consider venison should be hung?' he then asked. 'Provided,' I stipulated, 'that the weather be cold – for venison is a temperamental flesh which in mild weather may turn off with alarming rapidity – I allow three weeks and rub daily with ground ginger and black pepper'... I got no further. Mr Holmes leaped to his feet, 'Say no more,' he said, 'you know your subject Mrs Hudson and I congratulate you. Just bear in mind that twice *per diem* is a wise precaution in the matter of wiping and seasoning cut pieces, as is the practice of driving a skewer well along the bone, that you may ascertain by smelling the skewer thereafter, that it is still perfectly sweet!' I wisely forbore from telling my Master that he had not given me time to add this to what I had said, and thereinafter I set about obtaining a good haunch for his delectation and pleasure.

HOW TO ROAST A HAUNCH OF VENISON

Begin by wiping the haunch well with a clean cloth then, remembering that a haunch is not at all a fatty cut, bard* well with a larding needle and strips of raw unsalted pork fat. Then paint it all over, while it is cold and dry, with dissolved butter until a coat of this is clearly seen.

Make up a paste consisting of at least 1½ lb sifted flour and cold water to bind to a good rolling dough. Roll this out very gently upon a floured marble slab being careful not to stretch the paste in anyway whatever! It is the stretching which causes the paste to crack and split during roasting time. Then put into a fairly brisk oven (*Gas Mark 5*,

---

* From the French 'barder' – to cover a piece of meat, poultry or game with a slice of raw, unsalted pork fat from the rind, to offset the dangers of drying the parts during cooking time. F.C.

mid shelf, F.C.), allowing thirteen minutes to every pound when enclosing it in the paste as above described. Having estimated and noted the finishing time, withdraw the haunch twenty minutes before completion. Remove the flour and water paste and discard this (unless so be you have a dog who will consume the meaty paste with astonishing vigour) and baste the haunch with more butter. Sift flour lightly over all and return to the oven that the flour and butter may combine and brown delicately in the remaining cooking time. Dress the haunch upon a heated dish, surround with half sections of lemon that each serving may have one upon it, and be prepared to have the carving instructions ready to pass on if your employer be a young and inexperienced housewife.

TO CARVE A HAUNCH OF VENISON

Begin by making a sharp slice right across the knuckle end. This ensures a good flow of gravy. Then make your slices thinly right down the length of the haunch, remembering that the choicest part is where the fat is. This will be found to be chiefly upon the left side, from which derives the somewhat sarcastic nickname 'alderman's walk'.

TO BOIL A CAPON AS I DID FOR HIS GRACE THE DUKE OF HOLDERNESSE

ASSEMBLY

1 good fat capon; 2 quarts cleared, well-reduced chicken stock; ½ lb button mushrooms, scalded but left unskinned; one dozen very small, scraped, young carrots; 2 lb potatoes (peeled weight); 2 dozen shallots; a faggot of potherbs; salt and pepper.

PROCEDURE

Take a medium, preferably oval, fish kettle or sturdy iron stock pot. Into the centre, upside down, place an un-chipped enamel basin and set upon it an enamel plate just large enough for the capon to sit upon. Set the capon thereon in the pot. Bring the cleared, reduced stock to the boil, season with salt and pepper to taste, pour over and it should come just over the rim of the plate on the upturned bowl. Cover with a well-fitting lid, bring back to the boil and simmer for approximately forty-five minutes. Then slide down the sides, the mushrooms, their removed stalks, the onions and the carrots. Simmer again under the lid for a further half an hour. Add the potatoes and when these be ready, set the capon upon a large, heated dish. Then drain away all the liquor into a separate pan and set this over the open maw of your stove with a strong fire burning, that the liquor may reduce somewhat while you are arranging, in neat little piles about the bird, the mushrooms, carrots, shallots and potatoes. When all be so positioned, scatter fine-chopped, fresh parsley heads overall, together with a light sprinkling of salt and of black pepper milled fresh from peppercorns. Pour the reduced liquor into a jug for family occasions, that each member may take a small bowl of the liquor for soup before coming to the capon and vegetables with the remaining liquor as their gravy.

When this dish be intended for guests, reduce the liquor very strongly to a mere 1 pint. Add to it one ½ pint of thick cream and simmer both on until a nice pouring consistency is obtained. It may also be thought advisable to carve up the capon into neat portions in the kitchen, arrange them on a very large heated dish with the vegetables arranged as already explained, and then to pour the sauce over all that each person may help themselves to everything without delay. This Mr Holmes preferred.

MY WAY WITH JUGGED HARE

Serve this upon a chilly night in heated soup plates and let there be side containers of Red Currant Jelly, Red Cabbage, Mashed Potatoes and cut lemon slices.

ASSEMBLY

1 hare, left un-skinned for eight days after being shot, hanging by his hind feet in a cold place and with his head tied up in a piece of parchment (*foil, F.C.*); 1 quart old ale; 1 quart rich beef stock, well reduced; the thinly peeled rind of 1 lemon; nutmeg, ginger, cayenne pepper and salt to bring out the flavour to your desire; 3 port glasses of inferior port; flour in which to turn the joints; clean beef dripping in which to fry them; a faggot of herbs.

PROCEDURE

When the eight days be passed and the belly of the hare be green, skin him, gut him and be sure to capture all the blood into a basin, for it be precious for the sauce. Cut the hare up into neat joints. Set aside the liver. Dissolve about 6 oz dripping in a large iron frypan and when this sings with heat, turn the hare pieces thickly in flour and fry them over a very brisk fire until they be browned all over. Lift each one out into a large earthen or iron oven-pot. When all be fried, pour on the beer and stock, add the lemon peel, sink in the herb faggot and season with all seasonings lightly. The balance may be rectified in a further process when the time comes. Cover close, set in a slow oven (*Gas Mark 2/3, F.C.*), put at least one shelf below centre. Let it lie, cooking thus for several hours, that the flesh be ready to fall from the bones when taken up. When this is come about set all the hare pieces upon a heated platter, tent them over with oiled parchment (*aluminium foil, F.C.*) and slip into a cool oven to await your readiness.

Take up the liver into a very small stew pan and put with it about 1 medium ladleful of the pot liquor. Now cook with great gentleness, take up when tender and rub through a hair sieve that the resultant paste may be employed for the final thickening of your sauce. As soon as this paste be ready, pound it in a mortar with a fat piece of butter (*3 oz, F.C.*) and then work in the reserved blood. Thereafter work ladlefuls of hare liquor among it until the liver paste is all vanished. Pour into the pot, remove the herb faggot and the lemon peel. Stir about over fierce heat and let it bubble strong until it be of the desired sauce-consistency. Stir in the port, give it a moment or two to regain its proper heat and bubble well. Strain over the hare and arrange small tufts of well-picked water-cress about the rim of the dish.

MEAT

MEAT

A Ham Cooked the Way Mr Sherlock Holmes Liked Best
To Transform Slices of York Ham into a Delicious Dish
To Glaze a Ham
My Special Ham
A Carpet Bagged Steak
My Kidney and Oyster Pudding
Mutton Navarin
Mutton Chops in Dressing Gowns
My Roast Leg of Mutton
Hotch Potch
Pish-Pash
My Boiled Salted Brisket of Beef
My Parchment Baked Pork Chops
Topsy-Turvy Pie

A HAM COOKED THE WAY MR SHERLOCK HOLMES LIKED BEST

ASSEMBLY

1 York ham (anything else would be unthinkable for Mr Holmes); 4 fat twists of sweet hay knotted loosely together; 1 gallon good pork bone stock; 1 pint rough cider; one 1-inch stick of cinnamon; 4 torn bay leaves; a dozen parsley stalks, (all the flavour is in these and NOT the heads); 4 peppercorns.

PROCEDURE

Place the ham in a roomy container and cover completely with cold spring water. Leave to steep for a clear twenty-four hours. Remove, place in the sink and scrub well under the cold tap with a really hard-bristled brush. Then place in a fish kettle or some such container which possesses a well-fitting lid. Tip over the bone stock and the cider. Sink in the hay (which imparts a special sweet flavour to the ham), further immerse the bay leaves, parsley stalks, cinnamon and peppercorns, cover and raise sharply to boiling point. Steady off at a gentle simmer and maintain for one and a half hours. Turn ham over. At this point slip a piece of wood underneath to ensure the skin-side has no chance of catching on the base. Replace the lid and maintain until the rind, when turned over again, peels back easily. Lift out carefully, drain and set on a very large dish. Then remove all the rind. Discard it and leave the ham overnight to become completely cold. By this time a certain amount of natural juices will have escaped and formed themselves into a jelly on to which some fat will have dripped down. Remove this. Place the ham upon a ham stand and gather up the clear jelly into a pan. Allow this to dissolve on the side of the stove and then stir it over some broken ice (*ice cubes*, F.C.) until it becomes syrupy. Pour over the fatty top of the ham and if it does not create a complete film the first time, spoon up and over until it does.

Note: Mr Holmes, like my previous employer, spoke out very strongly against what he regarded as the iniquitous habit of coating the tender fat with gritty crumbs. These he claimed 'wholly ruin the flavour of the fat and constitute a heinous innovation'.

TO TRANSFORM SLICES OF YORK HAM INTO A DELICIOUS DISH

Mrs Agnes Bertha Marshall, to whom I have previously referred, wrote this treatment in her weekly magazine *The Table* to which my Lady subscribed in later years. She gave me her copies to study. Later, when Mr Holmes engaged me, I was able to afford my own annual subscription. I have no hesitation in placing on record that this beautiful and talented cookery teacher had no equal. Alas, she died in what some have called Highly Suspicious Circumstances in either 1900 or 1901. There is further somewhat mysterious and contradictory information concerning this demise.

ASSEMBLY

1 quart of the liquor in which a York ham has been cooked in the manner previously described; 6 thick slices of York Ham; black pepper to season; 2 teacupfuls of thick cream.

PROCEDURE

Place the cleared liquor in a thick, clean pan and simmer until it is reduced to one half pint. Add the cream and simmer again until smooth and creamy. Place the ham slices in a very shallow container – one suitable for immediate contact with bare gas flame or coals from an open range – and pour the sauce over. Season with pepper, and just as soon as the ham is heated through dish up and dress with little triangles of crustless toast.

Note: Doctor Watson was so particularly partial to this dish that he would sit waiting for its appearance with a napkin tucked into his collar. When I carried it in he invariably rubbed his hands together in pleasurable anticipation and cried, 'Capital! Capital! There is nothing that I enjoy more, Mrs Hudson!'. I recommend serving it with a purée of well-seasoned potatoes and another of sieved spinach.

For these receipts see pp. 132 and 134 respectively.

TO GLAZE A HAM

When the ham be cooked tender, take him up and dry him completely. Remove the rind carefully leaving a nice even surface of fat beneath, and place in a meat roasting tin. Now blend together very thoroughly half of one small teacup of *thick* honey, 2 tablespoons dry, English mustard and as much orange curaçao as will blend the mixture to a firm spreading texture. Spread over the ham, slip immediately into a fairly fast oven (*Gas Mark 6, F.C.*) and let him be for thirty minutes. During this time place a long extremely thin poker, (*or a long steel knitting needle or skewer, F.C.*) between the bars of the fire (*gas! F.C.*) and let it become red hot. On removing the ham, and with renewals of heat for the (wiped) implement, criss-cross the top surface which will smoke and zing each time you lay the poker upon the glazed fatty surface of the ham.

MY SPECIAL HAM

When the Duke of Holdernesse came to us, Mr Holmes rang the bell some time beforehand and advised me of this fact. That Boy was below stairs. I returned thence, pausing to visit my bedroom where I removed my best black bombazine from its covers in my wardrobe, and, as it was a fine day first shook it out and then hung it upon my clothes line in the yard to dispose of the strong smell of moth balls, it having been unused for some considerable time. I also set out my new black boots, and my mother's hair brooch which my dear father left to me when he passed on. Then I continued with my usual preparations; making quite sure that That Boy clearly understood that upon the pain of immediate banishment for ever should he disobey me, he remained below stairs until given permission by me to show himself above them again.

On Mr Holmes' instruction I then prepared our best silver tray with sherry which Mr Holmes decanted personally into one of those round, flat bottomed decanters which he informed me were named 'ship's decanters', the shape being designed to stand steady when a ship was upon rough seas. Then I set to work upon My Special Ham. I determined to Be Prepared should this Distinguished Nobleman decide to partake of a light luncheon before departing. I had already prepared the necessary for a dish of white-bait (see p. 72) to precede it and Prince Albert's Pudding to follow (see p. 166). My Boiled Capon which would come between was now a-simmering gently upon the side of the stove. With a ripe Stilton upon the sideboard to eat with Bath Oliver

Biscuits and our best Irish crystal jug (*Waterford, F.C.*) filled with crisp celery, I decided this would do very well, it not being as it were a planned meal but, one to which his Grace had come by chance.

For My Special Ham receipt it is necessary to have young turnip tops and these, through the good offices of my friend the Carter I had obtained upon the very morning they were needed.

ASSEMBLY

1 small, wide-shouldered ham; 3 quarts veal stock, very strong and clear; 1 large onion quartered; 1 ditto carrot; 1 wisp of hay; 2 lb young turnip tops, washed very clean; 1 pint thick cream; 1 quart dry cider from the wood; 4 separated egg yolks; 8 peppercorns.

PROCEDURE

When the ham be thoroughly soaked that he may be sweet, place in a fish kettle with the hay, cider, veal stock and peppercorns. Cover with the lid, place over the open maw of a good, strong fire and bring fast to boiling point. Now skim very thoroughly and then close up the maw that the ham may simmer gently and steadily. When this balance be achieved thrust in the turnip tops and keep a-simmering until a small piece of the skin, when pulled, comes cleanly away. Raise up the ham by the inner tray to your fish kettle, let him drain over the pot and thus remove all the skin. Discard it, for regrettably I have yet to find a use for it. Take up the ham, enclose him carefully in parchment (*aluminium foil, F.C.*) and put him into the slow warming oven compartment. Remove the hay. Add to the liquor in the pot the onion and the carrot diced rough, and simmer open, upon the side of the stove 'til they be tender. By this time the liquor should be reduced considerably. Drain all the contents in a roomy colander. Remove the peppercorns from the drained remainders and then rub all through a tammy cloth (*tamis or sieve, F.C.*). Place the tammy material into a smaller, thick pan, add 1 pint of the drained liquor and half a pint of the thick cream. Set the remainder in a bowl and stir in very thoroughly the 4 egg yolks. Let the pan of cider and cream rest beside the stove until service. Then quickly stir in the egg and cream mixture, setting the pan over an outer one of hot water (*double saucepan, F.C.*), that your sauce may not curdle. Stir until thickly creamy. Draw right to the stove edge. Cut the ham thinly into slices, overlap them down a heated entrée dish and pour the sauce over, that the slices be completely submerged. Hand sippets of dry toast to accompany this dish which has gained considerable approbation from those who have eaten it by my hands.

A CARPET BAGGED STEAK

As porterhouse steak will cost you as much as 1s. 4d. per pound, it is advisable to reserve this dish for high days and holidays.

It was always my custom to acquaint my two gentlemen during their breakfast if I were intending to put this dish before them for their evening repast. Standing back respectfully, drawing their attention by a slight cough I would say, 'Mr Holmes, may I know sir if you have any anticipation of being late for supper tonight?' I was never able to complete. For with a jubilant shout Dr Watson would lay down his napkin and terminate for me, 'Carpet bagged steak Holmes, let us not commit ourselves dangerously today!'

ASSEMBLY

A very thick, solid iron frying pan of suitable dimensions for receiving and wholly containing 1 porterhouse steak; 24 cooking oysters, so opened as to retain their liquor in a small bowl; 1 peeled shallot; salt; pepper; ½ pint strong brown gravy; 1 lemon; a bunch of watercress.

PROCEDURE

Take your sharpest (*pointed*, *F.C.*) knife and lay down your porterhouse upon the wood of your kitchen table. Then cautiously and carefully, working from within 1-inch of each end, cut a 'mouth' in the flesh which takes the cavity to within 1-inch of the opposing side to the one in which you made your incision. With this done, rub both top and underside with the halved shallot working its juice and flavour well into the flesh. At this juncture place your thick iron frying pan upon the open coals that it may become white hot while being left perfectly dry. (*Gas Full On*, *F.C.*) Thread two needles with stout *white* cotton, double the thread in each and make a large knot at the paired ends of each one. Push in your oysters, so positioning them inside the centrally split steak that they are evenly distributed. Then sew up the incision, drawing the two halves close and neatly together and being sure to leave a long end hanging at the knot end so that this may be grasped with speed and ease when the steak be fried. When the pan is white hot, lay in the steak and let it sear violently for one minute. Turn over and repeat the searing again for one minute on the reverse side thus ensuring that all the juices are locked in. Now close up your stove opening, that the heat may be fairly strong, but not violently so and continue to cook for four minutes on each side. During this cooking time boil up your brown gravy, then draw to the side of the stove, turn in the oyster juice, taste, correct seasoning with pepper and add a very generous squeeze from half the cut lemon. When the steak be cooked as explained, put it upon a large piece of apple or pear wood set upon a dish. Arrange a tasteful bunch of well-picked and washed watercress at each end. Drive an ornamental skewer through the remaining cut lemon half and drive this at the slant into the centre of the steak. Take to table with a well-sharpened carver and carving fork, that the gentlemen may cut fat strips as they please. Remember to provide several neat fingers of crustless bread which they may lay into the escaping juices as they slice the steak. I would recommend no vegetables being served with this dish other than jacket-baked potatoes split, buttered and parsley-sprinkled at the moment of service.

MY KIDNEY AND OYSTER PUDDING

It was this receipt which won me the great honour of a Personal Call from Dr Watson's bride. This gentle lady appeared at the door of No. 221b and when I opened it put out a little gloved hand and inquired of me, 'Are you Mrs Hudson?'

When I acknowledged that this was so, she stepped in and withdrew a small notepad from her muff. 'Then,' she said, 'it is you whom I have come to visit. I have heard so much from my husband.' The pretty dear hesitated at the word, she was so new married she coloured up most charmingly, and then resumed, 'He has so extolled the virtues of your kidney and oyster pudding that I have ventured to come and ask if you would be so very obliging as to instruct me in your art of making this wonderful pudding.'

Well, I mean to say, who could refuse a request couched so flatteringly with just the right amount of hesitancy as to give me a very good idea of myself. I acceded to her request, asked madam if she would name a convenient day, and undertook to obtain all the necessary ingredients and to instruct her in the making of my pudding. 'Then,' said she, 'I shall be for ever in your debt. Now I know that this is a bachelor household but I may hope perhaps to prevail upon Mr Holmes to sit down with him thereafter and eat some of your pudding myself for luncheon.' Of course, anyone with such winning ways was bound to attain her objective, and thus it was that she came into my kitchen, took from her reticule a very small, and not at all adequate, apron and *learned from me*. It is, I do assure my readers, a *Very Simple Dish*.

ASSEMBLY

12 lambs' kidneys; 24 cooking oysters; 1 pint Espagnole sauce (see p. 84); 4 oz very finely chopped shallots; 10 oz sifted flour; 5 oz finely chopped, skinned beef suet (*packet suet, F.C.*); the strained juice of half a fresh lemon; a generous pinch of black peppercorns; some cold water; 1 heaped tablespoon baking powder.

PROCEDURE

Make up the suet crust first. Mix the flour with the suet and baking powder, bind to a firm, rolling dough with cold water. Roll out upon a floured surface to a $\frac{1}{2}$-inch thickness and line into a well-buttered 2 lb pudding basin. Trim off the edges level with the top. Now tie a cloth over below the outer rim of the basin, securing the cloth with fine string and allowing the four corners to fall well down to the table. Butter the top surface of the tied cloth carefully. Gather up the dough trimmings and re-roll into a lid. Place upon the top of the buttered cloth, cover right over with butter papers and bring the four corners up and over so that they further completely protect the dough lid. Immerse in a steamer over a base pan half filled with boiling water. Cover upper pan close with a well-fitting lid and allow to steam for one and a half hours. Meanwhile, prepare the filling. Skin and slice finely the kidneys. Open the oysters with a proper oyster knife, and over a bowl so that their liquid falls into the bowl. Add the oysters and the lemon juice. Place the sliced kidneys in a thick pan with the Espagnole sauce and simmer very gently over a low heat adding the prepared onions and the pepper. Cook thus for thirty minutes, then rest them on the side of your stove until the pudding be steamed. Unfold cloth, remove papers and gently lift off the dough lid. I find the best way to do this is to take two metal slices, butter them lightly and slide them beneath, then all may be done without the slightest fear of breaking. Turn the kidney mixture into the main, crust-lined basin, stir in the oysters and their fluid, lay on the dough lid and pinch the edges together very securely. Cover again with butter papers, tie down again with string and return to your steamer to simmer, allowing exactly six minutes from the time that the steam escapes freely from beneath the lid of your containers. To dish up, remove string, cloth and butter papers. Wipe basin carefully, pin a stiffly starched napkin around it and set it upon a silver dish. Then with a sharp knife cut a generous wedge from the lid, set this over the remainder and carry immediately to table.

MUTTON NAVARIN

I once heard Mr Holmes observe, 'In the ordinary way of it, I am of the considered opinion that cold mutton is grounds for divorce. In any circumstances a woman who puts cold mutton upon her table should be condemned to sit at it alone; but this dish of Mrs Hudson's is, I am compelled to acknowledge, very appetising, do you not agree?'

Alas, only, 'Mumble ... mumble ... mumble,' came from the good Doctor, but I could judge from the way his head nodded that this was intended as an affirmative. He, I should explain, had his mouth a trifle over-full for good manners at the time.

ASSEMBLY

1 well trimmed shoulder of mutton; some seasoned flour in which to turn and coat the removed pieces; drawn mutton fat in which to fry; good mutton stock; salt; pepper; a herb faggot; dry English mustard, Cayenne pepper, ground mace, ground nutmeg and ground cloves; 2 peeled but not crushed cloves of garlic, and pray let these be medium-sized for they must not be allowed to betray their presence, merely influence; 6 small round turnips which are really young; 6 lumps of sugar; $\frac{1}{2}$ lb red Lima beans.

PROCEDURE

Place the beans in plenty of cold water and let them lie overnight. In the morning drain them. Make up a supply, or draw upon that which has already been made, of seasoned flour (to be found on p. 217). Cut the trimmed shoulder into neat 2-inch lumps, turn them thickly in the seasoned flour and fry briskly over a vigorous fire until browned and thus sealed all over. Lift them and place one layer upon the base of a stout earthen casserole. Set the remainder aside awhile. Push in the two peeled garlic cloves. Scatter some of the strained, soaked beans over, and some of the turnips cut into halves, then into quarters and finally into three slices per quarter. Repeat with all your given ingredients until there remain no more upon your table.

Roll out your lumps of sugar in thick folds of brown paper. Toss them into a sturdy iron frypan with a walnut of butter. Let them turn the darkest possible brown and caramelise, for it is thus that you obtain true colouring with no substances therein which might prove deleterious to the human stomach. Add a little of your strong mutton stock and let all bubble up, then turn into the remainder of the stock and pour all over the casserole. Let it come to the rim only of the contents,

Meat

for thus will the contents of the seasoned flour both thicken and flavour for you. Place in a slow oven (*Gas Mark 2, F.C.*) and allow to cook until the meat is delicately tender. Then remove and bear to the larder. Then next morning remove every particle of grease from the upper surface, and about one and a half hours before the meal put back into your oven at the same temperature, that it may creep towards final heating and thickening. Please remember to taste before sending to table, that you may adjust your seasonings should they prove inadequate.

MUTTON CHOPS IN DRESSING GOWNS

ASSEMBLY

4 well-trimmed, lean mutton chops; 1 quart of good strong beef stock reduced by simmering until it is only ¼ pint; a generous pinch of salt and a small faggot of herbs; 1 finely chopped shallot; ¼ lb finely-chopped, unskinned mushrooms; two chopped, hard-boiled eggs; 2 rounded tablespoons sweet butter; 1 teaspoon strained lemon juice; 1 heaped tablespoon finely-chopped parsley heads; a quarter of a flat teaspoon salt; a good pinch of pounded-to-powder black peppercorns; 3 tablespoons heavy cream. A flattish dish or soup plate containing a thick bed of fine, soft, white breadcrumbs.

PROCEDURE

Pour half the reduced stock into a stew pan with a base just big enough to take the four interspersed chops. Pour over the remaining reduced stock, tuck down the herb faggot, add the pinch of salt, cover and cook over very gentle heat, drawing your stewpan to the side of the stove that nothing may be hard boiled. In fifteen or twenty minutes, depending upon the size of the chops, remove the chops and the herb faggot and simmer the liquor on until it be a glaze (*of syrupy consistency, F.C.*). Mix together the prepared parsley, shallot, eggs and the chopped mushrooms previously cooked for eight minutes in the butter and lemon juice. Bind all together with the cream. Spread this mixture very neat and thick upon the chops on one side. Press down into the crumbs. Spread the reverse side of each chop and press this side down upon the crumbs, so doing until both sides be liberally coated. See that your fire be well tended that the oven be hot and into it put the cutlets upon a buttered meat dish. Cook them so, for fifteen minutes and serve very hot upon a heated dish inside a border of my creamed potatoes (p. 133).

MY ROAST LEG OF MUTTON

So soon as I was to inform Mr Holmes that the meat course for his evening repast would consist of a Roast Leg of Mutton, so he would nod, take a puff at that great pipe of his and say through the enveloping cloud of smoke, 'Excellent, but pray Mrs Hudson let there be plenty of onion sauce!' It is my considered opinion that my employer consumed more of the latter than of the former, he being as you might say, an addict of Onion Sauce as he was I fear an addict of that dreadful syringe.

ASSEMBLY

1 medium leg of mutton; 3 very large carrots; 3 equally large onions and the same of celery heads, well-trimmed, and the outside leaves used for a soup that nothing be wasted; 2 rounded tablespoons of butter, and 2 flat ones of olive oil; 1 breakfast cup of boiling mutton bone stock; 1 quarter of a breakfast cup of wine vinegar; 1 bay leaf; 2 cloves of garlic peeled; 1 rounded teaspoon of salt; half one flat teaspoon of pounded black peppercorns.

PROCEDURE

Chop fine the onion, carrots and celery. Melt the butter and heat the oil with it in a thick stewpan. Draw to the side of your stove that the base heat be gentle, stir in the prepared vegetables, cover with a lid and leave them so, just giving the pan an occasional shake until all be golden and soft. Then stir in the stock, vinegar, torn bay leaf, whole garlic cloves and also the salt and pepper. Cover with the lid once more and allow to simmer for twenty minutes. Remove from the heat altogether, pour through a colander lined with a fold of muslin and allow drained liquid to become cold. Place the leg of mutton in a baking tin and set it in a fairly strong oven (*Gas Mark 6, mid-shelf, F.C.*). Leave it so for thirty minutes, then pour over the cold mixture and baste well. Repeat the basting every fifteen minutes until the mutton be cooked to the desired pink inside, preferred by my Eminent Employer, or right through if it be intended for less selective palates. Strain off the liquor, slice the meat upon the leg, so that the cut slices lie even and undisturbed in appearance save for the sliced, skin edges. Make your Onion Sauce while the leg be a-roasting.

MY ONION SAUCE

Rough-cut 1½ lb peeled Spanish onions, cutting them after into neat dice. Place them in a stewpan with 1 flat teaspoon of coarse salt and cover them meanly with boiling water. Cover all with a lid and simmer until the onions be quite tender. Strain them and let the liquor fall into a measuring jug. If it be more than one quarter of a pint in bulk then re-simmer it until this quantity is obtained. Add to it ½ pint of sweet milk and let it become heated on the very rim of your stove. Dissolve 1½ oz sweet butter in another stewpan. Stir in the same quantity of sifted flour and stir for at least three minutes thereafter, that the flour taste may be so cooked out from it. Add the milk gradually stirring and then beating after each milky addition until all be absorbed. Simmer on the side of the stove for twenty minutes, giving an occasional stir, turn in the cooked, chopped onions and stir them about. Thereafter stir in ¼ pint of thick, rich cream, taste, correct the seasoning if need be with more salt and pepper – onions are ever hungry for salt in their cooking this way – and at the last, just before dishing up, add a 1½-inch square, ½-inch-thick wedge of cream cheese. Stir it about until it vanishes into the sauce and hand it separate from the joint.

HOTCH POTCH

After an occasion when some Personage did us the honour of visiting us, and thus we had for our humble way of life a Very Elaborate Dinner, I would prepare, while doing my dinner dishes, a Hotch Potch for my little 'family' (*Baker Street Irregulars, F.C.*) to eat the next day.

ASSEMBLY

2 lb best end neck of mutton; 2½ quarts mutton bone stock; 6 young, scraped carrots, split lengthwise once; 1 small, white, tight cauliflower and its leaves, with the hard core stems removed; 1 very small, tight, white cabbage; 6 parsley stalks, since in them lies *all* the flavour; salt and pepper to season; 1½ pints shelled peas; 1 lb turnips; 10 shallots – onions will not do at all!

PROCEDURE

Trim surplus fat from neck, divide the pieces and trim again into neat cutlets. Pour boiling water over all prepared pieces in a roomy pan. Bring fast to the boil, allow to chill and carefully remove all risen top-crust of fat. Place meat pieces into a sturdy casserole. Strew over the chopped carrots, shallots, turnips, parsley stalks, coarse-sliced cabbage, sprigged cauliflower with chopped trimmed leaves and cover with the stock previously simmered down to 2 quarts. Place on the lid and put into a slow to medium oven (*Gas Mark 3, mid-shelf, F.C.*). Let it lie one hour. Add the peas and return that it may lie once more until all be perfectly tender. Taste, correct seasoning with salt and pepper, and if liked, a tablespoon of mushroom concentrate in fluid form. Drain off all but sufficient to *moisten* the remainder. Turn the liquor into a well-heated tureen and strew finely-chopped parsley heads liberally upon the surface to make all look pleasing. Send to table as a first course. Meanwhile, arrange the casserole contents agreeably upon a heated dish and border with nice, floury potatoes. Send to table as a main course.

Note: Such as be left of both courses may thereafter be mixed together, fine mashed, or for the meat fine-shredded, and then served to the kitchen as a left-over soup with stock upon the following day for midday dinner. This being what is ever taken below stairs.

PISH-PASH

This is a dish which for once I and Mr Holmes both appreciated, although it came from the good Doctor and he obtained it in India.

As he explained its coming about to me, it appears the English Residents were sadly lacking in those amenities which we more fortunate dwellers in a civilised country ever take for granted. They had outside their 'bungalows' raised up on stilts like storks, what were called 'compounds' *where the chickens roamed*. 'But,' I now quote Dr Watson, 'there was little to peck upon in hard packed sandy surfaces like these and thus the fowl were stringy and lean and rather tough.' 'So,' the Doctor continued, 'we hit upon a way of treating them other than in our *daily* (imagine!) curries, and some English lady, in years gone by, named the dish Pish-Pash.'

I must confess it is both easy to make and very palatable when made even with a very old boiling fowl.

ASSEMBLY

1 large old boiling fowl, plucked, drawn and divided with head removed, neck retained, also liver, heart and crop; 2 lb very thinly sliced, peeled, Spanish onions; 2 or more quarts milk; 2 torn bay leaves; 1

tiny pinch of turmeric; 1 blade of mace entire; salt and pepper; a little cream if liked; ½ lb Patna rice.

PROCEDURE

Cut the bird into small neat pieces using a pair of those frenchified Game Secateurs to divide the legs, thighs and wings. Strew the prepared onions, just a single layer, upon the base of a deep, tall, sturdy casserole. Lay thereon a layer of chicken pieces, sprinkle lightly with salt and pepper, scatter on a little of the rice and so proceed, using up all, and burying the blade of mace and the two pieces of each torn bay leaf therein. Place neck, liver, heart and giblets in a pan with the well-smashed-down carcase of the old fowl. Use the flat side of a chopper for this. Cover liberally with cold water, bring to boiling, skim and then simmer for one hour. Strain off the resultant liquor into a clean pan and then simmer this down to one quarter of a pint. Mix with 2 pints of milk and pour all over the casserole's contents. Replace the lid and cook slowly in a mild oven (*Gas Mark 2, one shelf below centre, F.C.*) until all the milk has been absorbed by the rice. Now add a further pint of milk and continue covered-cooking until rice has again absorbed the milk. So do with more milk until the rice is soft and swollen and both the bird pieces and the rice are perfectly tender. The consistency at this stage should be soft but not runny. There should be no incidence of escaping fluid run out upon the plate when each portion is laid thereon BUT nor should the mixture be sufficiently dried out for it to doughy. To obtain this former, you merely cook on *after* all is tender for a short while and at precisely the same heat until the surplus moisture is taken up. For the latter you beat in according to your purse, single cream or more milk in which circumstance you only allow such longer time in the oven as is needed to heat the chosen addition. According to instructions from Dr Watson I served my gentlemen with this set upon heated soup plates and I also set spoons and forks for them to use for the eating of it.

MY BOILED SALTED BRISKET OF BEEF

One of the strictest orders (and the most tiresome I may say) I ever received from my Famous Employer concerned those ragamuffins to whom he gave the name 'My Baker Street Irregulars'. They were nothing more than street-Arabs and decency forbids me to give details of their appearance in a book devoted to Clean Cookery.

I must therefore confine myself to stating that, from the very first time I ever set eyes upon that Wiggins and his disreputable companions, I made my own rules and Mr Holmes made his.

Hands and necks had to be scrubbed, hair washed, dried and all submitted to inspection before I would consent to feed any of them. I also found it imperative to include their ears. I will say no more. Then and then only would I put food before them, which they devoured on all occasions as if they had not broken bread for a week! Nor would I permit broken boots to be scuffed against the rungs of my kitchen chairs. Boots on the floor, heads bent for Grace was the order of every day for them; then food. Each boy had to carry his plate and mug (I obtained tinned ones for *them*) to the sink to wash, dry and replace. Gradually I began to instil in them some semblance of manners but it was uphill work!

Then Mr Holmes took a hand. Coming to the landing he called out, 'Cease this bedlam! I cannot have the house invaded in this way.' He halted them upon the stairs. Wiggins, the infant ringleader, looked up startled by this remonstrance. 'From now onward,' Mr Holmes said severely, '*they* report to you Wiggins, and *you* to me.'

I regret to state that this had not the slightest effect. On the next occasion, up those seventeen steps they scampered once again. In six years, though he shook a long finger disapprovingly and said, 'Now you children,' it was without the slightest effect and apparently my employer never seemed to have the slightest expectation of producing any.

When I was warned of their coming in, I would often give them a really filling dish of boiled beef and dumplings for which I used, not the good silverside which I salted and sent upstairs, but cheap beef brisket. I gave it them with potatoes boiled in the liquor, and also onions and carrots. I heaped it all into soup-plates and watched the mountains vanish with elbows out and shocking sucking sounds of street-Arab approval.

Here is the way of it:

Six days before service obtain a whole brisket, lay it upon the kitchen table and cut away all the surplus fat. Put this aside to render down, strain and thus put it to Other Uses.

Roll the piece up tightly, drive two skewers in, $1\frac{1}{2}$-inches from the base and one 1-inch from the top. Tie a piece of stout trussing string to the skewer's loop and draw the string around tightly until you can secure it again to the same loop. Do the same with the other skewer. Half fill a very roomy container with cold water. Put in handfuls of grated rock salt and stir well, adding more salt until an egg will float therein. Immerse the brisket. Wedge it down so that he rise not above the water level, using a piece of clean firewood. So leave in a cold place for six days. Take up, set in a deep pan or jam kettle. Immerse the now salted beef with cold water, cover and bring to the boil rapidly over the open fire (*full gas flame, F.C.*). When the liquor be boiling close the open maw and draw the pot away towards the stove sides until a steady but not fierce simmer be obtained. Maintain until meat be cooked one hour. Immerse at least 18 peeled Spanish onions of medium size. Add at least 8 fat carrots, scraped and split lengthwise each one into four strips. Cover again and cook on until both vegetables be tender. Lift them out, drain them, set them in their vegetable dishes, cover and put to wait in a cool oven (*Gas Mark* $\frac{1}{4}$, *F.C.*). Immerse $2\frac{1}{2}$ lb peeled old potatoes for the last 25 minutes of cooking which should be about now. When potatoes are tender, lift out, drain and keep warm as with the other vegetables. Take out the meat, put under a cover in its serving dish and keep this warm too. Return the pan to the open fire (*full gas, F.C.*) and as the liquor boils strongly immerse the dumplings (see following receipt) and let them simmer fairly hard. Place them around the meat, pour the liquor into a fat jug and serve. I always gave the poor little wretches a mug of this liquor each; albeit I could never teach them to keep their noses out of the mugs.

THE DUMPLINGS

Mix 1 lb of sifted self-raising flour with 6 oz of fine-chopped, skin-free mutton suet which be ever much better than beef for this purpose. Mix in 1 rounded teaspoon of best baking powder, 1 level teaspoon of kitchen salt and bind to a light, firm paste with cold water. Roll into quite small balls, drop into the boiling liquor and only lift out when swollen up and well-risen to the top. I ever cut one to try. Or if preferred the dumplings may go in with the potatoes to save time and then be removed after them.

MY PARCHMENT BAKED PORK CHOPS

Mr Holmes had a positive obsession for the number four. When I discovered this I ever made either four dishes for the tea table, four items for his breakfast or four courses for his evening meal. This latter of course persisted whenever he was so good as to appear for it, which was, alas, infrequent, for he had little or no sense of time and absolutely none of punctuality, which did create sore problems for me from time to time.

Thus, when making this dish I knew that four parchment parcels containing four separate smaller pork chops would be expected of me, rather than two very large ones.

ASSEMBLY

4 lean, neatly-trimmed pork chops of good thickness through the chop-eyes; 1 Bramley cooking apple; 4 teaspoons brandy; 4 dessertspoons thick cream; 4 tablespoons cider from the wood; pepper, salt and four small sprigs of rosemary spikes.

PROCEDURE

Cut your parchment sheet or rolls into four rectangles large enough to completely enclose the chops and their saucing and still leave enough for firm folds over across the tops and at the ends. (*Use oiled aluminium foil, F.C.*) Oil the parchments, lay down the chops centrally. Cover each with 1 part of the brandy, cream, cider, pepper, salt and rosemary. Peel, core and slice the apple extremely thinly in rounds. Lay these down over the assembly, using an equal amount for each chop. Fold as explained and bake in a moderate oven for twenty-five to thirty minutes, for pork be the one meat which must never be served until completely cooked through. Unfold the parcels, take out the rosemary which will by now have impregnated the entire dish, and slide the contents parcel by parcel on to a roomy, heated dish. Pick off the apple slices and set them in between the chops, letting the sauce lie where it has slid. Mr Holmes always expected triangles of crustless white bread to be fried crisp in pork fat and to be arranged about the dish.

TOPSY-TURVY PIE

This be another modest but filling dish which I would make in great quantity to fill those scallywags of Mr Holmes'.

ASSEMBLY

½ lb sausage meat; 1 large onion; 3 medium-sized tomatoes; 1 rounded tablespoon butter; 1 hard-boiled egg; 2 tablespoons olive oil; rough-puff paste (*use bought Jus-Rol, F.C.*), 1 flat dessertspoon Bovril; 1 teacup hot stock.

PROCEDURE

Slice the peeled onion fine, and dissolve the butter with the oil. Lay in the slices, somewhat to the side of your stove that they may cook yellow and tender without any fear of browning. Work in the sausage meat, season with salt and pepper, work in the stock and Bovril and allow to simmer for five minutes, turning and blending while you do thus. Peel and slice the tomatoes and butter the base of a Victoria sandwich tin liberally with some of the remaining butter. Slice the hard egg and lay these slices, interspersed with tomato slices, over the base of your prepared tin. Then turn the sausage-meat mixture over and pat and spread until very even. Cover with the paste crust rolled to a generous $\frac{1}{8}$-inch thickness and prick over the surface with a bodkin to let the steam out. Cook in a quick oven (*Gas Mark 7, one shelf above centre, F.C.*) until well risen and browned on top. When ready, ease off the pie base carefully, turn the pie upside down upon a hot dish and serve with a jug of good gravy and a big dish of jacket-baked potatoes split open and spread with the remainder of the given butter.

OFFAL

Offal

My Tripe
Haggis
Meg Dodd's Haggis
Cream of Sweetbreads for a Dinner Party
Potted Lambs' Brains in Clarified Butter
Some Uses for Potted Brains
Ox-Liver Made Delicate as Calves' Liver
How to Cook Liver and Bacon Properly
Pork Faggots
Scallywag Pie
My Devilled Kidneys

MY TRIPE

DR Watson was wont to say, rubbing his hands together at the table after tucking his serviette into his collar, 'Vulgar maybe, but I LIKE TRIPE and above all I like Mrs Hudson's tripe.'

Now in my very young days I had many occasions for being thankful that half a penny would purchase me a bowl of steaming tripe from a Hoxton street vendor. I would wrap my mittened fingers around the white tin mug with the Royal blue rim in which it was served to me, and thus warm them and sniff up the odour which at that time I thought quite splendid. In later years when my palate became accustomed to more recherché dishes I reflected often upon the merits of tripe cooked in a more luxurious manner. When in the service of Mr Holmes I heard Dr Watson speak wistfully of his desire for a 'steaming mug of tripe'. I set to work with, of course, *proper honeycomb tripe and not that single rubbish*! Eventually, after several attempts which did not satisfy me I found out the secret of this plebeian British Delicacy and gave it to my gentlemen who professed themselves well-pleased.

It is essential to grasp the two basic principles before embarking upon my creation. There *must* be twice the amount of onions to tripe and after the dish is completed, it must be allowed to go cold, rest for twenty-four hours in the larder and then be re-cooked in a mild oven for one further hour.

ASSEMBLY

2 lb honeycomb tripe; 4 lb peeled, very thinly sliced Spanish onions; salt to taste; black pepper to taste; cold water; milk and cream; 2 heaped tablespoons arrowroot.

PROCEDURE

Cut up the tripe into finger-thick strips and if these look long enough to be unwieldy between spoon and mouth, divide each one into more suitable lengths. Place together in a good iron pot with enough cold water to come 2-inches above these materials. Bring the water to the boil on a strong stove, close up its cavity that the temperature may be reduced and allow it to simmer very steadily but gently until the tripe is completely tender. Strain the liquor away altogether, back into your pan, and set the tripe and onions aside. Open up your stove again to full heat and boil the liquor so hard as to reduce it right down to a mere ½ pint. Return the tripe and onions to it. Add sufficient milk to make all moist. About 1 pint will prove sufficient. Stir until heated through once more. Slake the arrowroot in a small bowl with about 1 gill of thin (*single*) cream. Take a ladleful of the pan liquor and stir this in. Turn the arrowroot mixture on to the pan contents and stir until really quite thick, a little too thick in fact. Bring this back to the right consistency with a ½ pint of Jersey cream. Allow all to come to the boil once more, stirring carefully. Turn into a covered oven pan (*casserole*) and rest uncovered in the larder for twenty-four hours. Re-heat in a moderate oven and when required hand with bowls of My Tripe, crustless fingers of toast, well-buttered.

Author's Note

Can't beat it! Just interpret her coal stove with Gas, at Gas Mark 4 in the oven for re-heating. Stick to arrowroot, cornflour always *tastes* which just shows what a good judge Mrs Hudson was. *F.C.*

HAGGIS

Occasionally, and such occasions were all the more appreciated for their rarity, Mr Holmes, when faced with some particular dish would explain its origins in great length and with a wealth of detail, to which feasts I ever manoeuvred to be present until the end, by busying myself at the sideboard upon some pretext or another that I might add to my scant store of knowledge from my Great Employer.

It was thus I learned that Haggis was not Scottish! That it derived from Italy and that thence, as did almost all great French cooking, it travelled to France and thus to the British Isles. This latter only very occasionally however! Haggis it seems was a favourite dish with a great Roman called Apicus. His 'Haggis' was made into a boiled pig's stomach which he caused to be filled with a mixture of pig's fry and pig's brains, raw eggs and pineapples beaten to a pulp, all then very highly spiced and further flavoured by something called *Liquamen*. As to the constitution of *Liquamen*, although it revolts me to write it, I will do so in the interests of Food History. The intestines, gills and blood of many fishes, little and great were stirred together with handfuls of salt and thus set out in open vats to putrefy in the hot Italian sun. Once putrefaction was satisfactorily achieved the mess was blended with Roman wine and mixed spices and sold in the markets of Rome. It should be noted that *Liquamen* was made originally in Greece.

To complete my story, let me further explain what my Master discoursed upon so eloquently. The Scots, it seems, at least in olden times disliked pork excessively! So they recoursed to sheep when first the Haggis story filtered through to them. This it did via Normandy where in the eleventh century it was known as *Franchemoyle*. I do know the spelling be right upon these two strange items for I took my notes to Mr Holmes for correction and he complimented me upon my attention to what he had said. Then in conclusion, before dismissing me he tossed over his shoulder, 'Why not try your hand at a Scots Haggis Mrs Hudson. Doctor Watson and I both like one very well; but we prefer to eat ours with thin brown bread and butter than potatoes which I do regard as famine food, grateful upon the empty stomach but too filling to justify themselves otherwise.' This too I recorded carefully. Mr Holmes likewise astonished me as I again turned to go by adding, 'If you are lacking a good receipt, go to the British Museum and ask them for a copy of *Meg Dodd's Cookery*, no one recorded better counsel upon Scots cookery in olden times than Meg Dodd my dear Mrs Hudson.'

I obeyed Mr Holmes of course. Indeed, as I was ahead with my work, my gentlemen were dining out and there was but myself and That Boy to feed, I straightaway put on my bonnet and after instructing That Boy to listen for the upstairs bell, take his heels off my new-painted kitchen chair and scrub his nails which were in deepest mourning, I repaired to the British Museum and there found exactly what Mr Holmes had said.

MEG DODD'S HAGGIS

Clean a sheep's pluck* thoroughly. Make incisions in the heart and liver to allow the blood to flow out and par-boil, letting the windpipe lie over the side of the pot to permit the discharge of impurities. Change water after ten minutes boiling. A half hour's boiling will be sufficient; but throw back the half of the liver to boil until it will grate easily; take the heart, half of the liver and part of the lights, trimming away all

* A sheep's pluck comprises the heart, liver and lungs of a beast when used for culinary purposes. *F.C.*

skins and black-looking parts, and mince them together. Mince also a pound of good beef suet and at least four good-sized onions. Grate the other half of the liver. Have a dozen small onions peeled and scalded in two waters to mix with this mince. Have ready some finely ground oatmeal, toasted slowly before the fire for sufficient hours until it is of a light brown colour and perfectly dry. Less than two teacupfuls will do for this quantity of meat. Spread the mince out on a board. Strew the meal over lightly with a high seasoning of pepper, salt, a little cayenne, all three mixed together well first. Have ready a prepared Haggis Bag, perfectly clean, and see over it that it may have no very thin part, else your labour will be lost by its bursting! Put in the meat with a ½ pint of good beef gravy, being careful not to fill the bag too full, thus allowing the meat room to swell. Add the juice of a lemon or a little good (*wine*, F.C.) vinegar, sew up the bag, prick it with a large needle when it first swells in the pot, to prevent bursting, and let it boil slowly for about three hours.

Author's Note

In the absence of a 'copper' for boiling our Haggis, we score by being able to steam them. Thus, if they do burst we are none the worse off and they waste nothing. *F.C.*

CREAM OF SWEETBREADS FOR A DINNER PARTY

ASSEMBLY

4 large throatbreads (for a party of eight); flour; boiling water; cold water; salt; pepper; 1 lb small button mushrooms; 1 pint unwhipped, thick cream; 16 rounds of brioche bread, each measuring 2½-inches in diameter; 8 very thin slices of truffle (1 *truffle*, F.C.); the strained juice of 1 lemon; butter.

PROCEDURE

Wash the 'breads' thoroughly under a cold tap, removing as many of the little red veins as possible. Place 4 rounded tablespoons flour in a roomy bowl and beat down with cold water to an absolutely smooth paste. Have ready a kettle of boiling water. Pour this on to the cold paste, stirring the while. Continue stirring until the mixture thickens and clears, looking like the paste you would use for affixing paper to a wall. Turn all into a good-sized pan and immerse the 'breads' therein.

Offal

Set on a brisk fire and allow to reach boiling point. Withdraw from the fire and leave the 'breads' in their '*blanc*', as this paste mixture is called by professional chefs, until all is perfectly cold. Remove all remaining skins, and set on a flat piece of board. Cover with a piece of waxed paper and then another piece of board. Place heavy weights on top and leave in a cold place overnight. In the morning, slice the 'breads' into ½-inch-thick slices. Dissolve 2 oz of butter in a thick frying pan, slide in the *médaillons*, as they now are, and allow them to 'stiffen' on both sides. Throw in the cream, and the scalded but un-skinned, finely sliced mushrooms without their stalks. Simmer over a fairly strong fire until the sauce is thickened. Lift out the 'breads' and set on the made *croûtons*, having first strained off the mushrooms from the cream and set them as a base upon the croûtons. Place a single round of truffle upon the centre of each médaillon, bubble up the cream, taste it, season to taste with salt and black pepper. Pour overall on the heated dish. At the moment of service a little freshly milled fresh parsley heads may be strewn about the sauce, and lemon squeezed overall.

The Croûtons

Beat 1 egg into 5 fluid oz of sweet milk, add thereafter 1 fluid oz of thick cream and beat again. Slide the bread rounds through this mixture but on no account let them lie an instant in it or they will collapse into fragments! Immediately after passing each one through, slide it into slightly smoking hot oil and allow to puff and turn golden brown on both sides. Drain and use.

POTTED LAMBS' BRAINS IN CLARIFIED BUTTER

ASSEMBLY

To fill a 2 lb stone jar with this mixture you will require 14 lambs' brains and 1 lb sweet butter; salt; white pepper and a pinch each of nutmeg and cinnamon.

PROCEDURE

Blanch the brains exactly as I have explained in my preceding receipt for Cream of Sweetbreads. When these are cold, remove every fraction of skin and veins, and mash with a fork until you obtain a smooth paste. Into this paste stir 5 oz of just-melted butter and the seasoning to taste.

The Sherlock Holmes Cookbook

Melt the remaining butter in a small pan over a very low heat. As this bubbles up, skim off the bubbly foam until all you have left in the pan is a very still and perfectly clear mixture. This is *Clarified Butter*. Smooth off the top of your potted brains. Pour on the clarified butter and when this is quite set, tie down with parchment and store in a cold dry place. (*Use aluminium foil and a refrigerator. F.C.*)

SOME USES FOR POTTED BRAINS

1. Spread very thickly upon the base and around the sides of individual vol-au-vent cases. Drop a small raw egg into the remaining cavity in each. Cover with a top-coating of thick cream. Sprinkle with salt and pepper and place in a brisk oven fairly high up for about ten minutes or until egg is just set. Only experience can give you perfect results and you should ease away the cream with the handle of a teaspoon in order to ascertain if the egg white is properly set; but at all costs avoid hard cooking the eggs or this delicacy will be ruined!

2. Spread the potted brains thickly upon neat crustless squares of *brioche* bread. Overlap paper-thin slices of *un-skinned* cucumber until the brains spread is completely covered. Season with salt and pepper and serve to gentlemen at tea time.

Note: Observe that the cucumber is NOT skinned. Thus may it remain perfectly digestible to the most delicate of stomachs.

3. Make small crustless sandwiches of 1 slice brown and 1 slice white buttered bread with a thick spread of Potted Brains in between. When required, dip each sandwich into Fritter Batter until completely coated. Slip into slightly smoking hot oil and deep-fry until puffed and richly browned. Set upon a d'oyley-covered dish, sprinkle each with salt and a dash of cayenne pepper and border your dish with crescents of lemon alternated with small sprigs of parsley, fried crisp in hot oil for thirty seconds.

FRITTER BATTER

Beat 4 rounded tablespoons flour with gradual additions of cold water until paste is the consistency of thick, rich cream. When required, whip in one separated egg white very stiffly. Beat into batter and use when smooth and fluffy.

OX-LIVER MADE DELICATE AS CALVES' LIVER

In my father's house we were never able to afford calves' liver, so, together with many other little subterfuges, we learned the way to make coarse ox-liver highly appetising and at far less cost, even taking into consideration the outlay for the milk employed.

ASSEMBLY

2 lb ox liver; 1 pint milk; 1 flat teaspoon soda-bicarbonate.

PROCEDURE

Slice the liver to the thinness desired for subsequent cookery. Pour into a roomy basin the 1 pint milk and blend in the soda-bicarbonate. Immerse the liver slices in this mixture. Leave for at least thirty hours. Remove, wash slices under a cold tap. Wipe and use. The milk will be seen to be port-wine coloured and rather dirty-looking. Discard it, unless you happen to possess a large dog. In this case pour the milk into the dog's bowl and the dog will lap it up greedily. Proceed with whatever form of cooking is desired.

HOW TO COOK LIVER AND BACON PROPERLY

It is all too little known among home cooks that all the nutriment, especially the iron content, is *cooked out* of liver which is cooked until it is firm and dry. Liver *must* be just cooked through and no more. Therefore, for grilling, you should first dissolve sufficient butter in a plain grill pan (with no grill rack), to cover the base of the pan. No more. Then you should tow your prepared slices of liver through the melted butter *on both sides*. By this time the grill heat will have developed sufficiently for you to commence cooking. Let the slices cook until they are just well-coloured and slightly browned – but only slightly please. Turn them over and repeat for only half the time taken so far. Lift out, drain and set on a heated dish. Place the chosen number of bacon rashers at No. 3 Cut, on your grill rack. Affix this over the grill pan and thus raise the bacon to high up near the flames. Watch it carefully. As soon as the bacon humps up in little hills and valleys, turn over and repeat. Thus will your bacon be done to a turn and will not fly apart at contact with a table fork. You will observe that by now the surplus bacon fat will have fallen into the base pan residue of liver juices and butter. Cut some triangles of crustless bread. Draw them through the mixed fats etc. on both sides, then brown each side lighly under the grill and use with alternate sprigs of watercress to border your dish of properly cooked liver and bacon.

PORK FAGGOTS

These were not much appreciated by either Mr Holmes or Dr Watson but are worthy of inclusion if only on the grounds that many of the police officers who came and went from our house at very odd hours were wont to put their faces around the kitchen door and inquire of me, 'You don't happen to have any of those faggots of yours on the go do you Mrs H?'

As you may imagine, I therefore made them as frequently as I could obtain the materials.

ASSEMBLY

The liver of 1 pig, its lights and its fat from around the intestines; 2 lb onions; a quartern loaf with all crusts sliced away then made into crumbs; sufficient milk to soak the crumbs pappy; 1 dessertspoon coarse salt; 1 teaspoon freshly-ground black pepper; $\frac{1}{4}$ of a nutmeg; 1 pounded blade of mace; 1 dessertspoon each of dried, crumbled sage, basil and marjoram; the flead* from a freshly killed pig.

PROCEDURE

Pass twice through the mincing machine the liver cut into neat pieces, the quartered, peeled onions and the lights. Turn the mixture into a roomy bowl and work in the breadcrumbs, herbs and seasonings. Cut neat squares from the flead, place as much of the mixture as may be enveloped by each flead square and fold each so that the corners completely enfold the filling *underneath*. Place side aside in a roomy meat-baking tin and bake in a moderate oven (*Gas Mark 4, mid-shelf, F.C.*) until the meat be thoroughly cooked inside and the flead wrapping nicely browned and bubbling with pork fat which has escaped. Leave in the tin until cold. Separate with the set fat adhering to each. Serve either hot with a good brown gravy and apple sauce or cold with a mixed salad.

* The fatty jacket which is removed from the interior of pigs. Each is then hung on a coathanger on a clothes line and thoroughly dried out! *F.C.*

SCALLYWAG PIE

I ever thought, privately and to myself, of those so-called Baker Street Irregulars of his (Mr Holmes) as those 'Scallywags'. Be that as it may, I inadvertently let slip this nomenclature of mine in the presence of my employer and while awaiting his orders for the day. Mr Holmes laughed, shuffled a mass of papers into even greater disorder and observed, 'You know Mrs Hudson, you really should create a Scallywag Pie for those young rascals. You can do it easily. I place no limit upon your culinary powers *when* you decide to put your mind fully to the subject.' This last was a nasty dig; but I had asked for it, having forgotten how he liked his scrambled eggs to be more than normally moist – wet in fact – and had presented some for his breakfast that morning with which he was displeased! However, after this exchange I considered the proposal and the more I thought of it the more it pleased me, if only in the interests of economy. I therefore thought around all the most economical and suitable subjects to utilise for such a pie and eventually came upon the ideal ones by sheer accident, as so often happens.

I was purchasing meat and on my way to my best butcher in Mortimer Street which was famous by reason of it containing Mrs Marshall's School of Cookery. On my way I chanced to pass a stall at which a busy trade was being conducted in the sale of pig's fry, and rabbits. Now pig's fry consists of pig's hearts, lights, liver and sweetbreads, all sold in small pieces at sixpence per pound and, as a matter of interest to the reader I will add that a nice young rabbit, skinned and cleaned, sold 'entire' that is to say with the head left on and the interior still retaining the liver and kidneys (after being cleaned) cost me one shilling. This I considered most advantageous as *my* poulterer was in the habit of charging me one shilling and sixpence which is a difference so great as to arouse the Highest Suspicions of Profiteering. Here then is the pie which eventually emerged from Mr Holmes' remarks.

ASSEMBLY

One medium rabbit cut into neat joints and rolled in flour; 2 lb pig's fry also turned in flour; salt; pepper; 1 herb faggot; 4 hard-boiled eggs; 1 lb sifted, self-raising flour; 6 oz good, clean, firm dripping; 1 egg-in-shell; a glass of very cold water; 1 measured flat teaspoon of salt; 1 oz stale, grated fine cheese ends; 3 oz dripping; 2 bay leaves; 2 lb carrots; 2 lb onions; 1 pint bone stock; gelatine.

The Sherlock Holmes Cookbook

PROCEDURE

Commence with the paste that this may chill upon a piece of cold slate, stone or marble in a shady place (*refrigerator, F.C.*) until required which ever facilitates easy rolling thereafter. Shake the flour through your dredger, together with the salt, upon a cold piece of marble and form it into a ring upon this surface. Into the ring place the dripping, whole shell egg, salt and cheese and then, with the fingers, and drawing in more and more flour gradually from the encircling border, work up to a good rolling dough adding small amounts of water with some restraint lest the paste become over-soggy. Fold into a clean, floured napkin and set in the cool as already explained. If so be you have a spare piece of cold slate it be not a bad thing at all to lay this over the top of your paste parcel as a further insurance of coolness. Take the dripping and set to dissolve and sing in a thick iron pan over a fairly brisk fire. Fry the floured pieces of fry and rabbit until they be stiffened and brown all over. Then pick them out and place them in an iron pot or other suitable receptacle for oven-cookery. (*An earthenware casserole is best, F.C.*) Add to them the carrots chopped small and the onions likewise. Throw over a mere 1 pint of good bone stock, sink in your herb faggot, cover and let be in a very moderate oven (*Gas Mark 3, mid-shelf, until all is perfectly tender, approximately two hours. F.C.*). Take from the oven, allow to cool down sufficiently to handle without discomfort and then take every scrap of flesh from the rabbit pieces – including from the head, the cheeks, tongue and brains. Drain all the liquor into a separate pan, it will not be much above a $\frac{1}{2}$ pint by now. Make it up with cold water to $1\frac{1}{2}$ pints and place therein all the rabbit bones and the dried bay leaves. Let them simmer for an hour on the side of the stove. Meanwhile, mix up the pig's fry, rabbit flesh and vegetables so that they be evenly distributed and fill to half way into a large family-sized pie dish.* Quarter the hard-boiled eggs lengthwise and lay them, cut side downwards upon the bed of mixture. Add the remaining mixture to reach to just below the rim of the pie dish. Now sink in your pie funnel centrally. Then, when the simmering stock be really flavoursome strain it, taste it and correct the seasoning rather strongly with salt and pepper. Then stir into it until completely dissolved three leaves of gelatine (*between $\frac{1}{2}$ and $\frac{3}{4}$ oz powdered gelatine, F.C.*), then let it await the cooked pie. With no moisture over the contents,

---

* Remember please that families were much larger in those days and a really large pie dish is needed unless you prefer to make two smaller pies and then slip one away into the freezer for future use, which is what we do after the pies have been baked. *F.C.*

affix your paste cover. Roll out the paste to a ¼-inch thickness. There is enough meat substance within to support this for hungry lads. Lay it over and trim off the edges neat, for nothing be more disagreeable to anyone than a double over edge of baked pastry with nothing beneath to complement it! Make a cross in the centre above the tip of the pie funnel, fold back the four corners to let in a little ventilation and brush the surface with good, sweet milk. Bake in a fairly brisk oven (*Gas Mark* 5, *F.C.*) until well browned on top. Remove from the oven and pour your made liquid through the funnel-top so that the pie be thoroughly lubricated with a mixture which, when cold and set will be like jelly and will enable you to cut it into large wedges. Of course there is a disadvantage in this. Those scallywags, faced with their pie, and seeing in it the possibilities of coarse eating, were immediately for picking it up in their never really clean hands and biting off huge mouthfuls. This I would not tolerate.

MY DEVILLED KIDNEYS

This should always be done with lambs' kidneys as I do most seriously consider that pork kidneys be far too indigestible to impose upon the human stomach at the breakfast hour. This indeed is why I ever encourage the eating of porridge as a first breakfast course; it forms a warm and comfortable lining to the stomach which is thus protected when more alarming comestibles are sent down. Not that I ever had much encouragement in this from my employer who did not express himself with any particular grace upon the subject. However, he had been known to, I might almost say *wolf* half a dozen kidneys so prepared after he had been out all night upon a case. Then, comfortably attired in his dressing-gown and red morocco slippers, freshly shaven, he would positively attack them.

ASSEMBLY

A minimum of 12 kidneys for two persons; 4 bay leaves torn in halves; 16 very small shallots, boiled in salted water until cooked but still firm; 16 medium sized mushrooms divested of their stalks but left unskinned; a bowl of My Devil (*for which please turn to p.* 39, *F.C.*), and a small bowl containing olive oil and a pastry brush.

PROCEDURE

Skin the kidneys. Cut them almost through so that they only remain hinged but are therefore not completely severed. Thread one upon each of two long, metal skewers in such a manner that they remain flat or 'spatchcocked'. Then thread on a piece of bay, a small shallot, a mushroom, another kidney, mushroom, shallot and then another series this time with a piece of bay and so on until half are used upon each skewer. Brush all over on both sides very liberally with olive oil and set over a gridiron over a well banked-down fire in your stove. (*Grill them fairly slowly. F.C.*) Thus let them cook slowly for about two minutes. Turn them, repeat the procedure then remove them and coat them very liberally with My Devil and return them to the gridiron to complete their cooking. Place the remainder of the heated Devil in a small, heated, sauce boat, and set each skewer-load upon a split length of French Roll. Arrange a sprig of parsley at each end and so send to table.

VEGETABLES

VEGETABLES

For the Proper Cooking of Garden Peas
A Good Potato Soufflé
Potatoes for Service with a Goose Roasted My Way
Potato and Cheese Cakes
Potato Purée
Proper Potato Purée
My Creamed Potatoes
Roasted Chestnuts for a Goose
My Glazed Onions
Spinach Purée
A Dish of Salsify
Country Cousin

VEGETABLES

YOU may know a good cook from an ignorant one by the way she treats her peas! This I have staunchly maintained was no more than the truth, which Cook used to say shaking her head in rightful disapproval at the very word 'boiling' in a receipt book.

So now, without any further reference to my teacher I will expound upon Proper Methods having duly given the credit to the One who taught *me*.

Peas and lettuces are in abundant, modestly-priced supply at precisely the same season of the year. It is rare for the latter to have no bruised outer leaves when offered for sale even in the best of greengrocers and the purchaser will disregard this flaw if the hearts of the lettuces be firm and stout.

FOR THE PROPER COOKING OF GARDEN PEAS

Remove all the outer leaves only from one or two lettuces. Wash them carefully, drain them and be sure to take off any brown bits. Use them to line out any lidded pot which may safely be put into an oven. Hold back one fourth of these and tumble upon the lining of lettuce leaves 2 to 3 lb of shelled peas. Add thereto 1 rounded teaspoon castor sugar, 1 flat teaspoon cooking salt, 1 flat eggspoon freshly milled black peppercorns and then swill with 4 fluid oz inexpensive, dry, white cooking-type wine, (*or clear bone stock may replace the wine, F.C.*). Cover all with the remaining lettuce leaves, then with the pot's lid and place in a moderate oven (*Gas Mark 4, mid-shelf. F.C.*) and leave for one and a quarter hours. Remove pot, lift off lid and discover therein some unsightly, dwindled brown leaves which is what the lettuce will have become. Dredge all out leaving peas in their own liquor. Serve from an entrée dish with small triangular sippets of toast to form a border or, for dinner parties, strain the peas, keep warm. Place the strained liquor in a pan with half its own bulk in thick cream and simmer down to a good sauce consistency over a fairly brisk fire. Return to the peas. Separately, fry any odds and ends of back bacon dry in a frying pan after dicing them up small. Mix into the sauced peas and serve.

A GOOD POTATO SOUFFLÉ

It is only essential to understand exactly how the potatoes should be prepared for a soufflé, for the veriest beginner to cookery to obtain a good soufflé from them. So if you will please turn to my explanation on p. 132 for Proper Potato Purée and follow the directions there set out.

For a soufflé take 1 lb of the aforementioned potato purée, beat with it 2 separated (*standard, F.C.*) egg yolks and add seasonings of salt and freshly milled white peppercorns – black would render this dish unsightly to the eye. Blend into the mixture 1 flat tablespoon fresh-chopped, fresh parsley heads, 1 oz finely chopped lean and fat of ham and then, when your soufflé mould is well buttered and your oven hot (*Gas Mark 7, one shelf above centre. F.C.*), beat thereto the fairly stiffly whipped whites of 5 (*standard, F.C.*) eggs. Level this mixture off in the mould. There is no need for you to bother with a buttered paper around the outside of the mould. Bake for seventeen minutes, dish and serve immediately.

POTATOES FOR SERVICE WITH A GOOSE COOKED MY WAY

(*see p. 77. To Roast a Goose Digestibly.*)

Let us first be specific. A good goose may weigh around 12 to 14 lb or more, if so be the bird has been penned and force fed as certain of the Smithfield merchants do, although I am of the opinion that this is a somewhat inhumane practice originating with those Frenchies! If we say 12 lb that may estimate the overall cooking time as being 195 minutes, or if you prefer – three hours fifteen minutes. Taking this for an example the potatoes will need to be inserted in the oven, above the bird, one hour before cooking is completed. But first you must prepare them.

PROCEDURE

Peel stout King Edward potatoes with great fineness remembering that

Vegetables

all the goodness lies just under the fine skin as my dear father always reminded me when, in later life, I questioned his never eating potatoes other than roasted in their jackets! If they be large ones cut into even sizes, but not too small. Then bring to the boil a half-filled medium pan of water, stir in 1 teaspoon salt and immerse the potatoes. Clap on a lid and cook for exactly seven minutes, drain, immerse in cold water and finally wipe. When the one remaining hour of goose-cooking time arrives, pour some of the removed goose fat into a deep pie dish, immerse the potatoes and see that they are completely submerged in the fat. Put *above* the goose in your oven and let them be. When you remove them with the goose and drain them out of the fat you will find they have become coated with a richly flavoursome dark brown potato-texture, one which is unique to this method of cookery.

POTATO AND CHEESE CAKES

A good way for cutting the sharp edge of growing boys' appetites as I soon learned with Our Young Limb! who could as easily devour a platter of meat did I not ration it out with good, filling, side sundries!

ASSEMBLY

3 large or 6 small, floury potatoes; 1 oz butter; 1 oz grated stale cheese ends; salt and pepper; 1 egg; a little milk.

PROCEDURE

Peel, boil, strain and mash potatoes finely. Return to pan and stir dry over side of stove until surplus moisture is expelled, then mash in the butter and cheese, season well with salt and pepper and beat in the egg. Butter some patty pans, drop spoonfuls of the mixture thereon, smooth the tops off with a knife until smoothly rounded, brush with the milk and bake in a fairly hot oven for fifteen to twenty minutes. (*Gas Mark 5, one shelf above centre. F.C.*)

POTATO PURÉE

ASSEMBLY

2 lb large, old potatoes; 1 oz butter; 2 small eggs; salt and pepper to season; 1 rounded tablespoon freshly chopped parsley heads; a little milk.

PROCEDURE

Having made sure that your potatoes are of a really floury nature, scrub them in the jackets and bake them so in a fair oven (*Gas Mark 5, mid-shelf. F.C.*) until they 'yield' when squeezed. Divide each one, scoop the flour into a roomy basin and crush down with a fork until every small piece has been pulverised. Turn into a saucepan and with a wooden spoon stir, over the side of the stove, until every scrap of moisture has been expelled. Stir in the butter, beat up the eggs, then beat into potato mixture with the parsley and gradual additions of a few drops of milk. Final mixture should come to a peak without collapsing.

Note: There are many variations thereafter. A cheesy mixture may be obtained by the adding of 2 rounded dessertspoons of finely grated Parmesan cheese. A meat-flavoured mixture results from adding 2 oz finely chopped chickens' livers, after sautéeing these in a little butter in a small pan. Alternatively, chopped, cooked gammon may be treated in the same fashion. On special occasions you may well wish to replace the milk with thick cream.

PROPER POTATO PURÉE

Scrub $2\frac{1}{2}$ lb old potatoes. Put into a slow oven (*Gas Mark 2, one shelf below centre. F.C.*) and let them be until they are soft when squeezed gently. Halve them and scoop the flour into a sieve. Rub down fine into a dry saucepan. Place over a low fire and stir with a wooden spoon until any infinitesimal particles of moisture are expelled. Work into this pasty mixture 1 oz good butter and a pinch of both salt and pepper. Use like this for my Potato Soufflé receipt on p. 130.

If wishing to use the potatoes for presentation as MASHED POTATOES, then pray add 1 egg yolk and 2 tablespoons thin cream to the mixture.

This may, if liked, be further enhanced by 1 rounded tablespoon of fine-diced lean ham and the same of freshly-chopped, fresh parsley heads. It is with this enhancement that I shape my mashed potatoes into a neat, flat-topped mound with a large table fork and then surround with freshly cooked sausages for *SAUSAGES AND MASHED POTATOES.*

MY CREAMED POTATOES

ASSEMBLY

1 lb old, preferably red-skinned potatoes; the yolks of 2 eggs; ½ oz Gruyère or Emmenthal cheese; ½ oz Parmesan cheese; ½ oz butter and 2 oz butter; 4 tablespoons thin cream; salt, pepper and nutmeg to flavour.

PROCEDURE

Steam the peeled potatoes but pray do not boil them, for this ensures the quality of your finished dish will be diminished. When steamed, pound them down until they are perfectly smooth and return them to a clean pan. Stir them with a wooden spoon, over a low heat, at the side of your stove, until they are perfectly dried out and the spoon almost stands erect in them. Then beat in the egg yolks, the 2 oz butter, the thin cream and the seasonings to taste. Finally beat in the cheeses and set the ½ oz of butter to melt in a little dish. Set your potatoes in their border, fork them up as explained in my parent receipt for Fricassée of Eggs (see p. 32) and then brush the surface all over very lightly with the melted butter.

If desirous of browning the potatoes before sending to table then be advised and withhold the parsley until after so-doing lest it be frazzled brown.

ROASTED CHESTNUTS FOR A GOOSE

'I shall pay for this Holmes,' said Dr Watson, eating a great many chestnuts with great rapidity, 'and all the goodness and digestibility of Mrs Hudson's goose will be nullified by the richness of these which I frankly admit I find irresistible.' Then turning to me he would inquire, 'have we any bismuth in the house Mrs Hudson?' In reply I would lay a bottle of bismuth tablets beside his cover and Mr Holmes would chuckle.

ASSEMBLY

Goose fat and chestnuts.

PROCEDURE

Cut a small nick with a well-sharpened knife in each chestnut, being sure to cut through both outer and inner skins. Immerse these, so prepared, in fast boiling water and allow them to simmer strongly until soft. Drain through a colander, allow to cool sufficiently for easy handling and then remove both outer and inner skins. Please do this with some care as I have learned that the high cost of the dessert luxuries, Marrons Glacés, is not at all the cost of either the chestnuts or the sugar syrup but the high incidence of breakages. I always set aside my few 'casualties' and use them to make chestnut purée for a brace of pheasants. When all are shelled treat exactly as for my receipt for potatoes for a roast goose (p. 130) but do not allow more than forty-five minutes in your oven, set beside the potatoes. Drain them very thoroughly thereafter and send to table in a d'oyley-lined silver entrée dish.

MY GLAZED ONIONS

This was an item learned many years before from my Lady's Cook, and for which Mr Holmes called immediately he caught one of his rare colds. 'Nothing like it for the common cold Watson,' he would declare, trumpeting into one of those bandanna handkerchiefs which he affected.

Take 12 even-sized medium to small onions and place them in a thick pan with 1 oz butter, 8 pieces of loaf sugar, 1 flat teaspoon of coarse salt and as much good, cleared stock as will come to just above them. Bring to boiling, and when this achieved damp down your fire or draw to the very rim of a fierce one, that they may simmer gently until cooked but still whole and not collapsed in any way. Strain off the fluid, set the onions in their dish to keep warm and reduce the liquor over a fierce fire until it resembles brown syrup. Pour this, very carefully, over the neatly arranged onions and send to table without any further adornment.

SPINACH PURÉE

Wash 2 lb spinach very thoroughly and tear leaves from stems. Pile all into a perfectly dry pan and set on the side of the stove. Stir on a low heat until the juices run so as to avoid any leaf scorching on the base of the pan. Then cook on until totally collapsed (*an overall eight minutes maximum, F.C.*). Rub through a tamis cloth (*sieve, F.C.*), return purée to wiped-out pan and stir in a walnut of butter, a pinch of cinnamon, salt and pepper to taste and finish with 1 oz finely-grated Parmesan cheese.

Note: When not serving with a creamy sauce, then 2 tablespoons of thick cream may be run over the purée when this is dished up.

A DISH OF SALSIFY

This is a vegetable which needs special culinary attention. Indeed I, in a measure, contradict myself by so saying, as *all* vegetables give of their best *only* when carefully cooked and *all* respond remarkably to careful treatment.

ASSEMBLY AND PROCEDURE

Take up 2 bunches of salsify, separate, trim off tops and bases, strew in a wide container and cover with a solution comprising equal parts of cold water and strained lemon juice. This is an arbitrary treatment if you are not to suffer the ignominy of blackened salsify upon your table which would, of course, be unthinkable! Let your salsify lie, either in stick or cut slantwise into 1-inch pieces which I prefer. When the time (15 mins) has elapsed, drain out the vegetable, cut if you have not done so before and place in a clean pan with $1\frac{1}{2}$–2 pints of boiling, salted water. Simmer carefully until tender but by no means collapsed. Drain very thoroughly in a colander. Stir into it 4 rounded tablespoons of butter, 1 flat teaspoon of finely chopped parsley heads and the same of scissored chives, season with salt and pepper to taste and turn into a heated entrée dish for service.

COUNTRY COUSIN

This is a herbal, savoury mixture which I used to be given when I was a child. It took the place of Yorkshire pudding and I would have a fat slice of it with good brown gravy spooned over it for middle day 'dinner' as it was called by poor country folk.

ASSEMBLY

1 egg; 6 oz sifted, self-raising flour; $2\frac{1}{2}$ fluid oz milk; $2\frac{1}{2}$ fluid oz water; 1 flat teaspoon salt; $\frac{1}{2}$ flat teaspoon pepper; 1 heaped tablespoon fine-chopped fresh parsley heads; the same of chives, and half the quantity of thyme.

PROCEDURE

Sift the flour with the salt and pepper into a roomy basin, make a well in the centre. Put in all the herbs, then break the egg on top. Mix the milk with the water. Pour a little on top of the egg and begin to work up, adding more of the fluid gradually and ever beating until a smooth, speckled, batter is the result. Have ready a small to medium pie dish into which you have previously put a very large knob of clean dripping (3 *oz, F.C.*). Having made this sizzling hot in a brisk oven, pour on the batter and put the pie dish well up in your strong oven for about twenty to thirty minutes depending upon the heat you have achieved. (*Gas Mark* 7½, *one shelf above centre, F.C.*)

Note: It was very filling and nourishing, so I used to give it to Mr Holmes' Scallywags on cold winter days.

CHEESE DISHES

Cheese Dishes

Stilton Cheese
My Potted Cheshire Cheese
My Cheese and Onion Pie
My Cheese Rolls
A Cheese Fondue
Racket (La Raclette, F.C.)
To Make a Good Curd Cheese

STILTON CHEESE

THIS is an interesting curiosity. Whether or not it is THE Stilton Cheese, only the individual palate may determine. Suffice that it was given to my great aunt Tabitha Jenkins when she was in the employ of the Lady for whom she worked upon the outskirts of Melton Mowbray. Her Lady was of an instructive nature and also, as were so many country women of her day, given to putting up cheeses with her own hands, assisted by the girls in her employ. It was during one of these cheese-making occasions that the Lady permitted Tabitha to learn the way of it which, my great aunt assured me she never forgot although she, like many girls of her station, was a poor hand at reading and writing. She committed it to her head, together with the story which, when I went into service, she told to me. The way of it was this:

The following receipt was used by a Mrs Poulton for Mr Cooper Thornhill who owned The Bell at Stilton and who charged half a crown a pound for it without disclosing its source. It was never allowed to be dug into, recalled Aunt Tabitha, indeed there was a local chant with which all such cheese servers were impressed, 'cut high, cut low, cut level', and thus never make a crumbly wall of deteriorating cheese as is the custom with some uninformed persons even today! All I can add is that the cheese so made tasted excellent and was in much favour with both Mr Holmes and Dr Watson.

And here is the receipt as my aunt repeated it to me:

Take the milk from a single milking of seven cows. Then take the cream skimmed from a single milking of seven cows and put in enough boiling water into the cream to bring it to blood heat. Salt the milk to taste. Bring both milk and cream together well blended. Put in sufficient Rennet to make both hard. Then wring out two pure linen cloths. Cut up the hard mixture in very thin slices. Lay half into each prepared cloth, tie all four corners and suspend upon a hook or bar for one hour. Take down and immerse in a tub of cold rainwater. Let them lie one hour. Then hang them up again until they have dripped dry. Place the contents of both cloths into a cheese vat well lined with a sheet of the finest butter muslin. Cover with a lid which fits over the cheeses inside but does not rest upon the sides of the tub. Place a light weight upon the lid. Gradually increase the weights, on the hour every hour for twenty-four hours, first removing and draining the cheese in the tub each time before adding more weights. If it be not pressed enough to have a firm but creamy consistency then press on up to a maximum of thirty hours. Thus you may withdraw it from the vat. Remove the muslin with great care and neatness, replace in clean muslin drawn very taut and even and totally enclosing it and so place upon your store shelf in your cheese room at the same temperature as you would for wine, 54 degrees.

Author's Note
The author does not specify whether the results of this are White Stilton as I suppose or Blue Stilton due to increased length of time in maturity which latter I doubt. F.C.

MY POTTED CHESHIRE CHEESE
Whenever Mr Holmes was engaged upon one of his protracted cases and could not be persuaded to desist for long enough to eat a Proper Meal he would say hurriedly, 'Bring me a slice of bread, buttered with your own butter, Mrs Hudson and lay upon it a thick slice of your excellent Potted Cheshire Cheese. That will sustain me!'

ASSEMBLY
3 lb of the very best white Cheshire Cheese; 1 lb preferably home-made butter; one $5\frac{1}{2}$ fluid oz wine glass of Canary or dry Madeira; $\frac{1}{2}$ oz of mace pounded so fine it may not be detected; 2 oz clarified butter (see below).

PROCEDURE
Place the cheese, cut into small pieces, with the butter in a mortar and pound with a pestle until it be smooth, add in the Canary or Madeira and the mace and pound well again that all may be incorporated evenly. Press into a large stone jar or pot and cover with clarified butter. Tie down with a piece of parchment and keep in a cold place.

TO CLARIFY BUTTER
Melt the butter very slowly in a small pan. Allow to bubble and skim off the bubbles until only clear liquid remains. You will need at least 7 oz to obtain 2.

Cheese dishes

Author's Note

Canary wine was much venerated from Elizabethan times to the mid-nineteenth century. It originated from the Canary Islands and was wiped out by the *phylloxera*. F.C.

MY CHEESE AND ONION PIE

It was often my custom to tuck a wedge or two of this pie into the Railway Train 'tiffin' baskets required by Mr Holmes for his journeys.

ASSEMBLY

1 lb puff pastry paste; 1 lb white Cheshire Cheese; ¼ lb butter; ¼ pint dry white wine; ¼ pint thick cream; freshly ground black peppercorns to season; 2 well whipped eggs; 1 lb extremely thinly sliced onions, fried until soft and golden over a very slow fire in a thick iron skillet with 2 oz of extra butter and a tablespoon or two of olive oil to stop the butter from blackening.

PROCEDURE

Pound down the cheese with the 4 oz butter until smooth and season fairly strongly with the black pepper, then work in the wine very carefully and gently and thereafter work in the cream and eggs in the same manner. Do all this while the onions are frying, for they take quite a time over a necessarily slow fire to become soft; and also roll out half the paste very thin and use to line into a medium-sized pie dish bringing the paste right up to the rim and wetting this beneath with a little cold water. When the onions are fried, drain them of any surplus grease and then beat them into the cheese mixture. Fill into the pie and affix a pie funnel centrally that the paste lid may be well supported. Roll out the remaining half of paste until it be of the size of the pie dish's top surface. Lay in position again moistening the edge, this time of the under paste with cold water. Pinch edges firmly between finger and thumb to flute them all round. Make a small cross in the top where the pie funnel presses. Fold back the corners, brush the top all over with a little extra cream and bake in a strong oven until well-risen and a rich golden brown. (*Gas Mark 7, one shelf above centre. F.C.*) Let it be quite cold before cutting.

MY CHEESE ROLLS

These represent a sturdy savoury to put before gentlemen at a quiet dinner by themselves.

ASSEMBLY

Some trimmings of puff paste; Gruyère or Emmenthal cheese; mustard; some de-rinded bacon rashers; 1 egg; 1 tablespoon thick cream; 2 tablespoons thin cream; black pepper fresh ground from corns.

PROCEDURE

Roll out your puff paste trimmings upon a very lightly floured board to a mere $\frac{1}{10}$-inch thickness and cut, say, half a dozen neat pieces measuring 6-inches by 3-inches. Beat up the egg and strain. Then blend into it a generous seasoning of black pepper, and both the given creams. Brush the paste pieces with this mixture. Cut some extremely thin slices of the chosen cheese and make each to be a $\frac{1}{2}$-inch smaller all round than each paste piece. Lay one upon each. Brush again with the egg mixture, lay down a rasher of bacon upon each, and brush these again with the egg mixture. Roll each up and seal the edges against the main body of each roll with a further brushing on of the egg mixture. Finally set each upon a baking sheet which you have passed under the cold tap first and then shook off the drops. Brush all the rolls' tops with the last of the egg mixture and bake in a strongish fired oven until puffed and richly browned. Dish in a napkin and send immediately to table decorating the ends of each roll if desired with a sprig of Fried Parsley.

TO FRY PARSLEY

Pick fat sprigs of fresh, dark green parsley heads, wash them in cold water and pat them dry in a cloth. When your deep pan of hot oil is beginning to throw off a faint haze throw in the sprigs singly, let them be for so long as they take to frizzle crisp which is a matter of seconds, lift them out, drain them well and use as explained.

Author's Note

This method of treating a baking sheet for the baking of puff paste is classic and employed today by the finest *pâtissiers*. F.C.

A CHEESE FONDUE

ASSEMBLY

$\frac{1}{2}$ lb very finely sliced Gruyère cheese; 1 egg-cup of cooking Kirsch; 1 generous pinch nutmeg; 1 heaped teaspoon potato flour (*fécule de pomme obtainable from Harrods or Fortnums*, F.C.); 2 separated egg yolks; 2 fluid oz unbeaten, thick cream; $\frac{1}{4}$ pint dry, white cooking wine.

PROCEDURE

Place cheese and white wine in a thick pot on the side of your stove where the cheese may melt extremely slowly. (*Lowest possible gas, with ordinary asbestos mat between pan-base and flame. F.C.*) When cheese is dissolved, stir well. At this point have ready the egg yolks stirred smooth with the cream; the potato flour stirred smooth with the nutmeg and Kirsch. Stir the egg/cream mixture into the cheese mixture, then stir in the Kirsch mixture. When all is smooth and thick and creamy, set over a spirit stove on the dining table with a basket containing squares of crumbs of bread. Then each person spears a piece of the bread upon a fork, swirls it around in the mixture and pops it into the mouth.

RACKET
(*La Raclette, F.C.*)

Mr Holmes as you will know, had occasion, well nigh disastrous once – to visit Switzerland. There, in one of what he called 'Cantons', he acquired this receipt for me. I always ensured success with it by building the sitting-room fire with exceptional care so that, well banked down, and with a top layer (over small glowing coals) of coal dust, I took the precaution of moistening this last with a few drops of paraffin that it would catch well and throw out a tremendous heat. This done I then took half a small Wensleydale in its rind and set it upon a fire-defiant platter before the tremendous glow. Indeed, Mr Holmes, as ever on return to the house in inclement weather, would stride to the hearth and stretch out his long thin hands to the blaze. Then if it were 'Racket' night he would exclaim, 'Powerful enough to roast an ox!' Dr Watson would echo, 'By Jove you're right Holmes!' and I would proceed with my arrangements. They were of the simplest. The cut face of the cheese being set towards the fire it would begin to soften and thus would slide in melting rivulets down on to the platter. Therefore it behoves any who copy this to bear in mind that the platter should be a large one. When a sufficient accumulation has formed on the platter, heaving and bubbling like some lava in a volcanic crater, bring in a couple of floury potatoes on each heated plate as I did. Then my gentlemen would scoop up the cheese lava until it totally enclosed the potatoes and eat the mixture with forks taking fingers of buttered toast which I set beside them both as well. As soon as all the lava cheese was gone I would return its cut face to the coals and so continue until my Master cried out, 'Enough Mrs Hudson, pray desist or we will fail to do justice to your dinner this night!'

TO MAKE A GOOD CURD CHEESE

Make a junket, by raising to just above blood heat 1 pint of sweet, new milk and stirring thereto 1 teaspoon of rennet. Pour into any container until set, which will be brief indeed, and meanwhile prepare for its further reception. Place over a fine hair sieve two folds of butter-muslin and when the junket be set, take it up gently in small spoonsful and lay it upon the muslin, making sure there is a receptacle beneath to catch the whey which will then flow down into it leaving the curd quite dry. Take up the curd into a further bowl and beat thereto half the curd's weight in thick cream. Take an ordinary sieve and line this out with four folds of butter-muslin making quite sure that the four corners hang low over the sides. When all be in, tie the opposing corners over into strong knots and thereby hang the curd cheese from a hook in a cool place. Let it hang so for twenty-four hours. Take down and turn into a clean basin. Add to it 3 heaped tablespoons of fine-chopped or scissored fresh chives, the same of fresh parsley and one tablespoon of fresh sage chopped extremely small. Adjust the seasoning with salt and black pepper, fresh-ground or pounded down and also add 1 rounded teaspoon of paprika powder. Shape into a neat shape like a round Victoria sponge – only much smaller – and so send to table with fingers of hot, buttered toast.

A few sandwiches, made with one slice brown and one slice white buttered bread for each are very good when filled with this spread which must then be covered close and thick with fairly fine-chopped, well washed, picked and dried mustard and cress.

Author's Note
Not to be tried with modern 'long-life' milk please. *F.C.*

PUDDINGS

PUDDINGS

A Tale
On Steaming Properly
Mr Sherlock Holmes' Plum Duff
Six-Cup Pudding for Simple Everyday Use
Proper Pancakes
Cook's Pancake Batter
Queen of Puddings
Steamed Apricot Pudding
My Apricot Sauce
Titsy-Bitsies
Puff Pastry
Spotted Dick
Apple Fritters as They Should Be Made
Fanchette for a Dinner
My Aunt's Simple Cherry Pudding
A Dish of Wine Cherries in Summer Time
The Prince Regent's Pudding
Rum Sauce
Crusades
Bachelors' Pudding
Kaiser Wilhelm Pudding
Kaiser Sauce
Prince Albert's Pudding
Apricot and Pistachio Sauce
Semolina Pudding which Be Not a Penance to Eat
Italian Pie

A TALE

WHEN in an expansive mood – which was not all that often I fear – Mr Holmes was wont to recount to Dr Watson at the supper table in his famous sitting-room, commencing with a, 'You had better listen to this too, Mrs Hudson,' – the tales of how a great number of the world's most famous dishes were the results of culinary accidents.

One of his most famous expositions concerned a certain Count de Rumfort who invented something which he called *Soufflé Surprise* or Norwegian Omelette.

As I had heard Mr Holmes speak in his erudite fashion on many occasions concerning this Count who was a scientist, I was puzzled to know how this would be reconciled to the culinary art. However launching himself upon his discourse Mr Holmes explained: 'Count de Rumfort was at the time living in Paris where he was conducting some experiments upon heat-insulation. One such morning the Count suddenly dashed from his laboratory, cried out to his wife, "Clap on your bonnet my dear, we are going shopping," and he led her away to the nearest market where they made a singular small set of purchases. To wit, 1 Camembert Cheese, 1 dozen eggs, 1 large block of ice. With these he and Madame hurried home, where, under his instructions, the Countess separated egg whites from yolks and put the whites in a large bowl on the window-ledge of a north-facing room, so as to keep them cold and in a draught, this being the pre-treatment which ensures they whip best. Meantime, the Count busied himself chopping up the large block of ice into little bits. With this done he set the Camembert upon a metal dish, put it in the charge cave and completely buried it in the ice. There he left the cheese for several hours. Then he again summoned his wife and requested her to whip up the whites extremely stiffly while he stacked the kitchen range – or whatever the Frenchified equivalent is to our good English stoves. When the oven of the French contraption was as hot as could possibly be achieved, he snatched the cheese from under the ice, smothered it in the stiff-whipped egg whites and slipped it inside the oven.

'That night, while dining with his wife in a Very Famous Restaurant the Count told the proprietor what he had done, ending up with, "And when several minutes later I removed my dish, the meringue was well browned around the cheese but the cheese remained ice cold and frozen solid!"

'The proprietor then asked permission to bring his chef into the restaurant when the Romforts had finished dining, in order that he too could hear this amazing tale; but in the meantime the proprietor repeated it to the man who appeared very excitedly at the table carrying with him the first *Soufflé Surprise*. He had replaced the Camembert with ice cream, added sugar to the egg whites, and set the ice cream upon a base of sponge called *Genoese*. And now he set the resultant confection before the Countess.'

Mr Holmes would always conclude one such tale by announcing, 'And so that there may be no mistake about it Mrs Hudson, I will come down tomorrow morning and show you how it was made.' It was then that he explained to me that there was a much more elaborate version made with a particular kind of masking paste – a mingling of sugar syrup and egg yolk which was then introduced to the whipped meringue.

'But,' he said, 'it need not concern us, this suffices and is sickly-sweet enough for us to serve should we ever have to entertain a young member of the fair sex!' This was before Dr Watson had met his future bride, so perhaps my Great Man was also clairvoyant, as has been suggested.

Within five minutes, if your oven be right the soufflé will be found to be richly browned all over. Serve immediately upon a larger metal dish with pretty d'oyleys previously set upon it. It is perhaps fanciful; but Most Agreeable to a Young Lady, if a pre-made flower nosegay or spray be set in readiness to be laid against the larger rim of the (cold) outer dish when dishing up. On cutting – as the Count had proved with his Camembert cheese experiment – the ice cream will be found to be perfectly hard still inside. Which is quite remarkable!

Author's Note

With a modern Gas Oven – the author would never cook by anything else – this is the one occasion when the oven needs to be pre-heated. Do so for fifteen minutes, then allow only a maximum three and a quarter minutes baking on the highest shelf. The correct name for this much

Puddings

overrated pudding is *Omelette Norvégienne* and it should be made an indictable offence for it to be called by the bastard name of 'Baked Alaska'! There is no more heinous offence in classic cookery than for a great dish to be given a wholly inaccurate or false name. *F.C.*

ON STEAMING PROPERLY

The container should be covered carefully with oiled parchment (*aluminium foil over buttered greaseproof, F.C.*) and placed in a pan in which the water should come two thirds up the sides of it. Watch until the water re-boils after immersion. Then put on the pan's cover, draw slowly to the side of the stove until the desired steady simmer is obtained and let the contents so cook for the time stated, keeping a careful watch lest – if the time be very long – the water diminishes too low.

MR SHERLOCK HOLMES' PLUM DUFF

Care MUST be used if featherweight results are to be continued. The currants must be carefully dried in a small handful of flour and rubbed clear with a dry cloth. The flour must be self-rising and three-times sifted. The suet must be pure beef suet chopped extremely finely. Very cold water must be used to bind the mixture to a firm dough as if it were then to be rolled out for pastry. The cloth in which the pudding is tied after assembly must be fine-grained Holland, lined out with well-buttered butter papers. These are the notes I made when Cook first taught it to me and I have found them of the Utmost Importance.

ASSEMBLY

6 oz superfine sultanas; 10 oz self-raising flour; 1 small pinch of salt; 5 oz fine-chopped beef suet; cold water to bind.

PROCEDURE

Sift the flour into a roomy basin. Work in the prepared suet with the fingers (I need scarcely add that these must be spotlessly clean). Then work in the sultanas making sure that these are well and evenly distributed. Make a well in the centre, put in about 2 fluid oz water and start working up with a table knife adding more water sparingly to achieve a firm dough. Shape dough into a ball, enclose loosely in several buttered papers, overlapping to allow room for expansion during boiling. Tie loosely but securely in a Holland cloth. Lower into the boiler, sufficiently filled to ensure complete coverage and allow the pudding to boil steadily for two and a half hours. Unwrap. Remove papers on a well-scrubbed kitchen table. Set the Duff upon a silver entrée dish. Dust lightly with Dark Barbados sugar. Hand separate bowl of this sugar when carrying round the Duff (previously sliced at the sideboard) and also hand a well-polished silver cream jug containing Jersey cream.

Author's Note

Today such a pudding is steamed for three hours under a loose covering of buttered papers and an outer covering of aluminium kitchen foil. Make a pleat in the centre of the paper so that when pressed down all round the basin and secured with a rubber band, the pleat begins to open up across the centre thus allowing ample room for expansion. Use packet suet of good quality and if you can achieve the right sugar and cream so much the better! *F.C.*

SIX-CUP PUDDING FOR SIMPLE EVERYDAY USE

This was much liked by That Boy, whom I restricted to three helpings after it had been offered in the dining-room, until when he remained at table drumming his heels in impatience to get at his share.

ASSEMBLY

1 teacupful of each of the following ingredients: flour, chopped suet, fine white breadcrumbs, raisins – stoned and chopped, currants, skim milk; 1 small pinch carbonate of soda; 2 teaspoons wine vinegar; 1 egg.

PROCEDURE

Warm the milk to blood heat, dissolve the soda in it and allow to cool a little before stirring in the vinegar. Mix all dry ingredients together in a roomy mixing bowl and make a small hole in the centre. Pour in the milk mixture and work up with the hand at some speed, adding the beaten eggs, as this is not a mixture which requires much 'working upon'. Place in a buttered basin, cover with butter papers, then tie on the cloth and so boil in the copper or in a large pan for at least two and a quarter hours.

PROPER PANCAKES

Even when I was a very young apprentice in my Lady's Cook's kitchen I learned the foolishness of that malpractice called 'tossing a pancake'. As Cook observed sagely, and I later discovered to be so from the lips of that Greatest, Mrs A. B. Marshall, 'If a pancake is thick enough to toss there is only one place to toss it my girl – into the dustbin!'

When I first learned the way of making proper ones I was stood against the table watching Cook make the batter for which I have not found a proper receipt in any English or Scottish receipt book save only Mrs A. B. Marshall. When she had done, Cook took away the batter and put it under a plate in the larder. 'Not,' she explained, 'because it needs to wait, for it may be made and used immediately, but because it is for testing YOU my girl.' She then made me make another batch, from memory and this time she stood over me watching how I worked, with a wooden spoon, in a wooden basin and working first with some gentleness so that the batter be not made springy, finally when really very thin, working fast and vigorously. These things done, Cook took down two small flat-based, shallow-rimmed iron pans and set them upon the stove where it was but of gentle heat. 'Let them be until you are ready for the making,' said she, 'that the iron may become hot.' Then, from the larder she fetched out a piece of fat from uncooked, unsalted pork. 'This is all the grease that you require,' she informed me next. 'When your pan be hot you "polish it" with this piece of fat and a great deal of elbow grease. The pan be ready when he "sings" at the first fatty application.' Thus did she 'learn me' as I then called it before my education was taken in hand by my Lady. Well, we went to work, she with one pan and me a moment behind her all the time to watch her movements and working side aside.

First came the elbow grease, then, with batter as thin as thin unwhipped cream I saw she picked up her pan slightly to tilt it away from her and thus poured in the thin batter from the near side so that it run like a very thin, smooth film over the hot, greased base.

'We don't want lumps and humps down the middle of *our* pancakes!' she commented.

Then we both set the pans back again on the moderate part of the (closed) stove top and waited only a moment until the thin rims were set. 'Now you can see my lass,' Cook pointed out, 'as how no one could toss a pancake this thick what didn't want a flop like a dump of soggy bedclothes in the middle of their pan,' saying which she wiped a metal spatula with the piece of pork fat, slid him under the very thin pancake and quite slow-like and easy, turned him over.

'Now only a few seconds on the underside,' she instructed, 'for it needs no more, and then out with it on to an oiled, upturned afternoon tea plate and under another plate covered with a wet cloth into the very coolest part of your oven to keep warm without crimping up the edges.'

I split my first one, I made a sorry mess of my second too, and beyond clicking her tongue cross-like at the waste of batter Cook let me be. Thus on my third I managed to make a creditable turn-over and on my fifth a pale, even, very thin pancake just like Cook's.

After that I had no trouble with my pancakes for she 'learned me', as she said, 'right and proper'.

COOK'S PANCAKE BATTER

ASSEMBLY

2 eggs (*standard*, *F.C.*) and 1 extra egg yolk; 5 oz sifted self-raising flour; some milk, or better still thin cream and milk; 2 tablespoons olive oil and no other.

PROCEDURE

Sift the flour into a roomy basin. Make a well in the centre, drop in both the raw eggs and the extra yolk, the olive oil and a few tablespoons of milk. Use just enough to stir to a very thick batter. Do not beat at this juncture. Then add a little more milk and cream – spoon and spoon about, or just milk for everyday occasions and stir in gradually increasing the speed as the mixture thins until you are beating steadily and fast. When the batter is of the identical consistency with thin, pouring cream, you stop and employ the batter as I have explained. This was how we always made Mr Holmes' pancakes on Shrove Tuesday and it was quite remarkable how That Policeman fellow always happened to be passing upon some trivial query or another just before I was dishing up my gentlemen's luncheon on Shrove Tuesdays. It was ever so. He would be arriving on the doorstep, That Boy would be taking him up and then coming down to tell me, 'He's here again same as last year Mrs H.' and I would tell him resignedly, 'Set another place boy and only use the second best napkins because he wipes those whiskers of his in such a manner as filthies every table napkin he gets a hold of, him being a savage person and of no good table manners.'

Then I would set to and make more pancakes so that, when the time came to dish up, sure and certain that bell would be pulled and up would go the boy to come back and say briefly 'ee says like always'.

My readers may deem it an exaggeration on my part, but I undertake that more than once I have made eighteen pancakes for That Policeman fellow who has scoffed them back like they were winkles for his tea.

Mr Holmes was what you might say 'unorthodox' in his manner of eating pancakes. Not for him the pieces of lemon and the castor sugar in a nice silver dredger. Oh no! He ruled, 'Lemon slices are for Lapsang Suchong tea, and I will have a small jug of fresh orange juice and a bowl of Barbados (called 'pieces' by the Grocery trade) sugar, rich, thick and very dark brown for preference although the light brown is preferable to the white!'

Mr Holmes was in fact Immensely Particular, and what I believe those Frenchies call 'a gourmet'.

QUEEN OF PUDDINGS

ASSEMBLY

8 oz fine, white breadcrumbs which are very soft; $7\frac{1}{2}$ oz superfine castor sugar; the grated zest of 1 medium lemon; 2 eggs (*standard, F.C.*); 4 extra oz castor sugar; 3 oz sieved apricot jam; the strained juice of the lemon; milk; $\frac{1}{4}$ oz butter.

PROCEDURE

Place the crumbs in a basin, add milk sparingly until all becomes a pap. Remember this must not be too wet – just pappy. Butter a medium sized pie dish. Add into the basin the separated egg yolks, lemon juice and rind, also sugar and sieved apricot jam. Turn into the prepared pie dish, level off neatly and bake, uncovered, in a slow oven (*Gas Mark 3, one shelf below centre. F.C.*) until set. Remove and cool. Whip separated egg whites until only just stiff. Whip in 1 oz from the extra 4 oz sugar. Whip on for four minutes. Stop whipping altogether and just stir/fold in the remaining 3 oz of sugar. Either pipe through a forcing bag with a 'crown' nozzle affixed or just spread over evenly and pull up to *level* peaks with a fork. Return to a really cool oven (*Gas Mark 1, same shelf as before. F.C.*) and leave until meringue is a pale biscuit colour on top. Serve from the pie dish with a nice paper pie frill affixed round the rim to conceal this and the sides of the pie dish both of which would be unsightly at the table.

STEAMED APRICOT PUDDING

ASSEMBLY
3 oz sweet butter; 3 oz superfine castor sugar; 4 very large eggs or 5 less large ones; 3 oz apricot jam, first rubbed through a fine sieve and then weighed thereafter; a little extra melted butter; 3 oz sifted, self-raising flour.

PROCEDURE
Brush the interior of a 2 lb pudding basin carefully with melted butter. Beat the given 3 oz butter until almost white, very light and completely free from streaks. Add the sugar and beat again to the same texture and appearance. Separate the yolks from the whites of your eggs. Add a spoonful of flour to mixture, then first yolk, beat and so continue until all are incorporated. Now blend in the sieved jam carefully and thoroughly. Whip up the egg whites until you may turn the container upside down and they will remain securely in the bowl. Add these fast, beating well but not with a heavy hand. Cover with a butter paper and cloth (*aluminium foil and a rubber band, F.C.*), and tie securely with strong twine just below the rim of the bowl. Boil for one hour ten minutes under a lid, making sure water never comes more than two thirds up the basin. (*Steam one hour forty minutes. F.C.*) Serve with My Apricot Sauce.

MY APRICOT SAUCE

ASSEMBLY
5 oz sieved apricot jam; 2 tablespoons inexpensive sweet white wine (*or water, F.C.*); a few drops Apricot Brandy; 1 tablespoon fine chopped, blanched sweet almonds.

PROCEDURE
Place all in a sauce saucepan on the side of the stove (*over low heat, F.C.*) and allow all to become piping hot *after* unmoulding the Steamed Apricot Pudding. Pour the sauce over the pudding and send to table.

TITSY-BITSIES
These were the delight of the nursery folk where I was previously employed. They are speedily achieved and at very little expenditure. Cut

two to three dozen fat cubes of crustless bread. Place 4 oz golden syrup in a small pan over a low heat and stir thereto 1 tablespoon softest brown sugar, the strained juice of 1 orange and 2½ oz sweet butter. When 'singing' hot, drop in the bread cubes, stir about that they may become uniformly brown and steeped for exactly seven minutes. Turn into an entrée dish and hand thin cream for pouring upon each portion. Be sure to supply small bowls for service, they would spread messily upon plates.

PUFF PASTRY

Wherever serious cooks are gathered together there you will find discussion and debate as to the very best way in which to achieve this rather recent discovery. If this be not known to my reader it may be as well to recount the happening of it as told to me by my Lady who, being much joined to Foreign Connections, entertained someone with a Most Peculiar Name whom my Lady had the goodness to inform me was a Very Famous Cook. From him did she hear the tale and I now tell it as my Lady told it to me and Cook.

It transpired that in a restaurant in Paris there was a young apprentice cook to whom my Lady gave a fancy sounding name which quite escapes me,* and the head cook bade him one morning put up some pastry paste for his instructor's immediate use. The boy began his Assembly. Into the kitchen came a person with whom the Head Cook was very familiar so he straightaway drew him into his private sanctum sanctorum and here regaled his friend with a bottle of wine.

In the kitchen the young man worked away at his task. He sifted the flour on to a marble slab. He weighed out his butter, wrung it in a cloth to expel surplus moisture and set it against a corner of the slab. He sprinkled salt upon the flour, worked it in with his finger tips, took up ice-cold water obtained from the charge cave and, making a central cavity in his flour, poured in some cold water to which he added a squeeze of lemon juice. All as he had been taught. Then he bound up the flour with more water until he obtained his smooth rolling dough.

This was when he saw to his horror that the butter was still set upon the corner of the slab and he had wholly omitted its incorporation in the flour mixture. He cast a horrified glance towards the Head Cook's room, of which he saw thankfully that the door was still fast closed. He thought for one frantic moment, then straightway rolled out the dough fast into a long strip. Then he took up the butter lump and laid it in

* Commis-Chef.

the centre, pressed upon it to flatten it a little with his pin and then folded it up, half-turned it round, hesitated, decided to stop and with another terrified glance towards That Door he rolled again and half turned, and rolled again. In all he rolled and rolled until there was no sign of butter showing through the mixture. Then and then only did he wrap it in waxed papers and put it in the charge cave. Then he leaned back and mopped the perspiration from his brow. It was all of one hour later when the Head Cook came out again, with his friend to whom he bade good-bye. Then straightaway he walked across to the young man demanding, 'My pastry, where is my pastry?'

In fear and trembling the boy fetched it, saw it rolled out and put on a sheet into a hot oven. When the head cook opened the oven door he saw that the paste had risen as it had never done heretofore and he snatched it from the heat calling everyone to gather round and see this marvel of the culinary art. Then he turned on the boy, grasped him by the shoulders, shook him violently and in a voice of great strength demanded that the boy tell him what he had done to produce this wonder. And that was the origin of puff pastry according to the tale my Lady told me.

You now know the way of it, so I will merely set down for you the proportions and certain other niceties which have developed in the making of it since that first accidental discovery.

PUFF PASTRY

ASSEMBLY

15 oz very finest flour, sifted three times on to a very cold surface with salt therein; 14 oz sweet butter, treated as explained in my tale above; 1 generous pinch of salt; strained juice of half a very small lemon; VERY cold water to bind.

PROCEDURE

Gather your fingers into a posy and with this push out the mound of sifted flour into a ring. Put into this ring the lemon juice and a little cold water and begin to work up centrally with two knives, adding more water and drawing in more flour gradually until a firm dough of good rolling consistency is obtained. Dust more flour over the marble surface. Roll out the paste into a long strip, say 20-inches by 7-inches wide. Then take up the butter, and having wrung this well out in a cloth pat into a 5-inch rectangle and lay it centrally upon the paste.

Puddings

Fold the top over. Fold the base over the top, and be very careful to roll the edges together after each fold every time such are made, as this is vital. Having enclosed the butter, give the paste a half turn on the table, always to the right, and then roll with little jerky movements into a long strip once again. Always jerk roll as it is thus that the air bubbles may be persuaded into the dough and indeed you find them developing if you work this way. Fold again, half turn, and rest in your charge cave (*refrigerator, F.C.*) for twenty minutes. Then repeat all over again at twenty minute intervals, thus giving to the paste seven rollings in all, and ever beginning with the half-turned paste from the previous rolling at the top and away facing you as you work. To ensure no mistake in this, drive a thumb indent into the top before putting into the charge cave each time.

SPOTTED DICK

It was ever Dr Watson who was the lustier trencherman. Mr Holmes was a far more dainty eater, but the one compensated the other – for while, if I may be excused the vulgarity, Dr Watson 'tucked in', Mr Holmes would pounce upon the subtleties or any omissions, thus keeping me upon my toes. In the matter of such sturdy puddings as this one, thanks to Dr Watson there was seldom more than enough left than would provide portions for That Boy and me.

ASSEMBLY

10 oz sifted, self-raising flour; 1 heaped tablespoon baking powder; 5 oz fine chopped, skin free suet (*use from a packet, F.C.*); 4 oz currants which are well cleaned first to remove any grocer's impurities, by rubbing in a piece of clean linen and with a dessertspoon flour scattered over; cold water to bind; a bowl of soft brown (pieces) sugar; a jug of melted butter.

PROCEDURE

Sift the flour and baking powder together into a bowl. Run the prepared suet in through the fingers until evenly distributed. Do likewise with the currants. Bind to a firm, rolling dough with cold water and press into a fat sausage on buttered papers, completely and loosely enclose in same, then wrap in a clean white cloth, also loosely, and tie the ends with stout string. Lower into the copper containing boiling water and so stoke your fire that this is maintained for two hours. Unwrap completely. Set upon a heated dish. Let the side accompaniments be handed separately.

Author's Note

Steam in a buttered basin with buttered paper and foil on top for two and a half hours. *F.C.*

APPLE FRITTERS AS THEY SHOULD BE MADE

I never make these fritters without recalling my wonderful experience of sitting among the pupil-audience for one of the great Mrs Agnes Bertha Marshall's cooking classes. We all crowded eagerly together in benches which were so raised about a cleared area below, that even the ones on the topmost rung were well able to see this lovely and gifted lady as she cooked and instructed throughout a memorable day. She wore a charming morning dress with, as I recall, a very elegant braided ruff about the hem. Yet so orderly and so precise was she that never a speck fell upon the floor to soil that pretty hem. Nor did she wear what any of us working cooks would consider to be an apron; but only a little fancy, frilled thing which she tied about her slender waist.

Now I had ever made my batters with egg, milk and a little water. Mrs Marshall soon showed me the error of my ways. First she prepared the apples, sound Bramleys of course, by paring away the skin extremely finely and then using one of the modern apple core removers to thrust down centrally and withdraw again with all the core therein. These she then sliced a half inch thick so that they resembled apple rings, just fresh ones instead of the dried ones with which we were all familiar. She then summoned a member of the audience to assist her. 'Pray prepare the steeping agent,' she requested of this person whom I longed to be but was too shy for such exposure to all those pairs of eyes. This consisted of the strained juice of 1 lemon to offset discoloration, followed by 2 large tablespoons of inexpensive cooking brandy and 1 tablespoon of sugar. 'Now,' Mrs Marshall explained, 'we will leave those steeping for thirty minutes.' Mrs Marshall, really she was a very pretty woman, then said, 'Now we will make a batter which will really puff them up beautifully every time.' So saying she measured off 4 heaped tablespoons of superfine self-raising flour into a basin. Then she made a well in the centre, put in 1 tablespoon of olive oil and thinned the mixture down to a very thick batter consistency *with cold water*. Having so done she covered this springy paste with a plate and let it lie until the thirty minutes had elapsed, when she gave her assistant 2 egg whites to whip stiffly, proving that they were so, for all of our

Puddings

entertainment, by turning the bowlful upside down over her elegantly dressed hair. Finally she folded and cut the egg whites into the stiff batter, thus making it a trifle looser. Then the apple rings were drained over a sieve so that the juices ran down into a small bowl. Each apple ring was then drawn through the batter until completely coated. For this she employed the blunt end of a wooden skewer and thus lifted the ring into her deep pan of almost smoking hot, pure olive oil. 'You must so regulate the oil heat,' she explained, 'as to ensure the batter and apple are cooked right through,' adding, 'they *are* done when a rich golden brown.' She dredged them on pieces of crumpled tissue paper, set them in a fine line, overlapping down a silver dish covered with a dainty paper d'oyley and, at the last, passed a sieve of icing sugar over the tops, tapping the side with one finger as she did so to ensure even distribution. To my surprise she then poured the soaking fluids into a very small copper saucepan, added 2 dessertspoons of apricot purée, stirred both over a strong heat – she performed with a modern gas stove – and when hot poured in another tablespoon of brandy and turned it into a pretty chased silver jug. 'And thus send to table,' she ended. The dish was then passed round for all of us to inspect. It came with an additional bowl of sifted icing sugar. I was one of the lucky ones who was able to taste a morsel and since then I have ever made my Apple Fritters – if I may coin a phrase – *à la Mrs Marshall* – and they have always won the highest praise both from my two gentlemen and from any guests who have perchance arrived timely upon the luncheon scene.

FANCHETTE FOR A DINNER

We celebrated the engagement of Dr Watson to his young lady with a dinner at which I served this dainty pudding. The bride-to-be was so charmed with it that she later asked of me if I would show her the way of it. This of course I did, remarking, with due respect, how quick she was and how deft her delicate fingers.

ASSEMBLY

¼ lb superfine castor sugar; the yolks of 12 eggs; ¼ lb finest self-raising flour; 1 pinch salt; 1 teaspoon *Noyau*;* 3 egg whites (not too fresh please); 3 oz superfine castor sugar again; ½ lb my Melting pastry

* This eau-de-vie is obtainable today from Edouard Robinson in Old Compton Street, Soho. F.C.

The Sherlock Holmes Cookbook

paste (please turn to p. 197. Follow the recipe for the paste with the following amendments – delete cayenne and Parmesan cheese and add 3 oz castor sugar); a delicate mixture of candied fruits for decoration;* ½ pint double cream.

PROCEDURE

Make up my paste. Then be sure to rest on a cold larder slab for at least one hour (*thirty minutes in domestic refrigeration, F.C.*). Roll out the paste to a little under ¼-inch thickness and line out a round tin like a giant patty pan of 9-inch diameter. This may be obtained from the Purchasing Department of Mrs Marshall's School of Cookery, 31/32 Mortimer Street, London W.1.† The flour adhering to the under-side will be all that is required. Roll off the edges so that they lie against the flutes of the tin. Put in your large circle of grease-proof paper. Turn in a sufficiency of dried pulses to come to the rim and bake in a fair oven. (*Gas Mark 5, mid-shelf sixteen minutes. F.C.*) Take out, remove the paper and pulses. Return the shell to a very slow oven for five minutes to dry out the base. Now turn your full attention to the filling. Mix together the flour and sugar, work in the egg yolks, at first with the back of a wooden spoon, later, when the mass is blended use a loop whisk and beat very steadily for five minutes. Turn into the top of a double pan over hot water in the base pan, add the salt and cream and stir carefully over a steady heat until the mixture be thickened very much and made perfectly smooth. Add Noyau. Cool it down thoroughly by plunging the upper pan into a bowl of crushed ice and stir on. When the cream be cold, turn into your pastry shell and level off neatly. Whip up the given egg white very stiff indeed, draw a little of the stiff foam to one side of its bowl and slice in the second amount of given sugar. Then draw in very gently. Place in a forcing bag with a decorative, wide-mouthed pipe affixed and cover the entire upper surface with a sloping, rosetted dome of piped meringue. Put into a very moderate oven once more, (*Gas Mark 1, lowest shelf. F.C.*) and let it lie until the meringue has hardened much and turned the faintest pale beige in colour. Withdraw and chill. At the moment of service decorate the meringue top tastefully with candied fruits, such as pieces of candied apricot, pineapple and greengage.

* Crystallised fruits to us. *F.C.*
† Closed down finally in 1945.

MY AUNT'S SIMPLE CHERRY PUDDING

My aunt always drummed into me that it was worthless to attempt this simple pudding save when fat black cherries were in season.

ASSEMBLY

3 lb stoned cherries; 1 small handful soft brown (pieces) sugar; 5 fluid oz good claret; 3 oz unsalted butter; the yolks of 4 eggs; 12 sponge cakes. This pudding is always improved if these last are left to become somewhat hard before using. (*Use a packet of bought ones, they'll be stale! F.C.*)

PROCEDURE

Butter a medium pie dish and lay therein the sponge cakes, cutting up such as do not fit to make them do so. Whip the egg yolks thoroughly, beat into the claret. Melt the butter and pour upon the sponge cakes. Strew the cherries over. Press down. Scatter the sugar on top. Then pour over the egg and claret mixture. Leave standing for half an hour. Then and then only place in a mild oven (*Gas Mark 4, mid-shelf. F.C.*) and bake for thirty minutes. Serve hot with a jug of thin cream; or serve cold with a decorative top of whipped, thick cream.

A DISH OF CHERRIES IN SUMMER TIME

ASSEMBLY

2 lb stoned, fat, black cherries; 10 oz home-made blackcurrant jelly; 4 tablespoons cooking kirsch; sifted icing sugar in a separate bowl.

PROCEDURE

Place the cherries and every drop of their juices into a stone jar, shake over only 2 tablespoons of your sifted icing sugar and place in a very, very slow oven with a saucer on the top of the jar, that they may draw well for the space of one hour (*floor of oven, Gas Mark 1, F.C.*). Meanwhile, set the jelly in a stewpan against the very rim of your stove to melt slowly and become quite smooth. Stir in the kirsch, work in the cherries, taste and add more sifted icing sugar with discretion, sending the rest to table in a silver sugar-dredger. You should also send up, when your dish of cherries be perfectly cold, a bowl of whipped cream forced into a spiral in a crystal bowl.

The Sherlock Holmes Cookbook

Note: Here be an example as to how to present my Rout Biscuits as a side dish at a luncheon. They make an admirable accompaniment.

THE PRINCE REGENT'S PUDDING

This did come to me by a turnabout way, for it was a cousin of mine who gave it to me. He was a valet in chamber to one of the gentlemen in the Palace and this gentleman let the receipt lie upon his table, quite open and for all to see. My nephew copied it. Thereafter the gentleman concerned remarked quite casually while my cousin was dressing his hair, that he was in a hurry, as he had to bear the receipt to Queen Alexandra who had expressed her approval of it to a mutual friend.

ASSEMBLY

4 oz fine soft breadcrumbs; 4 oz sifted self-raising flour; 4 oz desiccated coconut; 4 oz cleaned currants; 2 large eggs; 3 oz castor sugar; $2\frac{1}{2}$ oz fine chopped, seeded raisins; 4 tablespoons thick unbeaten cream; 5 fluid oz or $\frac{1}{4}$ pint sweet new milk.

PROCEDURE

Mix all the dry ingredients together very thoroughly. Whip the eggs up well, whip in the milk. Add, through a well in the centre, to this dry mixture and include the cream thereafter so that, if by some mishap you have mis-weighted your ingredients too spare, you may abstain when a thick, well-bound mixture has resulted. Turn into a well buttered basin which has been further dredged with fine castor sugar and the surplus tapped off. Cover with several butter papers laid on very loose. Then, with clean linen, tie securely with strong twine about the rim. Take up the four corners of the cloth and knot them centrally. Lower into your boiler and boil for two and a half hours. Serve with Rum Sauce.

RUM SAUCE

ASSEMBLY

$\frac{1}{2}$ pint cold water, preferably rain water boiled; the strained juice of 1 lemon; 2 thin-skinned oranges and the grated rind of 1 orange only; just over a $\frac{1}{2}$ gill or $2\frac{1}{2}$ fluid oz of white rum; sugar to taste; a greengage-sized piece of very sweet butter; as much potato flour dissolved in cold water, taken from the half pint, as will make it quite thick. I always use

Puddings

2½ heaped teaspoons, but the teaspoons vary in size, so make in this instance as much as this but thereafter stir in gradually that you may abstain when the liquor is sufficiently thick.

PROCEDURE

Boil the remaining water with the rum, lemon and orange juices, and add thereto the 1 grated rind. Dissolve the potato flour as explained, stir in and thereafter stir in the sugar to please, and the butter, until the sauce be very clear.

CRUSADES

I cannot now recall where in the world I obtained this receipt, but it is ever a popular one.

ASSEMBLY

12 rounds of ½-inch-thick milk loaf with no crusts whatever thereon and all stamped 3-inches in diameter in circles; a liberal supply of melted, very sweet butter; apricot jam in purée, i.e. rubbed through a fine sieve; flaked almonds which have first been browned by strewing over a dry baking tin and setting in a hot oven for a few moments, when the upper part be brown, turn all over and repeat the browning; fine chopped pistachio nuts.

PROCEDURE

Take a very sharp knife with a tapering point and cut out the centres of your bread rounds so as to leave a neat, central cavity in each one and a border of only a ½-inch in width. Press down a little, then fry briskly in 'singing' hot melted butter. Drain and set upon a heated dish. Swiftly fill the cavities with the jam and employ a small brush to brush more purée over the rims. Encrust these thickly with the browned almonds. Scatter fine-chopped pistachio nuts over the jam centres and so send to table. I always serve a plain lemon sauce in a jug with these dainties.

BACHELORS' PUDDING

This is an appropriately named pudding to put before hungry bachelors in winter time – if so be they can ever be relied upon to appear at the time which they declare roundly upon departure will see them home again.

ASSEMBLY

4 oz fine, soft breadcrumbs; 4 oz currants shaken in ½ oz flour and this shook off in a clean cloth thereafter; 4 oz cooking apples, being the peeled, cored weight; 2 oz superfine castor sugar; 3 fresh eggs, and if so be you are doubtful pray place them in a roomy basin of cold water. If any rise to the top and float, be sure to extract them and take them back to the grocers for replacement; the grated rind of 1 medium lemon; 1 small teaspoon self-raising flour; a generous grate of nutmeg. Some people will put a generous pinch of salt in with this but I will have none of it.

PROCEDURE

Chop the prepared apples fairly roughly. Place the breadcrumbs in a roomy bowl, mix in the chopped apples, currants, sugar, lemon rind and nutmeg. Sift through the fingers until very evenly distributed. Beat up the eggs thoroughly. Make a well in the centre of the dry mixture. Turn in the beaten eggs, work up thoroughly, cover with a clean cloth and let be for thirty minutes. At the end of this time scatter the self-raising mixture upon the top and work it in. If so be the mixture is a trifle too thick for easy working, add a small quantity of sweet, fresh milk. Turn into a well-buttered 2 lb pudding basin. Cover the levelled-off top surface with buttered butter papers. Tie down in a cloth. Set in a steamer over plenty of boiling water in the base pan. Cover close and let simmer gently but steadily for three hours. Hand melted butter sauce in a sauce-boat and if considered desirable, fresh cream in a nice jug.

MELTED BUTTER SAUCE

Place 4 oz sweet butter in a small thick pan and set by the side of your stove that the butter may melt slowly without bubbling. When it is completely dissolved, stir in 2 very high-heaped tablespoons of soft brown (pieces) sugar and a generous squeeze of strained lemon juice.

KAISER WILHELM PUDDING

It was told to me that the poor little boy with the crippled hand had a great fancy for this pudding, which was served to him on frequent occasions in whatever passed in his foreign country for a proper nursery.

ASSEMBLY

2 oz ground almonds, rubbed free of any little lumps; superfine castor sugar to taste; 3 good-sized eggs (*standard, F.C.*); one $\frac{1}{2}$ pint very best thick cream (from a Jersey cow be ever best); 1 tablespoon fresh, strained orange juice (try to use the juice of a blood orange in winter time); a few blanched almonds; some shredded candied peel.

PROCEDURE

Separate the egg yolks from the whites. Beat the yolks to a pale batter with 1 huge-heaped tablespoon of castor sugar, then beat in the ground almonds very thoroughly, work in orange juice and then the cream, already part-whipped to the stage where it just flops from the whisk. Do this a little at a time whipping thoroughly after each addition. Whisk up the egg whites very stiff indeed, whip in 2 more tablespoons of sugar, and blend them into your mixture – carefully, completely, but without violence so as not to whip out the air you have whipped in. Have ready a mould, prepared in the following manner. Butter it very liberally, scatter shredded, peeled, blanched almonds and candied peel (*the standard diced kind does well enough, F.C.*) and finally sift a little castor sugar over. Turn in the mixture, level off the top very even, cover with buttered, butter papers, then with a cloth, and place in a steamer over plenty of boiling water in the base pan, that it may steam gently by the side of the stove and not bubble very fierce, for not less than one and a half hours. When it be done and carefully unmoulded on to a heated dish, make the sauce which is to accompany it; but have all your preparations for this sauce done while the pudding is being steamed.

KAISER SAUCE

ASSEMBLY

4 good-sized eggs (*standard, F.C.*); 4 half egg-shells filled with sweetish Hock; 4 generous teaspoons superfine castor sugar; 1 teaspoon cold water; 1 egg-shell brandy.

PROCEDURE

Put the water, brandy and Hock into the top of a porage saucepan over hot water. Set over medium top-of-stove heat and allow to become hot. Meanwhile, whip up the eggs and sugar to a smooth, pale batter, scrape into the pan and whip, whip until all rises to a thick foam, never ceasing to whip for one instant. Serve in a sauce-boat and pray remember this sauce requires a ladle.

PRINCE ALBERT'S PUDDING

You may well inquire as to how I came to know His Royal Highness' Pudding, so I will give my explanation, somewhat shady though it be! The truth is that my friend Bessie Spears, having been in Royal Service these many years did obtain it from one of the chefs at Sandringham, she being in the state of walking out with same. Bessie then entrusted it to me with strict injunctions never to give it to anyone else, which of course I never have done until now. Bessie came to stay with me for a night at my cottage and we discussed the matter most earnestly together. In the end she decided that no harm could come after this long time either to her or to me through the telling of it. One cannot be too careful even so, when it comes to Royalty.

ASSEMBLY

Fine, soft crumbs from a milk loaf, as much as will form a firm pap with a ½ pint of warmed cream; the very finely chopped thin-cut peel of 1 large lemon; 2 oz castor sugar; 1 pinch of ground cinnamon; 4 eggs; 2 fluid oz each of orange-flower water and Maraschino.

PROCEDURE

Take a plain round Charlotte Mould (*7-inch soufflé mould, F.C.*) and butter it well on base and sides with cold butter. Cut foolscap paper to fit the mould all around the sides, then butter it upon both sides and fit it in so that the two ends overlap slightly. Now put about 1½ cupfuls of your crumbs into a bowl, pour on the warmed cream, blend and stir until a loose pap is formed and then stiffen this pap with more crumbs until it be firm. Work in the sugar, cinnamon and lemon peel. Stir in the Maraschino and the orange-flower water. At this point observe the texture, which should now be brought to about the consistency of a strong batter. If it be more runny, then you have one last chance to add more crumbs. Do so. Finally beat up your eggs very thoroughly, work them into the mixture, turn into the prepared container and steam until set, this should be so, if a steady simmer is maintained, after between one hour twenty minutes and one hour twenty-five minutes. The accompanying sauce is described below.

APRICOT AND PISTACHIO SAUCE

Place 1 lb good apricot jam in a stew pan and add thereto the finely peeled, finely chopped skin of 1 lemon, 2 oz castor sugar, 1½ gills cold water and a salt spoon of Marshall's Saffron colouring. Allow to heat through and eventually boil up together. Place in a small basin 1 oz potato flour with 1 gill cold water. Stir these together, pour on to the boiling contents of your stewpan and stir rapidly with a wooden spoon until perfectly clear and thick. Cook so, stirring over a low heat for ten minutes. Then stir in 12 shelled, skinned, fine-chopped pistachio nuts and 1 tablespoon apricot brandy. Rub through a tammy cloth (*tamis or sieve, F.C.*) on to the unmoulded Prince Albert Pudding having removed the foolscap paper band with care. Hand a separate sauceboat of Boiled Cream which should be brought to the boil and so maintained for five minutes with a further tablespoon of apricot brandy stirred in.

SEMOLINA PUDDING WHICH BE NOT A PENANCE TO EAT

What makes the recalling of this simple pudding memorable to me is that I had already prepared it for my master's luncheon when I observed from my kitchen window that yet another hansom had drawn up before our steps. Mr Holmes was ever a prodigious taker of hansoms, so I was not unduly disturbed by this event until I observed, stepping from the cab that Mr Lestrade from Scotland Yard who was indeed a frequent visitor. Hurriedly divesting myself of my apron, I bade That Boy remain below stairs and hurried up myself to meet the two gentlemen on their coming in.

'Ah Mrs Hudson, good day to you,' exclaimed my master. 'Would it be beyond you to provide luncheon for both of us?'

'Indeed no sir,' I responded, for I regarded it as something of a challenge that I must always be ready to meet these surprise catering problems. 'I rather fear though, sir,' I added, 'that the fare is but simple.'

As was his way, 'How simple pray?' inquired my master, so I told him.

'I have a good bowl of broth. There is a jugged hare in the oven and knowing you have a fancy for them sir, some semolina fritters with jam sauce and cream to follow.' You can imagine my surprise when a broad grin spread over our visitor's face. 'Semolina fritters,' he exclaimed, 'why I haven't had them since I was a boy.'

The only glum face in our household that day was That Boy's for I told him, 'No fritters for you my lad. I have just enough made for above stairs; but if you behave I will fry up some of that cold plum duff for you and give it to you with hot syrup,' which somewhat restored him to countenance.

ASSEMBLY

4 fluid oz sweet white wine; $4\frac{1}{2}$ fluid oz cold water; $4\frac{1}{2}$ oz semolina; 2 eggs; butter for frying; jam.

PROCEDURE

Oil a small piece of marble and set a plain pastry cutter beside it in readiness. The cutter should be $2\frac{1}{2}$-inches in diameter, plain and round. Put into a thick stewpan the wine and water. When they boil, shake over the semolina, and stir until the mixture is very thick and smooth. Stir in also the sugar. Turn the mixture on to the prepared marble slab, press out to a $\frac{1}{2}$-inch in depth and leave until quite cold. Then with a pan of boiling water beside you, dip in the cutter, stamp out a round and so repeat until only trimmings remain. Gather these up, re-press them into a $\frac{1}{2}$-inch depth and stamp out the remainder. When the time comes to use them heat enough butter to cover the base of a frypan over a fairly brisk heat. Put in the semolina rounds and fry them a moment or two. Add 4 tablespoons of preferably black cherry jam, but any other kind will suffice for this dish. Turn the fritters – as they have now become, that they be fully impregnated with the jam and slightly crisp on their outsides. Range them down a narrow heated dish and so send to table with a jug of hot cream. It is a sign of a bad and ignorant cook if so be she finds herself compelled to serve cold cream with hot puddings, through ignorance of the simple fact that cream boils excellently.

ITALIAN PIE

This was another receipt which, after she had tasted it at our table Mrs Watson begged for me to teach her. The way of it is simple. Nor is it costly to make, so I considered it a wise dish to add to a young bride's records!

ASSEMBLY

Puff pastry; $\frac{1}{2}$ pint thick cream; 5 eggs; soft milk-breadcrumbs – as much as will come halfway up a medium pie dish; 6 rosy pippins, peeled, cored and sliced fine; the grated rind of 1 thin-skinned orange; 6 oz fine white sugar; $\frac{1}{4}$ pint claret.

PROCEDURE

Line out a medium pie dish with fairly thinly rolled-out puff paste, trim off the edges neatly. Put the cream into a basin and stir in as much breadcrumb as will make a very thick paste. Beat into this the orange rind, 2 oz of the sugar and the well-whipped eggs. Beat all thoroughly and let it lie. Place the pippin slices upon the raw puff paste, sprinkle with the sugar, pour on the wine and spread the breadcrumb mixture neatly over the top. Place in a fairly brisk oven (*Gas Mark* 5, *mid-shelf. F.C.*) and bake until the paste be richly browned and puffed up and the top slightly springy to the touch.

AFTERNOON TEA RECEIPTS

Afternoon Tea Receipts

Macaroon Gâteau
Brandied Peaches
My Special Dough-Nuts
My Lardy Cake
Dripping Toast
Ginger-Bread
Sand Cake for Mr Mycroft Holmes
Proper Cucumber Sandwiches
White Christmas Cake
My Seed Cake
Milk Scones
Girdle or Griddle Cakes
Self-Raising Flour
My Walnut Bread
Scots Ginger Nuts
Hermits
Rout Biscuits

MY AFTERNOON TEA RECEIPTS

INSPECTOR Baynes and young Stanley Hopkins from Scotland Yard were the only two of the many police officers who came to Baker Street with my Complete Approval. They were both decent God-fearing men. I speedily discovered that they were loath to take tea above stairs, but much preferred to be invited below to take their tea in my small parlour. This was adjacent to my kitchen and therefore ideal for the service of freshly-baked items which had no time to deteriorate between oven or griddle and the table. So when I was privy to the fact of their coming, I made a point of answering the door or, if That Boy went before me, of ordering him to ask the two men to wait for me. Then I would lead them to Mr Holmes and on the way quietly inform them that their tea would be waiting in my parlour if they would be good enough to step down after they had concluded whatever was their current business with Mr Holmes.

This became a regular occurrence and it was remarkable how many visits to my Master coincided with the tea hour. Indeed, on one such occasion, when I came from my parlour to my kitchen, where those Scallywags were awaiting Mr Holmes' pleasure, I found the whole gang of them giggling and sniggering in a Most Unseemly Manner. My inquiries as to what caused this vulgar mirth caused That Boy, always bold out of reason, to say, 'We think Inspector Baynes is gone on you Missus,' and seeing my face at these words he straightway ran from the room. I pretended that I had not heard, considering this the most seemly course of action; but am bound to confess that when I had replenished the tea pot and returned with it to the parlour my cheeks were burning. The Inspector made matters worse by observing, 'You have a fine colour today ma'am. It suits you as well as your fine cookery suits us.' The poor man, clearly knowing no better, then blew upon his tea, an action which quite made me shudder. But even so both he and young Stanley Hopkins did enjoy their teas.

Inspector Baynes had a very sweet tooth, and I, having not made *MACAROON GÂTEAU* for a very long time, and intending it for Mr Holmes' dinner at which he was expecting some Important Friends; did what I ever do on such occasions, refreshed my mind in the way of it by making one beforehand. This is as good a time as any to repeat the lesson which Cook ever drummed into me. 'Never,' she would say, 'attempt any dish at which you are not experienced when cooking for a dinner party. Make one in advance and so be sure that you know exactly what you are about, then submit your dinner menu to your employer with confidence.'

MACAROON GÂTEAU

ASSEMBLY

1 metal flan-ring, 8-inches in diameter; 24 macaroons; 1 pint stiffly whipped cream; a little apricot brandy; some sieved apricot jam; flaked almonds; 1 oz sifted icing sugar; the strained juice of 1 small lemon.

PROCEDURE

Oil the flan ring very carefully. Set it upon a piece of parchment (*foil, F.C.*) upon an ordinary baking sheet and oil the base of the parchment very thoroughly also. Crumble up the macaroons fairly fine into a roomy bowl. Blend the icing sugar into the whipped cream, then add apricot brandy to taste. Sprinkle the lemon juice over the crumbled macaroons and then work in three quarters of the flavoured cream which be enough to make a firm paste. Put the mixture into the prepared ring and press it down inside. Press very close against the oiled sides of the ring. Smooth it off very neat and put it upon ice (*refrigerate overnight, F.C.*) until it be very cold and firm. Gently ease off the tart ring and with the aid of two metal slices lift the cake on to a turn-table which be slightly smaller than itself. Brush over the sides with sieved apricot jam and then press as many browned, flaked almonds as will hold, until the sides are completely masked with them. Place the remaining cream in a forcing pipe with a piping nozzle *No. 5 crown* and pipe decorative squirls and curlicues over the top to make all pretty. Set – again with the aid of two slices – upon a d'oyley-covered glass pedestal dish and hand a bowl of brandied peaches (see p. 175) separate. These I did not give to the worthy Inspector!

TO BROWN THE FLAKED ALMONDS

Strew a generous handful of flaked almonds over an ordinary, dry, baking-sheet and set into a brisk oven for a few minutes to brown, stir them occasionally that they be browned all over, cool and use.

BRANDIED PEACHES

ASSEMBLY

12 fine, ripe peaches; the thinly peeled rind of 1 lemon (I advise taking off the peel and then extracting the juice from it, being thus able to use the peel for the dish of peaches); $1\frac{1}{4}$ pints cold water; $\frac{3}{4}$ lb granulated sugar; 1 vanilla stick (*vanilla pod*, *F.C.*); brandy; peach brandy.

PROCEDURE

Place the peaches – a few at a time – in a roomy bowl and pour on boiling water to cover them. Leave a few minutes. Have ready a silver knife, for any other will ruin the flavour of this fruit, and likewise a bowl containing cold water, and add thereto two handsful of chipped ice (*ice cubes*, *F.C.*). Plunge in the peaches and when they are cold peel them very carefully. Then halve them and remove the stones. Put the sugar and water together in a wide, shallow pan with lemon juice and peel and set upon the side of your stove that every grain of sugar may dissolve before the syrup is permitted to boil. Then bring to the boil, remove peel, add the vanilla and sink in the peaches. Keep the pan to the stove side that the peaches may poach very leisurely lest bubbling cause them to break as they become cooked.

When they are clear – which denotes their perfect condition – lift them into a glass dish into which you have set a silver spoon that the dish may not crack by the heat of the fruit. Boil up the syrup hard until it be down to a mere $\frac{3}{4}$ of a pint. Stir in equal parts of apricot brandy and ordinary brandy to taste, cool a little, pour over the fruit and cover them close with parchment (*aluminium foil*, *F.C.*), that an exposed peach, top or side, does not darken by exposure and so ruin the appearance.

MY SPECIAL DOUGH-NUTS

Let it not be thought that I made a habit of such indulgences to mere Officers from Scotland Yard. This episode, of the tea party with my

The Sherlock Holmes Cookbook

MACAROON GÂTEAU, was exceptional, but it did serve to make the officers very interested in coming to Baker Street around the tea hour. Pleasing these officials therefore justified the use of my Master's more luxurious ingredients. However, as young Stanley Hopkins remarked upon more than one occasion, 'Apart from your fancies Ma'am, your featherweights is what are so remarkable.' He was, in his own clumsy way, pointing the difference between such delicacies as Macaroon Gâteau and items of simple bakery such as Lardy Cake and Special Dough-nuts. Now Lardy Cake is very simple to make, but it needs care and it has ever been a matter of puzzlement to me that Some Cooks be afeared of yeast work which I have ever found very straightforward, provided of course there is no slovenly skipping of kneading, or in time left for proper proving.

ASSEMBLY

½ oz fresh bakers' yeast (*that dried stuff is hopeless for such work, F.C.*); 1½ fluid oz warm milk, and also 5 fluid oz of the same; ¼ oz superfine castor sugar, and also 2 oz of the same; 2 oz sifted self-raising flour, and 10 oz self-raising flour; 6 egg yolks; 3 oz softened butter, see that it be not *oiled*; the grated rind of ¼ of a good-sized lemon; 1 tablespoon rum; some apricot jam; some extra sifted self-raising flour for kneading; some extra raw egg white for sealing the dough-nuts and also some extra castor sugar for turning the completed ones into.

PROCEDURE

Dissolve the yeast and ¼ oz sugar with the 1½ fluid oz warmed milk, stir in the 2 oz flour and work down (here is care needed) until every small lump has disappeared and all is as smooth as a well starched serviette. Cover this 'ferment' as I was taught to name it. Leave it be upon the table in a warm kitchen. Whisk the egg yolks with the 2 oz of castor sugar in a bowl set over a somewhat larger bowl containing hot water to come half way up the sides. Whisk (again do not skimp) until all is a foamy, feathery batter and *then* whisk in the softened butter, the rum and grated lemon rind. Examine your ferment and if so be it is all risen and bubbly, tap it violently, that the bubbles and seethings may subside. Add the egg, rum, etcetera mixture to it and then the 5 fluid oz milk. Work up carefully and thoroughly with a wooden spoon. Then do the same with the remaining 10 oz flour. Cover close with a thick piece of blanket and set in the warm to prove itself and rise until twice its original size. Turn it upon a floured board, knock it back with a few vigorous taps from your closed knuckles and then knead it until very smooth. The action for this is to hold the hands straight and vertical to the board and about a foot apart and to slap the ball of subsided dough from one palm to the other, interspersing this with a few vigorous thrusts from the 'heel' of one hand; this being the fat pad below the thumb. When all be well slapped, kneaded and absolutely smooth and shiny, roll it out upon your floured board until it be a mere $\frac{1}{3}$-of-an-inch in thickness. Cut all into rectangles measuring 3-inches by 4-inches. Spread 1 heaped teaspoon of apricot jam along the 4-inch side of each rectangle. Roll up like a sausage roll and seal the open edge with raw egg white brushed on very thick. When done, set each one upon a floured cloth, cover with another cloth and leave to make their final 'proving' for thirty minutes. In that time heat a deep, wide pan with a fry-basket inside and also a 4-inch depth of pure olive oil or pure lard, it matters not which be used of these two. Let the oil temperature rise to just below the point when it throws a faint haze upon the surface, and then fry your dough-nuts two or three at a time. It is here that you may fail if not observant. The first time you attempt this receipt of mine I do most earnestly suggest that you first fry one. By its inward condition when it has turned to a rich golden brown outside and cut open, you may adjust your errors in judgment at the cost of one dough-nut. If the inside be undercooked, then reduce the heat of your oil for frying the rest. IF the inside be fully cooked by this time then you will have judged rightly. As each one be fried correctly, tip straight into castor sugar and roll about, that each may be thickly coated with the sugar. Although I say it myself, these are well worth taking a little trouble about as they really are about the best that I have ever eaten.

MY LARDY CAKES

By my way I ever made three and not just one – and if so be neither my Master nor Dr Watson expressed the wish for more than 'buttered crumpets only please Mrs Hudson'; or perhaps Cinnamon Toast, or their other great favourite – as it was below stairs, too – Dripping Toast; then I would put one Lardy Cake upon my parlour tea table and wrap the other two for my guests to take home. The Inspector never failed to rub his hands at the sight of one and exclaim, 'How you do spoil us dear Ma'am.' I thought the use of the 'dear' was slightly uncalled for, my never having made the slightest gesture of encouragement towards him. But there you are, men will be men.

ASSEMBLY

2 lb 3 oz white bread flour; 19 fluid oz water at blood heat; $19\frac{1}{2}$ fluid oz milk at blood heat; $\frac{1}{2}$ oz salt; 2 oz proper bakers' yeast; $3\frac{1}{2}$ oz castor sugar; $3\frac{1}{2}$ oz and 8 oz pure lard; 8 oz currants; 6 oz sultanas; 1 fluid oz extra of milk.

PROCEDURE

Begin by chopping the 8 oz lard into small pieces. This ever be easier done with a knife which is drawn through flour at intervals. Sift the salt and flour into a bread crock. (*Slightly warmed earthenware container is best. F.C.*) Then put the yeast and castor sugar into a small bowl and stir them together vigorously until they liquefy and become quite smooth. Leave for a moment while you rub the $3\frac{1}{2}$ oz lard into the flour until it is so very fine grained as to be near-invisible, then mix in the dried fruits. Add half the blood heat water to the liquefied sugar/yeast mixture. Stir about and add half the blood heat milk and stir about once more. Make a deep well in the centre of the flour and tip in yeast mixture adding from second half of mixed, blood heat milk and water as much as needs be to obtain a good, smooth, pastry-paste-consistency dough. All this should be done by the hand. Cover close with a piece of blanket and set in the warm to prove until doubled in bulk. Turn out on to a liberally floured wooden surface. Roll into one strip measuring 18-inches by 6-inches. Dab the upper surface all over to within $1\frac{1}{4}$-inches of all edges with the chopped lard pieces. Fold the end nearest to you over to the middle of the strip and the opposing end over to the *fold* of the first thus obtaining a three-layer fold. Give one half turn upon the table, re-flour beneath and then re-roll to the given 18-inches by 6-inches and then fold in exactly the same manner once more. Then repeat all the turning and folding, but this time roll out again as long as possible which be very long indeed and let the finished, very long strip be 2-inches wide and 1-inch thick. Divide this strip into three equal lengths. Have ready three buttered and floured maximum 6-inch-diameter cake tins. Take up a strip. Coil it round and round upon itself until it resembles a very large Chelsea bun. Keep close and lift into a tin *which it will not fill*. Do this with all three strips into their three tins and cover all again very close with your piece of blanket and leave be upon the kitchen table with no more heat than is normal to your kitchen. Leave so until the dough be swollen and risen to fill each tin.

Afternoon tea receipts

Bake them all one shelf above the middle in a mild oven for thirty-five to forty-five minutes depending upon the strength of the oven's heat. (*Gas Mark* 3, *forty-five minutes. F.C.*) While these are baking, prepare your all-important glaze. Mix 5 oz soft brown (pieces) sugar with 2½ oz butter. Beat them well and spread over the tops of your three Lardy Cakes the moment they come from the oven. The heat of the cakes will do the rest of the glazework for you as they cool down.

DRIPPING TOAST

Pray do not think I am being foolish when I state that the quality of this item depends upon the quality of the dripping. The very best is, of course, goose fat dripping, so we will speak of this first. Everyone knows that goose can be a Most Indigestible Bird with an embarrassing tendency to 'repeat' on certain stomachs. Therefore, it may be useful to know How To Make Goose Digestible. The manner of it is simple. Set the bird upon a grid-iron (*grill rack, F.C.*) over a *deep* oven pan. Prod the goose all over very vigorously with forks until it be pitted all over with fork-holes. Set all in the oven and leave be for at least three-quarters of an hour. Let the oven be steady but only of medium heat. (*Gas Mark* 4–5, *mid-shelf height for bird on rack. F.C.*) Thus the cooking commences gently and as it develops so the fatty substances which form such a high proportion of these birds begin to bubble out and run down the sides of the goose. Thus does it do its own basting. But of course a certain amount of Sanguinary Juices escape also through these fork holes. These, in a steady trickle, gradually darken the skin as they slide down into the base pan until the goose becomes the colour of a horse chestnut.

When the goose be half cooked, examine the depth of goose fat and Sanguinary Juices which have run down into the base pan. If this be half-filled you must pour off some into a stone jar for storage in a cool place, as otherwise, by the time the goose is completely cooked these juices will overflow and could be dangerous as well as wasteful. When a jar is filled with such a mixture of fat and juice let it be until it is quite cold, then tie a parchment cover over and set aside in a cool place to use for Dripping Toast.

The best beef dripping is obtained by roasting a whole sirloin which ever has a central pad of fat in it. Thus, if roasted with just sufficient good beef bone stock to cover the base of the roasting pan to a depth of only ⅙-of-an-inch, you will again obtain a nice mixture of fat and Sanguinary Juices and the water will have quite evaporated by the time the sirloin be done. Store in the manner I have described for Goose Dripping and use either of them for Dripping Toast. I cannot leave this matter without making the observation that you can tell the standard of a good cook by the quality and condition of her dripping pots. If so be she has but the one and layer by layer pours on a sad mixture of fats and juices from game and poultry, beef, pork and suchlike; sure and certainly the perpetrator will be a dirty messy worker! Such extractions should ever be kept separate and kept *close-covered* (*with aluminium foil, F.C.*) lest perchance an inquisitive fly or even Dangerous Bluebottle fall in and be entombed!

The rest is simple. Cut new bread into crisp-crusted slices and leave the edges un-cutaway. Toast before a bright fire upon a good metal toasting fork and keep the slices *upstanding* lest they become flabby. Dissolve in a small metal container as much of your good, chosen dripping as you estimate may be desirable. Take each slice of hot, crisp toast and lay it down upon the liquefied surface. Take up when liberally impregnated. Sprinkle each lightly with salt and pepper, cut into fat fingers. Criss cross these fingers upon a water-plate* and send to table beneath a lid.

With such items would I regale my Scotland Yard Officers. I would likewise set upon the table a loaf of both My Home Made White and Brown Breads, a Jar of Potted Scrimps (p. 63), a pot of My Blackcurrant Jam (p. 236) and a pat of Sweet butter brought by the Carter from the farmer who was the son of my father's best friend. He alas, like my father, long gone to Higher Realms.

Likewise I would bring out a jar of My Potted Cheese, (p. 140) which, with some Scones, a dish of ham and pickles lest they be really hungry and a plate of little fancy cakes, was I believe the reason why that pair ever contrived to be around at tea time.

Now Mr Holmes' elder brother Mycroft also had a habit of presenting himself at the tea hour. Naturally, as befitted my place, I always made it my business to place before him some small selection of my tea time baking; but as he ate at all times with such Disregard for his Shape, I ever had misgivings about overfeeding him, he being of such enormous girth already. Therefore, as time passed I wooed him away from the richer items with such things as Sand Cake, Cucumber Sand-

---

* These water plates can still be picked up very inexpensively in antique or 'junk' shops. They are most commonly found in willow patterned china inset in a deepish copper or pewter base. Each one has a small vent with a screw-on cap. Remove the cap, fill the cavity between upper china and metal base with boiling water then screw back the cap. *F.C.*

Afternoon tea receipts

wiches and Ginger-bread; but as he would always spread slices of this last Very Thickly Indeed with our Farm Butter, I fear my efforts were in vain.

GINGER-BREAD

This be an abomination if it is not really moist, so I do assure my reader that This One Is and ever will be if the instructions are followed with the same precision as I have used in the writing of them.

ASSEMBLY

5 oz pure lard; 1 generous tablespoon Fowler's Black Treacle – none other will do; 7 oz sifted self-raising flour sifted with 2 rounded teaspoons ground ginger; 1 rounded saltspoon bicarbonate of soda dissolved in 2 tablespoons cold milk; $2\frac{1}{2}$ oz soft brown (pieces) sugar; 1 good-sized egg (*standard, F.C.*).

PROCEDURE

Put the lard and treacle into a small stewpan and allow to dissolve over the side of your stove. As soon as they be all melted, beat well off the stove. Set the flour mixture in a roomy bowl, make a well in the centre, pour in the treacle mixture, adding at the same time the bicarbonate and milk and the egg, well beaten with the sugar. Stir all around steadily until a perfect blend results. Turn into the prepared tin (see below), level off very even and bake in a mild oven (*Gas Mark 4, centre shelf. F.C.*). Take from the oven and while the ginger-bread is hot, ease the always-slightly-over-risen edges back, leaving thereafter in the tin until this be perfectly cold. I will speak more of this in a moment.

TO PREPARE THE GINGER-BREAD TIN

Line out a Swiss Roll Tin with foolscap. Brush well with olive oil and also brush oil around the sides of the tin.

Author's Note

Use a standard Swiss Roll tin measuring 10-inches by 14-inches by $\frac{3}{4}$-inch, line with fitting sheet of grease-proof and oil as Mrs Hudson explains. *F.C.*

The Sherlock Holmes Cookbook

I did discover, after trying various methods that the way to keep this ginger-bread moist for a Very Long Time was to leave it in the tin and to tie over parchment and then store in a cool, dry place. (*Use aluminium foil. F.C.*)

SAND CAKE FOR MR MYCROFT HOLMES

ASSEMBLY

8 oz sweet butter; 4 oz fine self-raising flour; 4 oz potato flour (*Fécule de Pomme obtainable from Messrs Harrods, Fortnum and Masons, Jacksons of Piccadilly and Selfridges. F.C.*); the yolks of 12 eggs; the grated peel of half a good-sized lemon; the whites of 12 eggs whipped stiffly; 2 fluid oz brandy; a little sifted icing sugar; 8 oz sifted icing sugar.

PROCEDURE

Beat the butter until it be almost white and very loose and creamy. Beat in the 8 oz icing sugar and again beat very well indeed. To skimp is to fail – remember. Add a little of the flour and potato flour both previously sifted together. Then add 3 of the egg yolks and again beat well. Thereafter add some more flour, then 3 more eggs and beat again and so on until both flour and egg yolks are all beat up to perfect, fluffy smoothness. Stir in the lemon zest, beat again and so likewise with the brandy, and finally the well-whipped egg whites which must be folded in carefully and thoroughly. Turn into one or more bun tins (*9-inches by 4½-inches by 2¾-inches, F.C.*) well-buttered and floured and bake in a moderate oven (*Gas Mark 4. F.C.*) until, when just touched lightly at centre, it be springy to the touch. To over-bake is to ensure a dry cake so go no further than I have explained. Turn upside down upon a cooling rack and so leave until cold. Turn right side up again and sift icing sugar thickly upon the entire top.

Note: Should this become stale then slice it into ½-inch-thick slices. Dissolve enough butter to coat a frypan to a depth of ⅛-inch, let the butter sizzle, slide in the slices, let them fry golden brown, turn them over and immediately put 4 fat tablespoons of golden syrup into the pan, by sliding it down the sides. As soon as the second side be golden brown, lift out and range slanting, one just at the base edge of the preceding one, add the strained juice of 1 small lemon to the pan residue and pour on top in a steady stream from end to end. Serve with a simple jug of hot cream and they will do very well indeed.

PROPER CUCUMBER SANDWICHES

Mr Holmes declared on many occasions, 'Cucumber sandwiches are capital fare, My Dear Watson. While others may think little of them I much prefer them to any cake!'

There is a trick to the cutting of the bread which you will do well to know. In my Lady's house it was ever the duty of the Parlour Maid to cut both the thin brown and white bread and butter for afternoon tea and also the slices to be made into sandwiches, and she always prided herself on the fact that her slices were always paper thin even with the newest of bread. The trick is to have beside you as you work, not only a Very Sharp Knife, but also a tall jug of boiling water. This I saw every day of my life being done. The Parlour Maid would plunge her sharp knife into the boiling water, speedily shake off any clinging drops and so slice easily and of transparent thinness. This dipping and shaking she did for every slice. Now I do it in like manner and I too can achieve paper thin slices. Set them out in two rows before you so that you may be sure you have the exact number of pairs that you will require. Remember too, that for the buttering you should work with well-beaten butter which be beat to a creamy texture. When you have so done cut your cucumber slices thinly. Always be sure to leave on the skins lest they become indigestible. It is the cutting away of the skins which causes the heartburn from eating cucumber. Lay the fine slices thickly upon one row of buttered bread slices. Sprinkle lightly with salt and fine-ground black pepper, lay the second row of buttered bread slices upon the first – cucumber covered now. Press down firmly, cut away the crusts and then cut each 'sandwich' into four triangular ones. Set them overlapping upon a d'oyley-covered dish and strew a neat border of cress around the outside. Remember the pressing. Nothing be more wrongful than to run the risk that cucumber slices should escape in the drawing room and make a mess of ladies' gowns.

WHITE CHRISTMAS CAKE

This was a novelty of which I read in Mrs Agnes Bertha Marshall's weekly magazine *THE TABLE*. I copied it out and determined to try it one day. Then quite suddenly, as was ever his wont, my employer was out all night upon a case, not just for one night but for several. He would dash home, give himself one of those dreadful injections, play upon his violin for some hours and then, as suddenly as he had returned he would thunder off once more crying out for a hansom and for That Boy who curled up under the stairs and fell fast asleep during these episodes. All this, you may imagine, upon an empty stomach, with only gulps of black coffee, and once a chop snatched from a tray I was carrying up stairs, this he bore away in his hand crying, 'no time to eat Mrs Hudson'. The last I saw of him on *that* occasion was brandishing the chop at the grinning cabby.

Then of course the inevitable happened and there followed several days when he lay abed. I would go in (after knocking of course) and would find him arms behind his head, staring at the ceiling. I took in trays and then I brought them out again. Finally I heard yet another thundering upon the stairs and he was off again! I was in despair and just about ready to pluck up courage and speak to the good Doctor – who was really very kind in spite of his faults of palate. There was little else I could do and not even this until I should see Dr Watson again, so, to keep my mind occupied, I set about Mrs Marshall's White Christmas Cake. I was just taking it from its cooling rack prior to swathing in pieces of Holland to store away in a tin when a shadow fell upon my work and I looked up to perceive Mr Holmes leaning against the doorway with his Inverness unfastened and his hands deep-thrust into the pockets. He looked haggard indeed but his eyes were bright and, imagine my astonishment when he remarked quietly, 'That looks remarkably good Mrs Hudson! Pray could I have a slice?' I tried to persuade him to go back to his room, telling him I would bring cake to him, but he would have none of it. I can see him now as clear as if it were yesterday, sitting in disarray upon the corner of my kitchen table munching cake, his long legs a-sprawl, and as the last mouthful vanished stretching out those long fingers of his and saying, 'Cut me another slice Mrs Hudson. That is a capital cake, I must say.'

From then on I ever thought of that cake as his 'Capital Cake' and ever had one put by in case he might ask for it.

ASSEMBLY

Prepare a 12-inch-diameter cake tin by lining it out with waxed papers on base and sides. Then brush the interior all over with good olive oil, being sparing with the oil but liberal with the 'elbow grease' as Cook used to say. Then prepare 7 oz sifted superfine self-raising flour; 7 oz cornflour and sift both together. Have also 12 oz unsalted butter; 12 oz castor sugar; 6 oz chopped angelica; 6 oz almond flakes; 4 oz chopped, dried walnuts; 12 oz chopped glacé cherries; 10 oz chopped, crystallised pineapple slices; 12 oz sultanas; 1 tablespoon rum mixed with 2 table-

Afternoon tea receipts

spoons brandy and 1 tablespoon strained, fresh, orange juice; the grated rinds of 2 small lemons; 6 eggs.

PROCEDURE
Cream the butter until almost white and absolutely free from streaks. Beat in the sugar and again bring the mixture to a very loose, light cream, adding in the grated rinds. Put all the other chopped items together with 1 oz of your flour mixture. Work them a little together to ensure they are evenly distributed. Put 2 tablespoons of the flour mixture on to your butter cream, beat it in, then add a little of the mixed fruits and an egg, and finally a few drops of the mixed fluids, and so continue until all ingredients are used up and your mixture is creamy once again. Put into the tin, level off the top and set the tin upon four folds of stout brown paper upon a baking tin. Put into a moderate oven for one hour, while letting your fire subside somewhat so that after the first hour the heat has somewhat reduced. Cook until the mixture, when listened to attentively, has entirely ceased singing or, if you must, insert a thin, steel knitting needle *off centre please* to see if it comes out wet or clean. If the latter your cake be done. (*Cook one hour Gas Mark 4, two shelves from the bottom, then reduce to Gas Mark 2 until completed. F.C.*)

MY SEED CAKE

Mr Holmes' favourite. Woe betide anyone who attempted to raid the cake tin when this cake was inside. On its next appearance, no matter how slim the slices which had been removed, Mr Holmes would cry upon the sight of it, 'Who has been at my Seed Cake, Mrs Hudson?'

ASSEMBLY
¾ lb sweet butter; 6 eggs; 1 lb very finest self-raising flour; 12 oz fine castor sugar; 1 small blade finely crushed mace; 1 mean, flat eggspoon grated nutmeg; a mean 1 oz caraway seeds.

PROCEDURE
First line out your cake tin on base and sides with grease-proof paper and then brush all over the interior with olive oil. This must *always* be done before any cake mixture is embarked upon. Beat the butter until it is very pale and absolutely free from streaks. Then add mace and nutmeg to mixture, then sugar, very gradually beating until again very loose and creamy. Break all eggs into a separate bowl. Beat these up very fine. Add a spoonful or two of flour to butter-cream mixture, then sufficient egg to beat until smooth, and so proceed using a few

drops of milk as deemed necessary for obtaining a mixture which just flops idly from a lifted spoon. Work in the caraway seeds. Turn into your prepared tin and bake in a moderate oven until it stops singing, when listened to attentively. (*Gas Mark 4, mid-shelf, one hour thirty minutes approximately. F.C.*)

MILK SCONES

If ever someone should be coming to afternoon tea, Mr Holmes would surely say, when giving me my orders, 'And be sure Mrs Hudson to let us have some of those capital Milk Scones of yours.'

The way of them is very easy too, but only the very best quality milk should be used and as you will observe, this should have a modicum of cream added to it for perfection.

ASSEMBLY

12 oz self-raising flour, sifted with 1 rounded dessertspoon baking powder; 3 oz superfine castor sugar; 2½ oz pure lard; 3½ oz unsalted butter; 4½ oz sultanas; 1½ fluid oz thick cream; milk.

PROCEDURE

Sift the flour and baking powder into a roomy bowl. Break up the butter and lard, rub them in very finely indeed, then sift in the sugar and thereafter the sultanas. Begin to bind this mixture with the cream and an equal quantity of milk, cutting both in with a small table knife and adding more milk as needed until a firm rolling dough is achieved. Turn on to a floured board. Press out lightly with your rolling pin to a mean ¾-inch thickness. Stamp into 2½-inch rounds. Then give a final shaping by working around them with the palms of the hands. Place upon a lightly floured baking sheet. Brush the tops with milk, scatter a little extra castor sugar upon each and bake in a fairly brisk oven. The time to remove them from the oven is all important. They must be cooked through – *but only just*, so I confess I do ever sacrifice one – which Billy then eats for me whatever its state – while he is turning the handle of my knife grinder, a chore he was always given when kicking his heels about the kitchen on a rainy day. When split open the test scone should be so light that if you grip it firm it breaks apart. It should be ever so slightly doughy from the pressure of the knife. That is the perfect stage at which to remove my scones from the oven. (*Bake them at Gas Mark 5, one shelf above centre. They should take approximately fifteen minutes. F.C.*)

GIRDLE OR GRIDDLE CAKES

The amount of these that Dr Watson could consume at one sitting had to be seen to be believed. Now I ever made mine in an iron griddle which I took with me to Baker Street when first I went there. It had been my mother's and her mother's before her according to my father's information. It made splendid griddle cakes! What I must stress in the making is that the surface texture is altogether wrong if any form of greasing is used other than a small piece of raw unsalted pork fat. This applies whether a griddle such as mine is used or whether it is necessary to use a large thick iron frypan. Set either upon the stove in sufficient indirect heat – that is, with the cover over the coals – for the pan to become singing hot. Then burnish it all over base and sides with the piece of pork fat, preferably on the rind for this enables you to take a firmer grip upon it.

ASSEMBLY

$\frac{3}{4}$ lb self-raising flour; 1 good-sized egg (*standard, F.C.*); 1 scant, flat teaspoon bicarbonate of soda, and the same of cream of tartar; milk; water.

PROCEDURE

Sift the flour into a roomy basin. Break the egg into a central hollow. Add 1 fluid oz of milk and the same of cold water and begin to work up the batter. Add more milk and more water in equal proportions to obtain a batter which just flops lazily from the lifted spoon. When of this consistency, and of course perfectly smooth and free from lumps, scatter the two powders over the top surface and draw them in with a gentle stir and fold movement with the spoon. On no account beat any more. By the time you have heated your chosen container the batter will be ready to use. Burnish the base and sides as I have explained, then drop small spoonsful, widely apart, on to the greased surface. Spread them out into neat circles with the back of the spoon. This needs a little practice so to begin with use a small table knife. Let them rest until small bubbles begin to break over the raw upper surface. Rub the piece of pork fat over a metal slice, slide it underneath each one and lift each quite high, that you may slap down upon the bubbled side. As you do so you will observe that the flap-jacks rise up immediately. Leave them until the same golden brown as the now upper side. Lift out and set, slantwise with one resting a little upon its predecessor, upon a cooling rack. When cooled either serve or store in an earthenware container with a well-fitting lid.

The above are plain flap-jacks. If sweet ones are found to be preferable then add, at the same time as the egg, 1 flat dessertspoon castor sugar.

If desiring sultana flap-jacks, then stir 3 oz of *pale* sultanas – these are ever the best quality – into the batter before adding in the two powders. Blend thoroughly before so adding those powders.

SELF-RAISING FLOUR

I have ever considered it a waste of God's good time to be a-mixing of baking powder with three-times sifted flour in order to aerate the flour for general use. I have also proved that it is not the truth to claim that only plain flour will make good Yorkshire Pudding or fine delicate pancakes. With very few exceptions I turn all my flour into Self-Raising Flour before putting it away in my flour crock, and can therefore sift it upon my table surface (for pastry pastes) or into a bowl (for whipping into cakes) without any time-consuming preliminaries. Here is my receipt which has stood me in very good stead throughout the years.

ASSEMBLY

4 oz ground rice; 4 oz bicarbonate of soda; 3 oz tartaric acid.

PROCEDURE

Sift all together three times. Now let us consider proportions. I have discovered, the only way which counts – by careful weighing with reliable scales – (for nothing is more injurious to quality in cookery than inaccurate scales) – that 4 heaped teaspoons equal 1 oz and so does 1 heaped tablespoon. So, you will know upon returning home exactly how much flour you have purchased. Allow 1 heaped teaspoonful of the above mixture to 1 lb of three-times sifted flour. If putting up a crock full, then buy for simplicity's sake, in 4 lb quantities and to each 4 lb bag add 1 heaped tablespoon in the manner explained. There are, however, certain bakery items which do require a greater proportion of raising agent so it is advisable to put up a tin of the concentrate to use additionally.

MY WALNUT BREAD

Pray do not ask me why, but Dr Watson was most partial to slices of this bread, fried in bacon fat and with No. 4 cut back bacon fried and

Afternoon tea receipts

laid upon the top. Mr Holmes on the other hand preferred to eat it in the normal manner, sliced thinly and buttered, or on winter tea time occasions, instead of plain bread or fingers of cinnamon toast. Oh yes, my gentlemen had their fancies and it was ever my duty to remember and cater for all of them which I endeavoured to do always!

ASSEMBLY

1 lb wholemeal flour; ½ lb salted butter; ½ pint milk; 2 level teaspoons salt; 2 generous pinches nutmeg; 1 generous pinch cinnamon; 8 oz rough-chopped, dried walnuts; 2 eggs; a mere flat teaspoon of castor sugar.

PROCEDURE

Sift your flour and spices together into a roomy mixing bowl. Rub in the butter very fine indeed. Work in the sugar. Then work in the walnuts. Beat eggs and milk well together. Make a well in the centre of the dry mixture, and work all up to rather a wet mixture. Half fill well-buttered rectangular bread tins and bake in a moderate oven for one hour or until bread responds with a hollow sound when rapped with knuckles. (*Gas Mark 4, mid-shelf. F.C.*)

SCOTS GINGER NUTS

I would often put a glass jar of these beside my Master's bed. As often as not they would remain untouched! But then, when I was beginning to despair of their ever winning Mr Holmes' nocturnal attention, lo the jar would be emptied and I would have to replenish it.

ASSEMBLY

Take 1 lb Fowler's black treacle – there is none other which equals it; 6 oz butter; ½ oz powdered ginger; 6 oz soft brown sugar called 'pieces'; 2 oz medium oatmeal; a further ½ lb treacle; a saltspoon of mixed spices; the very finely chopped, thinly-cut peel from 3 lemons; 1 lb finest self-raising flour; candied peel.

PROCEDURE

Put the 1 lb treacle into a stew pan with the butter and let it become warm by the side of your stove. To this stir in the sugar and when this has dissolved mix in all remaining ingredients, except flour. It is then advisable to turn the pan mixture into a roomy mixing bowl before you stir in the flour. When it be a smooth thick paste set aside and allow to rest for thirty minutes or thereabouts. Roll it out upon a lightly-floured board to a ¼-inch thickness. Stamp out into any fancy shapes or just plain 2¼-inch diameter rounds. Press a scrap of citron peel upon top centre of each one and bake in a moderate oven for twelve to fifteen minutes. (*Gas Mark* 5, *mid-shelf. F.C.*) Pray remember that these biscuits harden up after withdrawal from the oven and when cooling down, so do not over-bake.

HERMITS

When those Scallywags were about Mr Holmes' business and unlikely to have any food for many hours upon end, I would bake up a big batch of hermits and give these to them. They of course slipped them into their pockets, which must thereafter have been lined with crumbs! But there was no stopping them, particularly when the weather was cold for they assured me earnestly, 'They do keep us warm both outside and in, Missus.' This was reference to the fact that if Mr Holmes were in a hurry I would give them their Hermits straight from the oven, and in they would go to those ragged pockets, hot and crumbly and nothing I could say would make any difference!

ASSEMBLY

¾ lb stoned raisins chopped fine, the same of granulated sugar; 4 oz butter; 3 eggs; 1 mean flat teaspoon bicarbonate of soda stirred into 3 tablespoons milk in a teacup; 1 mean teaspoon (flat) grated nutmeg; 2 lb self-raising flour; 1 flat teaspoon each of ground cloves and ground cinnamon.

PROCEDURE

Rub the butter into the flour until the grains be so fine they are scarcely seen. Work in the fruit and sugar, and all the spices and run all through the fingers several times to ensure the most even distribution. Work up to a firm, rolling dough with the milk/bicarbonate mixture and beaten eggs. Roll out a generous ¼-inch thick. Stamp into rounds with a plain circular biscuit cutter of 3-inch diameter. Set them upon lightly-floured baking sheets and bake them fairly fast in rather a quick oven (*Gas Mark* 6, *mid-shelf. F.C.*).

ROUT BISCUITS

My last Lady always insisted upon a supply of these being kept in an air-tight tin for, as she so rightly said, 'They keep well and make a dainty addition to the afternoon tea stand, especially when callers arrive unexpectedly.'

ASSEMBLY

8 oz ground almonds; 8 oz sifted icing sugar; separated egg white; 1 oz fine-chopped angelica; 1 oz chopped glacé cherries; Noyau.

PROCEDURE

Mix the ground almonds and sugar together very thorough. Make a well in the centre. Put in a little raw egg white and work with a small table knife, gradually drawing in a very little more egg white until a very stiff paste is obtained. Moisten this down with a couple of teaspoons of Noyau which strengthens and emphasises the almond-flavour as no bottled essence can ever do. Pipe out the paste into little curlicues or fingers with a No. 5 crown pipe affixed inside a linen forcing bag (*use nylon now, this never sweats, F.C.*) on to a very lightly-buttered baking tray. Leave them be, uncovered, upon your kitchen table overnight, well away from any smuts which might deface them from the kitchen range. In the morning brush over the tops with a syrup of sugar and water. Dab mixed angelica and glacé cherries upon each and bake in a very hot oven (*Gas Mark $7\frac{1}{2}$, one shelf above centre. F.C.*) for a few moments until the piped ridges become brown. Do not let them stay long enough to become brown all over. The essence of these fancies is that while they look hard and like small fancy biscuits, yet they are still soft in the centres.

THE SUGAR SYRUP

Put 2 oz granulated sugar with 2 tablespoons water over low heat by the side of your stove to dissolve. Then boil it up, maintain for one minute and use.

SAVOURIES

Savouries

Bones for Serving with Mulled Ale as Beer and Bones
After Dinner Savouries
Baked Oysters in Their Own Deep Shells
Pope's Caps of Smoked Haddock
My Ham Ovals
Chickens' Liver Toasts
Devils Upon Horseback
My Sardine Cheeses
Doctor Watson's Madras Fritters
Spinach Pancakes
My Cheese Straws
Parmesan Balls
Bacon Rolls
Golden Bucks
Welsh Rarebit
Yorkshire Rarebit
My Own Cheese Biscuits

BONES FOR SERVING WITH MULLED ALE AS BEER AND BONES

ON those wintry occasions when the good Doctor brought a dozen or so of his medical cronies to Baker Street Mr Holmes would ask if it would be convenient to serve the assembled company with this pair of Old English Delights.

Never did I carry in my great china dish of steaming bones without failing to see the table on which I was to set them. The air would be so thick with the smoke of cigars, meerschaum pipes and suchlike. As regularly, a cheer would go up as I deposited my burden upon the ultimately discovered table, upon which That Boy had been sent scurrying ahead to lay down a triple fold of green baize to protect the polished surface. So now I will give the way for providing marrow bones for gentlemen.

Select only large beef bones which be well-filled with marrow. See that they be sawn up neatly by the butcher in pieces the size of a large man's clenched fist. Make up a paste of flour and water. Spread this thickly over each bone's cut to protect the marrow and hold it fast inside. Marrow has otherwise a distressing tendency to slide out into the boiling water. Lay a large clean piece of linen upon your kitchen table. Pile up the bones therein and tie them up bringing all four corners of the linen to top centre above the bones and knotting each pair securely. Remember also to have a long steel knitting needle handy for easing out those knots when you remove the very heavy, and extremely hot bundle from the copper. Once the bones are securely tied, thrust a broom handle through them and so lower them into your copper. You must previously ensure that the under-fire is burning brightly and that a large hod of good coals is set ready for regular replenishment. This I made That Boy do for me while I busied myself elsewhere. Let the bones lie, with the water bubbling strong above them for one full hour. Then remove them as explained and pile them on to one or more large dishes. Set a jug full of lobster prongs beside them for easy excavation, piles of hot toast for spreading the marrow upon, a roomy pot of made, English mustard and of course tankards for Mulled Ale for each person with each tied around with a clean white napkin and with a silver spoon inside each to offset the danger of cracking glass – unless you serve yours in Pewter Tankards.

AFTER DINNER SAVOURIES

Neither of my gentlemen were ever really content unless I terminated their evening repast – no matter at what hour this was taken – with an appetising savoury.

I was compelled to experiment until I found ones which met with Mr Holmes' approval – Dr Watson of course would eat almost anything just so long as it was hot and strong, so I fell into the habit of adding an extra dosage of cayenne pepper to his portion, if so be the item were not already covered by a Devil or included in its assembly one of his favourite Chutnees. The receipts which I include now were always among the most popular.

BAKED OYSTERS IN THEIR OWN DEEP SHELLS

ASSEMBLY

18 oysters; 4½ tablespoons thick white sauce (unseasoned if you please); 1 oz butter; the strained juice of half one good-sized lemon; fine, soft breadcrumbs be they white or brown; cayenne; black pepper; parsley for the garnish.

PROCEDURE

Commence by opening and bearding the oysters, which should be the small 'pie' oysters sold by all reputable fishmongers. Be careful to conserve the liquor therefrom. Wash the shells, wipe them carefully and then butter their interiors. Place 1 mean teaspoon sauce about the bottom of each – there being 4 full teaspoons to 1 tablespoon – then place 2 oysters upon each shell and mix the oyster liquor with the remaining sauce. Spread this amount evenly between the nine shells, sprinkle the tops thickly with the soft crumbs, and flick a few drops of lemon juice over each. Add a small, additional flake of butter to the tops of all nine and slip high up into a strong oven that they may be well-coloured on top in less than ten minutes. Set them upon a d'oyley-

Savouries

covered salver. Arrange a few sprigs of fresh parsley here and there and serve at once. I ever made an uneven number, for Mr Holmes was by far the smallest eater and the good Doctor always looked for a little extra.

POPE'S CAPS OF SMOKED HADDOCK

There be two stages to this item. For convenience I have put all the things for both into my beginning.

ASSEMBLY

For the paste
3 oz sifted, superfine self-raising flour; 2 oz butter; pinch of cayenne; 1 oz Parmesan cheese; 1 separated egg yolk; 1 teaspoon strained lemon juice; possibly a little water.
For the interiors
½ lb smoked haddock, cut neat and without bones; ½ pint milk; 1 oz butter; 1 oz Parmesan cheese; 2 tablespoons thick white sauce; 1 very generous pinch paprika powder; 1 egg yolk.

PROCEDURE

Turn the flour into a roomy bowl. Sift with the fingers, incorporating cheese with a pinch of both salt and pepper. Turn upon a piece of marble on your kitchen table, make a little hole in the centre of the tiny mound, tip in one half of the egg yolk – beaten, a very few drops of water and the softened butter. Work up with two small knives into a nice rolling paste, adding the lemon juice and a few drops of water if necessary. Rest upon the marble beneath a cloth for half an hour. Then roll out fairly thinly and stamp into 2-inch circles with a plain pastry cutter or wine glass. Prepare the filling by first cutting up the smoked haddock and poaching in the milk until cooked. Strain off the milk (use for a white fish sauce for some other fish dish), flake the haddock, then mix with the given second amounts of butter, cheese, paprika, sauce and half egg. Drop a sufficiency of this mixture upon each little circle, then draw the edges up to meet – having first wetted the four edges with cold water – making three of each one which gives the name to the dish of Pope's Cat or triangular one! Brush with a little raw egg and bake in a moderate oven for ten minutes. (*Gas Mark* 5, *one shelf above centre. F.C.*)

MY HAM OVALS

For this, please employ the pastry paste given for Pope's Caps of Smoked Haddock p. 197. In addition, pray assemble 6 oz cooked ham, chopped fine and remembering to mix fat with lean thereof; 2 egg yolks; ½ oz butter; 1 small shallot, chopped very fine; 1¼ fluid oz thick cream; 1 teaspoon fine-chopped parsley heads.

PROCEDURE

Roll out your paste too thick, as it were a large slice of bread and stamp therefrom small ovals. Lay these upon a baking sheet, prick over the top of each with a fork and bake in a brisk oven until turned a very pale biscuit colour. (*Gas Mark* 5, *one shelf above centre, ten to twelve minutes. F.C.*) Cool upon a suitable rack. Melt the butter in a small pan, and fry the prepared shallot until browned and soft, add thereto the prepared ham and stir over a low fire until all be quite hot. Withdraw from the fire, beat in fast the egg yolks mixed with the cream, stir with pepper until thick and of a reliable consistency for not dripping over the Ovals. Dome upon as many as it will spread adequately, sprinkle with the parsley and so to table.

Note: Remember that the Ovals, if in surplus, may be stored in an air-tight tin for later use and only then need warming in the low part of a very slow oven.

CHICKENS' LIVER TOASTS

When placing any mixtures upon buttered toast there is a way to the buttering which always ensures a perfectly even and quite un-torn surface which is sometimes hard to achieve if the butter be not of a sufficiently softened consistency. MY way is to soften and melt the butter in a shallow pan by the side of the stove and then to lay each toasted bread slice down upon it for a moment, which makes quite perfect buttered toast.

ASSEMBLY

3 chickens' livers; 6 very fine (No. 5 cut) slices of de-rinded back bacon; 1 oz butter; a pinch of cayenne pepper; 6 neat squares of toast, the size of a sandwich loaf slice, trimmed of all crusts; 1 saltspoon made English mustard; 1 flat teaspoon fine-chopped fresh parsley.

Savouries

PROCEDURE

Halve your livers, sprinkle them with pepper, then roll each liver half upon one end of a prepared bacon rasher and set upon a rack to broil over the open fire, turning them, that all may be done even and the little interior pieces of liver not done too firm. While this is proceeding mix the softened butter with the mustard and cayenne and spread equally upon your toasts. Set the rolls thereon and send to table nicely dished and garnished with parsley sprigs or well picked sprig-heads of fresh, crisp watercress.

DEVILS UPON HORSEBACK

This be the classic presentation of this English Speciality. First please prepare toasts as described on p. 198 for Chickens' Liver Toasts.

ASSEMBLY

8 de-rinded back bacon rashers; 8 stoned French plums (prunes preserved in port wine see p. 241); 8 peeled sweet almonds from Jordan (*if you're lucky! F.C.*); paprika, salt and pepper.

PROCEDURE

Toss the almonds in a little hot oil and turn in a mixture of paprika, salt and pepper. It is best to put this up in a little pot with a secure lid that it may be on call when desired for any dish. Mix 1 oz fine salt with 1 oz paprika powder, ¼ oz freshly milled black peppercorns and 1 flat eggspoon of cayenne. When the almonds be ready, put inside the stoned plums, close up and roll up in the bacon. Thread them upon a metal skewer and lay across the opened, well banked-down fire that they may broil all over thus. (*Use the grill. F.C.*) Then transfer the eight to *two* silver skewers. Lay each upon a buttered toast and dish tastefully upon a d'oyley-covered salver with sprigs of watercress.

MY SARDINE CHEESES

ASSEMBLY

12 fat Marie Elisabeth sardines, with tails and spinebones carefully removed and the opening equally carefully closed again upon a fine sprinkling of pepper; a small quantity of puff paste; 3 oz butter; anchovy paste; 1 egg; 2 oz grated Parmesan cheese; salt; cayenne pepper.

PROCEDURE

Roll out the paste very thinly. Cut into rectangles large enough to enclose one sardine apiece. Spread all rectangles lightly with anchovy paste. Melt the butter. Dip each sardine therein, roll thickly in the grated cheese, place one upon each paste square, brush the edges with a little raw egg white, overlay the paste and pinch all edges very securely together. Slip them by means of a metal slice into slightly smoking hot olive oil and let them fry to a good, rich golden brown. That the paste may be cooked right through, and not be raw in the middle, draw oil pan off the fire to the extreme side as soon as all the sardine cheese be within. When done, drain them and sprinkle on the remaining grated Parmesan cheese well mixed with a pinch or two of cayenne pepper. Send to table in a clean enfolding napkin that they may be piping hot when presented.

DOCTOR WATSON'S MADRAS FRITTERS

ASSEMBLY

4 ½-inch thick crustless slices of brown bread; 3 tablespoons of one of my chutnees; 1 oz butter; 4 slices cooked ham; fritter batter; parsley.

PROCEDURE

You may turn to p. 158 for the batter used by me for my Apple Fritters. Use it if you please. Stamp from the cut bread, rounds of 1½-inch diameter, spread each with butter and then cover with a spread of chutnee. Place a fitting circle of ham on top, pass each through your fritter batter, drop into slightly smoking hot oil, and as soon as all are in, remove pan to the extreme edge of your stove that the centres of the fritters may be perfectly cooked by the time the outsides are done brown. Garnish with parsley.

SPINACH PANCAKES

Please turn to p. 151 for my explanations as to making Pancakes, and to p. 134 for the proper cooking of spinach.

Now sieve 1 lb of cooked spinach and season strongly with salt, pepper and nutmeg. Put to it in a small, thick pan, 1 heaped tablespoon of thick cream, beat in 2 small egg yolks, and finally 1 oz of Parmesan

Savouries

cheese, grated fine. Let the mixture lie until quite cold, then spread over six fine pancakes, lay another six upon the tops, press down firmly, cut each in halves across the centre like to half circle sandwiches and pass through raw unbeaten egg white, then fine soft crumbs until very thickly coated. At the time that they are required slide them into slightly smoking hot oil, fry to golden brown, drain and set one overlapping the next upon a flat dish. Hand tomato sauce in a boat.

MY CHEESE STRAWS

I do most stoutly refute the merits of so-called cheese straws so thin in cheese and so hard baked that they be straws to the palate and no more! These, I can assure the cook–reader are truly appetising.

ASSEMBLY

½ lb puff pastry paste; a bowl of grated Parmesan cheese; pepper; salt; cayenne pepper; 1 raw egg white; 2 well-beaten raw egg yolks.

PROCEDURE

Roll out your puff paste to an ⅛-inch thickness. Cut into two matching rectangles. Lay one aside. Brush all over the other with raw egg white. Scatter very thickly with grated Parmesan and press down with a flat metal spatula to make it hold together. Sprinkle fairly with salt and black pepper, extremely sparely with minute flicks of cayenne pepper. Brush the upper side of the second puff rectangle with raw egg yolk, right to the edges and very thick. Turn over on to the cheesey top surface of the first rectangle. Press down with your rolling pin to hold firm and then cut into ¼-inch-wide fingers of the desired length. Some like to cut long strips and then twist them down their length to make their appearance fancy. Others prefer to cut short lengths and keep them straight. In this latter case you should join every fourth short length into a ring with raw egg yolk, and then when baking is done thrust one or two through each ring to give them a finished appearance upon their dish. All must be egg yolk brushed before baking, top and sides pray remember. All should be baked upon a cold-water rinsed baking sheet and put to a very strong oven that they may rise well. (*Gas Mark* 7½, *one shelf above centre. F.C.*)

PARMESAN BALLS

ASSEMBLY

6 oz fine soft white breadcrumbs; 6 oz grated Parmesan cheese; 2 eggs (*standard, F.C.*); 2 oz salted butter; one pinch of cayenne pepper.

PROCEDURE

Work crumbs and cheese with butter and cayenne to form a thick smooth paste. Shape into balls about the size of walnuts – in shell. Turn them in beaten eggs, then additional crumbs and fry in slightly-smoking hot oil to a rich golden brown. They be pretty to look upon if piled one above the other on a d'oyley covered dish to form a rising pyramid, the summit of which should be decorated with a sprig or two of fried parsley sprigs (*please see on p.* 142).

BACON ROLLS

ASSEMBLY

6, No. 5 cut, slices of streaky bacon with all rinds removed; ½ lb Gorgonzola cheese; ¼ lb puff paste; some grated Parmesan cheese; some paprika powder; 1 egg.

PROCEDURE

Cut each slice of bacon into two, lengthwise, then flatten and widen by batting with a meat batter (*or cleaned old flatiron, F.C.*) very vigorously but not so much as to split the strips. Roll a small piece of Gorgonzola, cut to matching width, inside each bacon strip. Roll out the puff paste on a thick scattering of Parmesan instead of flour, sprinkled with paprika. Cut up the paste into short strips the same width as the little rolls but only cutting each long enough to enclose each bacon over cheese roll. Place all upon a baking sheet, well spaced apart, brush over with beaten egg and bake in a moderate oven for twenty minutes. (*Gas Mark 5, one shelf above centre to give bacon time to cook thoroughly inside paste. F.C.*)

GOLDEN BUCKS

ASSEMBLY

¼ lb Cheddar cheese; 1 oz butter; 2 eggs; 2½–3 fluid oz old ale; an eggspoon of celery salt, and of pepper; 1 heaped tablespoon thick cream; 1 coffeespoon strained lemon juice; 12 drops of Worcestershire sauce – none other will do – and 2 small crust-denuded slices of ½-inch-thick buttered toast. Please turn for this to p. 198.

PROCEDURE

Mince or fine-chop the cheese. Put into a small stewpan with the butter, ale, celery salt, lemon juice and pepper. Beat both eggs and cream together and stir into the stewpan over a very low heat. Place within the stewpan a loop whisk and whisk away until the mixture becomes creamy and thick, whisk in the Worcestershire sauce and pour upon the toast pieces, each one on a separate plate. Garnish with sprigs of fresh parsley. Never confuse Welsh Rarebit with Golden Buck. The former may be browned and bubbled by a salamander (*grill*, *F.C.*) but the latter should never have this done to it.

WELSH RAREBIT

ASSEMBLY

4 oz thin-sliced Cheddar cheese; 1½ oz salt butter; 2 tablespoons old ale; a dash of Worcestershire sauce; 1 flat teaspoon dry English mustard.

PROCEDURE

Place all ingredients into a small stewpan and stir about continuously until very thick. Turn upon two squares of properly buttered toast and Salamander (*brown under grill*, *F.C.*) immediately prior to serving.

YORKSHIRE RAREBIT

Clearly this is a county of very hearty eaters! Follow the instructions for Welsh Rarebit above and when two of these be ready for salamandering ABSTAIN! Instead, cover each with a nicely fried rasher of curled up back bacon and lay thereon 1 soft-fried egg per toast.

MY OWN CHEESE BISCUITS

ASSEMBLY

3 oz superfine flour; 2 oz fine-grated hard Parmesan cheese; 2 oz salt butter; 1 teaspoon strained lemon juice; 2 separated egg yolks (*small*, *F.C.*); 1 pinch cayenne; 1 pinch of salt.

PROCEDURE

Sift flour and cayenne on to a piece of marble, rub in the butter, pour into central well all the remainder given, and work up to a firm dough, adding drops of water sparingly and only if considered really necessary. Roll out very thinly. Stamp into 1½-inch-diameter plain rounds, prick all over with a fork when laid upon a floured baking tray and bake in a cool oven (*Gas Mark 3, one shelf below centre, F.C.*) for just so long as it takes to lift one off with a metal spatula without it sticking. Let them lie flat upon a rack to harden and cool. From them may be made a number of good savouries suitable for handing around before dinner or for presenting two, three or more per person as a Savoury Course.

EXAMPLES

1. Coil one well-wiped anchovy fillet around upon each biscuit. Decorate with a rosette of cream lightly flavoured with a few drops of brandy.
2. Lay a slice of hard-boiled egg upon each one. Season a couple of tablespoons of very thick mayonnaise (*stiffened with a few drops of liquid powdered gelatine, F.C.*) with curry powder, a pinch of cayenne and a drop – no more – of lemon juice. Pipe over the egg on each biscuit.
3. Chop a slice of fat and lean of ham very fine. Blend with 2 dessertspoons of chutnee spread upon each biscuit and thereafter sprinkle very thickly with finely scissored fresh chives.
4. Mix 1 tablespoon of Bloater Paste with 1 tablespoon of concentrated anchovy purée. Add a small dessertspoon of curry paste and a ½ oz of well-creamed butter. Work all up, with 2 tablespoons of bought Mango Chutnee and pipe upon biscuits. Heat up low in a slow oven for a very few moments and send to table.
5. Take the contents of one lobster claw. Slice thinly. Lay upon biscuits spread with anchovy toast mixture (please turn to p. 211). Put a few drops of My Devil (p. 39) over each and heat by the side of the stove on a metal dish before sending to table.

BEVERAGES

Beverages

Sloe Gin
Scorcher
Mulled Ale
Buttered Rum
Ale Consoler
Mulls
Wine Posset
Churchwarden
My Bishop
Archbishop
Cardinal
Beadle
Negus
Bull's Milk
Black Velvet
Sherry Cobbler
Brandy Sour
King's Peg

SLOE GIN

MEMORIES are always present when I put up my year's supply of sloe gin. Nowadays, when I am free to wander the lanes near by and pick my own sloes, as I did when I was a small child, I think of those happy, busy, sometimes distracting days with Mr Holmes and Dr Watson with great wistfulness. However, all good things must come to an end and my way has been permitted to be very pleasant for the end of my days. When I feel what my dear father used to call 'as if I had a black dog upon my back', I always remind myself that none from the highest to the humblest can leave life alive! And that I have much for which to be thankful to my Maker.

ASSEMBLY

As many sloes as you will; gin of a reputable name (if such may be said of such a Dangerous Alcohol); a large darning needle; wine-sugar-upon-strings (*still obtainable if sought diligently as Mrs H. would say! F.C.*).

PROCEDURE

Take wide-necked bottles and make sure that the corks for them are firm and strong (*use bottling jars, F.C.*). Wash your sloes. Prick enough to come to the shoulder of each jar. Pray prick them thoroughly or your Sloe Gin will suffer! Drive a piece of wine-sugar down into the centre (*use preserving sugar, F.C.*). Then fill up with gin, cork down and store in a dry, cool place. Leave so for as long as you wish. It is far better to leave with the sloes than to rack off and bottle. Strain off the required amount into a quarter decanter and so serve in thimblefuls as a digestive after the evening repast. Beware of drinking too much of it. When five years old or more it becomes Highly Potent.

SCORCHER

Being a masculine establishment I was called upon occasionally to put up certain remedies for what Mr Holmes referred to as 'The Aftermaths of Revelry'. This is one such mixture.

Squeeze the juice of half a lemon, strain and turn into a wine glass. Stir in a liqueur glass of brandy and add a strong pinch of cayenne. Stir all well. It is to be drunk down in one gulp.

MULLED ALE

Many's the time that Mr Holmes, pondering upon a particularly knotty problem would come out of his room on to the landing and call down the stairs for me. When I answered him with the reply, 'Coming sir,' he would lean over the banisters and shout, 'Pray do not, but I have a stubborn problem which refuses to resolve itself, perhaps if you would be so good as to provide the usual lubrication I may be enabled to see some light.'

Thus did I know I was to make him a brew of ale. First, mounting the stairs, skirts in one hand, poker in the other, which I thought amusedly might surprise anyone whom I took unawares, I would enter that room, replenish the fire if so be it stood in need of attention and then thrust my poker in deep, thereafter exorting Mr Holmes, respectfully of course, to let it lie undisturbed and not attempt to poke at the fire with it until I had returned with my Ale.

ASSEMBLY

2 pints old ale; one 1-inch stick of cinnamon, pounded fine; 1 heaped tablespoon soft brown (pieces) sugar; 2 torn bay leaves; one 1-inch piece of root ginger bruised and in a muslin bag; 1 whole lemon sliced thinly with skin adhering but all pips removed.

PROCEDURE

Place all ingredients in a roomy copper pan and allow to come, very slowly, to boiling point. Remove the ginger bag, tie a stiffly starched, spotlessly clean, white table napkin around the pan and so carry in for service. There, remove the white-hot poker and grasping it firmly at the harmless end, plunge it vertically into the ale brew. There hold it quite erect as it foams and bubbles, fusses, whimpers and finally subsides. Without this last treatment the brew is quite worthless. When its temper has quite abated pour into glasses prepared as for CHURCHWARDEN (see p. 210).

BUTTERED RUM

When either of my gentlemen were afflicted with the common cold I would carry a glass of buttered rum upstairs to them in their beds and stand over them while they sipped it until all was gone, which did easily ensure a powerful sweating. Thus by morning they were quite restored to their normal health.

Place $1\frac{1}{2}$-inches of good rum into a tumbler, into which you have already inserted a long silver spoon. Add thereto $1\frac{1}{2}$ teaspoons strained lemon juice, 1 walnut-sized piece of sweet butter and 1 heaped teaspoon Demerara sugar. Fill to the brim with freshly-boiled, boiling water and stir about very thoroughly. This must be drunk immediately.

ALE CONSOLER

A very powerful brew not to be taken before going out into the cold again.

Place a quart bottle of old ale into a stewpan and heat through to just below boiling point. Add thereto 2 heaped tablespoons Demerara sugar; 1 level teaspoon ground-to-powder-ginger; the same of similarly treated cinnamon from the stick; a pinch of dried, powdered lavender. Have ready four good-sized eggs whisked to a high froth, stir about, stir in one claret glass of brandy, pour back and forth several times between two warmed jugs and serve swiftly.

MULLS

Whenever we were expecting visitors to an evening meal, at least whenever Mr Holmes considered them to be worthy of such attention, he would take the key which ever hung beside his desk and with it would descend to the cellar. After a sometimes protracted period he would then emerge with various ancient, cobwebby bottles and politely explain to me, 'I will deal with these myself Mrs Hudson.'

He was likewise very particular concerning the heating of good wines, saying, 'Pray let us exert extreme care in our selection of unimportant wines for mulling and the like. Nothing is more heinous than submitting wines of quality to such treatment.'

WINE POSSET

ASSEMBLY
1 pint sweet, new milk; ¼ pint dry, white wine; a generous pinch each of cinnamon, bay and lavender all pounded fine; the grated rind of half a lemon, sugar to taste.

PROCEDURE
Place both milk and wine in one stout stewpan together. Heat until the milk curdles – *which must be so*. Strain off the whey through a double fold of muslin. Liquefy the sugar in this by side-of-the-stove warming – gently; stir in the spices. Now rub the curdled milk through a tammy cloth (*fine sieve, F.C.*). Beat quite vigorously into the sweetened whey. Serve immediately.

CHURCHWARDEN

This was a warming 'cordial' which was much in demand when journalists of London newspapers did come in the late evenings to talk and smoke their pipes. This they did until the sitting-room at No. 221b was as thick as a London pea-souper.

Roast 1 good-sized lemon in an oven at very mild temperature (*Gas Mark 3, mid-shelf for twenty minutes. F.C.*). Place thereafter in a thick stewpan by the side of your stove and pour on to it 1 bottle of what Mr Holmes referred to when he handed it out to me as, 'a very ordinary red wine'. Measure off 1 pint freshly-made, weak tea and finally stir in, until completely melted, 4 oz loaf sugar. When all be just below boiling point pour into a punch bowl. Insert the ladle and set both upon a tray with tumblers wrapped in clean napkins and a silver spoon inserted in each lest the glass become cracked through the brew's heat when this be poured in.

MY BISHOP

Doctor Watson, as I have previously mentioned, was wont on winter nights to bring to us a number of his medical friends. Mr Holmes approved, for ere long he would be deep in a discussion of highly technical medical matters, mostly concerning poisons in which he seemed to show an almost morbid interest, though far be it for me to presume to criticise a Very Great Man. Such occasions would always signify that I would be called upon to make a steaming bowl of Bishop for their delectation and I would also send in during the evening a succession of Savouries, always hot ones and always either under a lidded entrée dish or in an enclosing napkin.

ASSEMBLY

1 punch bowl and ladle; 1 large, oily lemon well stuck with cloves; ½ lb loaf sugar; a generous grate of nutmeg from the nut – never from that powdered form; a 1-inch-stick of real cinnamon; a 1-inch-piece of root ginger bruised hard and enclosed in a bag made of butter muslin; 2 extra cloves; 3 generous pinches of allspice; ½ pint port; 1 pint claret (remember this may be made with whatever port and claret an employer hands to his or her housekeeper); 1 claret glassful of Cherry Brandy of which the best may be bought at Ye Sarre House, Sarre near Canterbury, Kent.

PROCEDURE

Roast and turn your clove-stuck lemon before a good fire until he be browned and sizzle-skinned all over. Pound together in a mortar and with a pestle, the sugar, spices and the thin-peeled rind of 1 extra unbaked lemon. Turn into a copper stewpan, add a ½ pint of sweet rainwater whenever possible, otherwise boil, chill and employ water from the kitchen tap. Add and heat up the wine mixture over the side of the stove making perfectly sure that it will not run the terrible risk of *boiling*. Meanwhile, drop the roasted lemon into your punch bowl and bruise him down with the bowl of your ladle. When your pan mixture be very hot, stir in the brandy, heat again and pour all over the lemon so that he may bob convivially in your Bishop. Thus would I carry the mixture in to loud cheers from the gentlemen. Then I would turn my attention to my savouries and send That Boy with them, in turn making sure beforehand that I had inspected his fingernails, ears and nose, for he was a messy boy having not been brought up right.

ARCHBISHOP

This be another warming brew which I was called upon to serve to similar company to that chosen for the service of CHURCHWARDEN.

Stick a Seville orange (no other will do) well with cloves that he be studded all over with them. Roast this *before* a good fire turning occasionally for a period of about thirty minutes. Cut the roasted orange in halves. Sprinkle the cut sides liberally with crushed loaf sugar. Heat through a bottle of ordinary white wine of a dry kind and in a stewpan, or upon occasions Mr Holmes has given me a bottle of medium sherry or dry Marsala instead. Place the orange halves in a punch bowl, pour on the heated wine. Return to the stewpan and allow to be re-heated until just below boiling. No hot wine drink may ever be allowed to boil.

CARDINAL

Another celebratory beverage for writing gentlemen.

Slice 3 tangerines which are close fitted to their skins and not standing away loose, which denotes AGE. Add $\frac{1}{2}$ oz bruised cinnamon stick, a small blade of mace, a pinch of ground-down nutmeg and 4 oz barleysugar purchased from a confectionary shop. This last must first be dissolved in 1 pint boiling water. Place all in a thick stewpan and cover close with a well-fitting lid. Simmer very gently for twenty minutes this being the exception to the – pardon the pun – Cardinal Rule. Strain clear, pressing down in the straining cloth (*sieve, F.C.*) with a wooden spoon. Add 1 quart of Rhenish wine (*Rhine wine, F.C.*), warm through, but now you do not allow to boil again.

BEADLE

This was ever the good Doctor's favourite.

Pound $\frac{1}{4}$ oz cinnamon in stick, with 4 cloves and $\frac{1}{2}$ oz powdered ginger all together. Add $\frac{1}{4}$ lb crushed loaf sugar and 1 pint freshly boiled, boiling water. Strain all through a tammy cloth (*sieve, F.C.*). Add this carefully to 2 yolks of eggs, beating the while very steady. Then add 1 glass of Raisin wine and 6 glasses of Ginger wine (*these 'glasses' are $6\frac{2}{3}$ fluid oz tulip wine glasses, F.C.*). Drink while very frothy, so remember to give one final whisk after whisking in the Raisin and Ginger wines.

NEGUS

This is one to which Mr Holmes and Mr Mycroft Holmes were both Very Partial.

Warm 1 bottle of medium sherry or Ruby-type port in a thick stewpan at the side of your stove. Have ready another stewpan into which you place 1 pint of boiling water and keep it hot. Take 1 thinly sliced, large lemon and set into a roomy bowl. Pour over it the hot wine. Add sugar to taste and do not let it be too sweet for gentlemen care not for great sweetness. Then add and stir in the boiling water, then 1 claret glass of brandy (6⅔ oz, F.C.) and 2 generous pinches of ground nutmeg. Serve very hot in glasses which have been treated as for Churchwarden (p. 210).

BULL'S MILK

This be one of the cooling beverages which I was called upon to put up by Mr Holmes when he had Convivial Male Gatherings upon hot summer nights, when the atmosphere in his room was so thick as to be unbearable by me when I went in with further trays halfway through the revelries.

This particular receipt is said to contain Quite Remarkable Restorative Qualities.

Place 3 tumblersful of sweet, new milk in a large jug. Add to it 1 claret glass of rum (6⅔ fluid oz, F.C.) and the same of inexpensive, inferior brandy. Then sweeten to taste with crushed loaf sugar, together with a generous pinch of both nutmeg and cinnamon and whisk into this mixture 3 lightly-whipped fresh eggs of good size. Set around with crushed ice in a big bowl with the jug of Bull's milk inset centrally and let it be for at least one hour. In this time pound down 1 lb ice splinters until they be well-crushed. Pour into the jug at the moment of service and pour into very small wine glasses. It be Very Potent!

BLACK VELVET

When Mr Holmes had occasion to entertain some of what he termed 'The Racing Fraternity', he instructed me in the manner of making this brew which I personally considered Extremely Nasty!

For each person present take one tumbler and into each put one third of the tumbler's capacity in Stout. Then with extreme slowness, just trickle in Champagne to the brim of each glass. Take a small stick and stir around with some caution. Let the imbibers take of it slowly and not attempt to drink it down like ale in one great gulp!

SHERRY COBBLER

Prepare in tumblers, one for each guest. Have ready a bowl of finely crushed ice; a jug of strained, fresh orange juice; a small dish of very thin-sliced, unpeeled oranges; a further bowl of castor sugar and a decanter of medium-dry sherry. Set upon a silver tray and present. Then each guest, or the host, for each guest, prepares each Sherry Cobbler in the following manner: Each glass a quarter filled with the sherry. To it add 1 generous teaspoon orange juice; 1 level teaspoon superfine castor sugar; 1 slice of orange; then fill to the brim with crushed ice. Stir about well before distributing.

BRANDY SOUR

Place in a jug 1 tablespoon plain sugar syrup;* add 1 teacup fine-crushed ice; the strained juice of 1 lemon; 1 gill of brandy of a common sort. Stir very thoroughly, strain into chilled wine glasses for service.

*The Sugar Syrup
Dissolve in ½ pint of water, ½ lb of loaf sugar, then boil two minutes.

KING'S PEG

I can only recall two occasions on which this was served at Baker Street. The first was upon the coming in of His Majesty the King of Bohemia and the second was when a friend of Mr Holmes called Carmody was to be wed that afternoon. Mr Carmody was exceeding nervous upon arrival and presently Mr Holmes summoned me. When to his pulling of the bell I made my appearance he said cheerfully, 'Mr Carmody is a trifle put out by his forthcoming nuptials and requires a little expert steadying Mrs Hudson. Pray make us some King's Peg which I have assured him will put him to rights most speedily.'

Place a bottle of dry champagne into a cooler packed with ice and twirl until sufficiently chilled. Pour the champagne into goblets which have been lined with 2 tablespoons of good brandy. Stir about and sip for immediate calming of the most tight-drawn nervous conditions. It was told me by my Eminent Employer that the name of this drink came from the plain fact that it was a much favoured one with His Royal Highness the Prince of Wales, later to be King Edward the Seventh. Upon being given a goblet of King's Peg, Dr Watson exclaimed, 'Good heavens Holmes, this is marvellous!' – which was ever a familiar cry upon the good Doctor's lips – generally about Mr Holmes' remarkable deductions.

ESTEEMED SUNDRIES

Esteemed Sundries

My Seasoned Flour
Basic White Sauce with White Stock and Wine
Basic White Sauce with Milk and Cream
Garlic Butter Sauce
Holland Sauce
Plain Lemon Sauce
Brown Sauce
Spanish Sauce
Anchovy Toast for Tea
The Proper Making of Coffee
Syrup of Coffee
How to Make Green Vegetable Colouring
How to Make a Parsley Ball
How to Make Mayonnaise
Mayonnaise for Decorative Purposes

MY SEASONED FLOUR

PUT up into a dry canister with a well-fitting lid and stand by the side of your stove upon a shelf that it may always be dry for immediate future usage.

ASSEMBLY

1 lb fine flour sifted with 1 oz ground rock salt; ½ oz pounded black pepper; 1 dessertspoon dry English mustard; ¼ oz pounded mace; ½ flat eggspoon cayenne pepper; 1 flat teaspoon nutmeg; ½ flat teaspoon cloves.

PROCEDURE

Mix all together and store as previously explained.

BASIC WHITE SAUCE WITH WHITE STOCK AND WINE

ASSEMBLY

1½ oz flour; 1 oz butter; ¼ pint dry, white wine; ½ pint white stock.

PROCEDURE

Place butter in a small, thick pan and when it be completely dissolved stir in the flour until this forms a paste like a soft ball in the centre of your little pan. Pour on half the wine. Ease the ball with a wooden sauce spoon that the fluid may run beneath and let it come to the boil. Then stir until the fluid be incorporated. Take up the pan and beat thoroughly. Add the remaining wine and then the stock in two parts following the exact waiting, stirring, beating procedure I have already indicated. Thus comes a perfectly smooth sauce which may be employed thereafter without any need to rub the same through a tammy cloth (*tamis or sieve*, F.C.) which is ever wasteful of time and labour in the doing and in the cleansing thereafter.

BASIC WHITE SAUCE WITH MILK AND CREAM

Following the instructions exactly as given for the Basic White Sauce With White Stock and Wine. Use the same quantities of butter and flour and only change the fluids to 8 fluid oz of good, sweet milk and 2 fluid oz of rich cream.

There are a few helpful rules which I would like to identify here in respect of these two sauces. The first is to run a small piece of butter through your fingers on to the completed sauce if you require it to have that sheen upon it which is the hallmark of good saucing.

The second is that you should never season either of these two sauces as you may require them to be incorporated into some already sufficiently seasoned item. Alternatively you may desire to utilise them with either sweet and savoury items!

The third rule is concerning crusting upon the top of sauces. To avoid this, take a piece of parchment (*greaseproof today, F.C.*), hold it under a running cold tap until it be thoroughly soaked, then shake off the surplus moisture and fit it like a skin over the surface of your sauce *if you are not intending to employ it immediately.*

GARLIC BUTTER SAUCE

This is a splendid foundation item upon which to draw for giving extra zest to soups, gravies and sauces. I always have it by me.

ASSEMBLY

1 head of garlic; 4 oz butter; 1 saltspoon salt; ½ saltspoon fresh-ground black peppercorns; the strained juice of 1 lemon; 1 extra teacupful of melted butter.

PROCEDURE

Peel every separate, detached clove of your garlic head and place in a mortar with the piece of butter, the salt and pepper. Pound down to a paste in which the cloves are perfectly crushed to pap. Then pound in slowly, drop by drop, the lemon juice and finally the melted butter. Turn into a jar covered with parchment (*aluminium kitchen foil, F.C.*) and tie down. Keep separate lest the strong odour of the garlic intrude upon some other preparation.

HOLLAND SAUCE
(Sauce Hollandaise, F.C.)

ASSEMBLY

10 separated egg yolks; 12 oz very best butter; 2 small shallots chopped extremely fine; 1 flat teaspoon each of fine chopped tarragon, and of parsley heads and thyme; 4 tablespoons dry white wine. (*Too much, halve ingredients, F.C.*)

PROCEDURE

Place all herbs in the very smallest pan you possess, add 4 tablespoons of dry white wine and set at the side of your stove that the herbs and shallots may thoroughly infuse the fluids and the fluids may be reduced very slowly to only 1 tablespoon. Place this in the base of a warmed double saucepan's upper pan with boiling water coming half way up the base pan. Toss in the egg yolks and begin whisking. From this moment onwards you will whisk unceasingly please, employing one hand for your loop whisk and leaving the other one free to take small lumps of the butter, which must be soft, and run them through the fingers on to the pan mixture. Now you must learn what is culinary teasing. It is the removal of the upper pan from the heat and the replacement of it at intervals so that the sauce may never be allowed to become much above blood heat. As you work so it will then thicken, by this you may know you are correct; but in your own interest exert the Utmost Caution, for the ingredients are scarcely ones which any honest cook would care to throw away. When all the butter is incorporated add a flick or two of salt to the very thick Hollandaise. Keep at room temperature until required.

PLAIN LEMON SAUCE

ASSEMBLY

½ pint boiling water; the strained juice of 2 lemons; as much castor sugar as tastes pleasing; 2 heaped teaspoons potato flour; 1 greengage-sized piece of sweet butter.

PROCEDURE

Stir the potato flour with the lemon juice until it is smooth, which is very quick indeed to come. Pour on to the boiling water, sugar and remaining lemon juice and stir fast until it thickens well. Stir in the butter in flakes and if so be it pleases you stir in 1 teaspoon of white rum.

BROWN SAUCE

This is a basic sauce which is of inestimable value to a cook.

ASSEMBLY

1 oz flour; 1 oz butter; 2 pints strong brown stock; 4 oz rough cut tomatoes and My Vegetable Mixture (see below).

PROCEDURE

Dissolve the butter in a small, thick stewpan, stir in the flour and continue stirring over moderate top-of-stove heat until this mixture becomes quite brown. Then stir in the stock, being careful to beat very thoroughly after each small addition. Then work in the prepared tomatoes and the Vegetable Mixture and simmer over very gentle heat until reduced to half its original quantity.

THE VEGETABLE MIXTURE
(*Mirepoix, F.C.*)

ASSEMBLY

1 medium, scraped carrot, then grated fine; 1 medium peeled Spanish onion, then grated fine; 1 sprig of thyme; 1 crushed bay leaf; 4-inch stick of celery white, likewise chopped fine; 1 oz butter; 1 fluid oz olive oil; 1 tablespoon Madeira wine.

PROCEDURE

Dissolve the butter with the oil and when both are hot fry onion and celery until just lightly browned, stirring gently the while. Add the remaining ingredients, simmer two minutes and add to your Brown Sauce.

SPANISH SAUCE

This sauce is a basic one which may be used for countless compound sauces as they are called in good kitchens.

Mix ¾ pint of Brown Sauce (see preceding receipt) with 1 fluid oz game stock which has previously been reduced by simmering until it is of the consistency of india-rubber. Add to these, over the stove in a small, thick stewpan, 4 unskinned button mushrooms sliced fine with their stalks, 4 fluid oz sherry and a generous pinch of castor sugar. Allow this mixture to simmer steadily, with occasional stirrings, until it has been reduced to a quarter part of its original whole, strain through a tammy (*Tamis = metal, from the French, F.C.*) and use as required.

ANCHOVY TOAST FOR TEA

One day Mr Holmes came in with a small parcel. He handed this to me saying, 'This, Mrs Hudson, is a purchase from Messrs Asprey in New Bond Street. It is for that superlatively good tea offering of yours, your Anchovy toast.' He stood over me while I unwrapped it to reveal a round dish with a domed lid. This I removed to discover beneath that the flat surface was considerably above the base.

Mr Holmes explained. 'You pour boiling water into this tiny cavity, after removing the screw,' – this he obligingly demonstrated for me. 'Then you replace the screw,' he did so, 'and when the container has had time to heat up you lay those excellent toasted fingers upon it and when it is filled close all up with this lid. Thus shall we have hot anchovy toast even though I may break off to delve into some reference book and be recalled with difficulty.'

Here is the way of it. Prepare a mixture by melting 4 oz of butter slowly and beating into it, off the fire, 2 separated egg yolks. Then shake in concentrated anchovy purée to taste, give the mixture a flick of cayenne pepper and put it upon a warmed plate by the side of the stove. Now make your toast, cutting the bread ½-inch in thickness, and removing all crusts. Lay each one down upon the anchovy mixture that its immersed surface may quickly absorb a sufficiency. Reverse the toast, cut into three flat fingers and so proceed, criss-crossing the fingers to the maximum height that the lidded container will contain.

THE PROPER MAKING OF COFFEE

My Illustrious Employer was also my instructor in the matter of making what he, who had a very Discerning Palate, considered to be really good after dinner coffee. When I had learned the way of it, which was exceeding simple, I used to leave all ready for Mr Holmes to make some for himself over a spirit lamp if so be he came back unexpected to the house in the small hours of the morning.

Take a sturdy enamel jug and see that he be not chipped, for such is dangerous and provides lodgement for microbes which be an abomination. Put therein 4 very high-heaped tablespoons of freshly ground superfine coffee beans. Boil a kettleful of fresh water. Pour from a height into the jug and on to the coffee. Take up the jug and set upon the spirit stove turned fairly low. Let the coffee surge up in the jug and cause a foam almost to the rim. Remove it and allow it to subside completely. Do this three times. Cover with a plate or saucer, leave for four minutes, strain into a coffee pot and serve with cream and loaf sugar.

Mr Holmes told me that this was the way those Frenchies made coffee and I am bound to admit it is the best method I have ever come across. I made mine of course over my coal stove and had the self-defensive habit, when Mr Holmes started that revolver practice of his, of making some coffee. Then to the bang, bang of his gun's deafening reports I would bear the tray to his room, knock upon the door (in the interests of self-preservation, for it be unmannerly to knock upon any doors other than those of bed, dressing or bathrooms). The sight of the coffee always persuaded my Master to desist this tiresome practising.

SYRUP OF COFFEE

I was at one time positively despairing of the terrible waste caused by my Master's absentmindedness. Coffee would be brewed for him at all hours of the day and night. Then when I came into his quarters the following morning I would find half-drunk cups of it, half-filled pots of it! It was more than my place was worth to give Mr Holmes coffee which had been heated up. Naturally I attempted so to do; but the roar of rage with which the first sip was greeted brought me hurrying back again to receive a Terrible Homily upon the error of my ways! Even so, it made me quite distracted. However, one day, when I was talking to my friend Mrs Hitchcock who was cook to my Lady's niece, she happened to remark that coffee syrup proved a positive God-sent boon to her when making glacé icing for afternoon tea sponges. This caused me to prick up my ears, for Mr Holmes was partial to coffee flavouring in both cakes and puddings. Mrs Hitchcock then explained, making me feel a perfect fool for not having thought of it myself. I never wasted any more coffee dregs!

To make the syrup, which keeps indefinitely in a well-stoppered glass jar on a dry goods shelf, simply put at least 1 pint into a tall saucepan, allow the coffee to boil – *yes boil!* and then draw the pan to the side of your stove and there let the coffee simmer, simmer until there only remains about 2 tablespoonsful. Pray add nothing to this, like sugar, for it would then upset the balance of a dish whose own ingredients will take care of the necessary sweetening. Put this into your jar, stopper it and put away. Thus, gradually, as coffee leavings accumulate, turn

Esteemed sundries

them into this for Syrup of which only a few drops are needed for glacé icing, or a teaspoonful or two to flavour a cake or pudding.

HOW TO MAKE GREEN VEGETABLE COLOURING

Pick over 4 lb of fresh, green spinach very carefully and remove all stalks. Wash, drain very thoroughly and place in a dry, thick pan over a lowish heat. There allow the spinach to collapse, as it will and to give up its own juices thoroughly. When it be a pap, place in a tammy cloth (*sieve, F.C.*) and wring out the drops into a bowl. When the spinach be useless and dry, pour the accumulated juices into a little bottle and cork down. This is proper, harmless, pure Green Vegetable Colouring.

HOW TO MAKE A PARSLEY BALL

I was ever irritated by the profiteering of greengrocers in winter over the price charged for parsley. I have been asked as much as a penny for a bunch of extremely small size. I therefore determined to revert to what my aunt always did in winter and make my own Parsley Ball from which I could take all the parsley I needed in winter time, at no cost whatever save the initial expenditure of one penny upon a packet of parsley seed.

Take a wire hanging basket of the kind used in the fashionable streets in summer time to depend from the awnings of great houses during the season. Line this with close-packed moss. Then fill up to the brim with fine loam on to which, having measured the amount you will require, you stir the contents of your seed packet. Press it down, but do so with a rounded shape atop, so that the 'ball' effect be true.

Just keep this basket regularly watered. Let it depend from a hook in your kitchen in a good light and nature will take care of the rest. (*You'll need more seed than you get in one packet today! F.C.*) After a few weeks – remember parsley seed is very slow to germinate – you will find your basket studded with tiny green spears. Within three months it will become a bright green ball. Just remember that this requires regular picking lest the leaves age and turn yellow before being put to some practical use in the kitchen.

HOW TO MAKE MAYONNAISE

The very best, straightforward, basic mayonnaise must be made with pure olive oil, superfine wine vinegar, ground down sea salt and ground down peppercorns. Mr Mycroft Holmes, whose opinion I respected concerning matters of the palate, always insisted on the inclusion of French Mustard which be entirely different from English Mustard, one being a paste and the other a powder, besides being of quite contrasting flavours. Mr Mycroft Holmes always brought me a bottle of the stuff when he went to France and those who are interested may like the name which I copied into my book many years ago *Gray Poupol de Dijon. La véritable moutarde de Dijon*, whatever all that foreign jargon signifies. To please Mr Mycroft I mixed my mayonnaise with this mustard instead of the good old English variety.

ASSEMBLY

1 pint pure olive oil; the separated yolks of 6 eggs; 1 rounded teaspoon salt; 1 mean, flat teaspoon pepper; 4 dessertspoons wine vinegar; plus, according to personal taste, either 1 rounded teaspoon English Mustard or that aforementioned French one.

PROCEDURE

Put the yolks into a roomy wooden bowl with the salt, pepper and chosen mustard and beat them through with a proper loop whisk until they become like batter which, I would remind you, is not done in five minutes! (*but it is with a modern electric mixer switched to full and left five minutes, F.C.*). Then begin to slide a fine trickle of oil on to this batter, whipping after each addition until the mixture becomes really thick. At this juncture whip in half the given wine vinegar. Then continue with the oil in a larger trickle – almost a stream is safe now – and so achieve, with the remainder of the oil and the second addition of wine vinegar, a really thick mixture which can be thinned down with cream as desired. Store it like my basic white sauces in a cold place, to draw upon when found necessary. (*Refrigerate for up to four weeks under wetted greaseproof. F.C.*)

MAYONNAISE FOR DECORATIVE PURPOSES

If you are accustomed to employing a forcing bag with a decorative pipe affixed for the purposes of embellishing salads and the like, then

Esteemed sundries
it is useful to know that for every 1 pint of mayonnaise, made as in my previous receipt, you only need to dissolve 2 leaves of gelatine in 2 fluid oz of water and stir this syrup in. Then beat it thoroughly and by the time you have assembled your dish and are ready to pipe, the mixture will hold the most delicate twirls and convolutions firmly.

PRESERVES

Preserves

Chutnee
Dr Watson's India Apple Chutnee
Dr Watson's Favourite Raw Chutnee
Wild Strawberry Jam
Wild Strawberry Tart
My Bitter Orange Marmalade
My Marrow and Ginger Jam
Dried Apricot Jam
My Peach Jam
Raspberry Jam
Blackcurrant Jam
Red Currant Jelly
Crab Apple Jelly
Quince Jelly
Rowan or Mountain Ash Jelly
Lemon Jelly
Gooseberry Jelly
Damson Cheese
To Preserve Runner Beans (Sometimes Called Scarlet Runners)
To Pickle Beetroots
Oxford Sauce
My Plums in Port Wine

PRESERVES

MR Holmes liked bitter orange marmalade. Dr Watson did not. His lady during their courting days was particularly partial to my Wild Strawberry Jam, for which I was wont to obtain a leave-of-absence day on which I would go into Kent, taking a train thereto and so to the station of Sevenoaks. There my nephew would meet me with a pony and trap. This I fear he obtained by manufacturing some story for his newspaper which he desired to 'follow up' in the vicinity and which necessitated the hiring of same from a local livery stable. Be that as it may, in this matter I considered it best to remind myself of the old proverb, 'let sleeping dogs lie'. He would bestow my picnic basket within, take from the trap a large leathern rug lined with scarlet flannel and wrap this around my knees when he had hoisted me into the seat beside him. Then, at a spanking pace, we would make our way out of the town on a warm summer's day. A few miles beyond we turned on to a cart track which wound between woodlands of great peace and tranquillity. The banks were thick with wild strawberries. Here we would fall to our knees and pick away, filling straw punnets with our treasures. From them I would also make Wild Strawberry Tart, employing thus the scum which I skimmed from my jam that nothing be wasted.

Here I must confess that I am particularly partial to a Marrow and Ginger Jam made with young, fresh marrows used before the skin and flesh become hard – which is when they should be used according to cookery books! I also required a quantity of apricot jam which I always made with dried apricots for my Apricot Purée used so much in my cooking. Then there was Blackcurrant Jam needed for sore throats, Blackcurrant Jam Tart and little tarts in particular; Red Currant Jelly for Dr Watson to eat with Jugged Hare, besides my needing it for glazing sweet items, notably Coconut Madelaines, after which there had to be all my chutnees, pickles, of which we ate a great deal as a household, and in particular my Pickled Onions about which I was perhaps unduly fussy.

The Sherlock Holmes Cookbook

All in all, preserves played a large part in my culinary activities, for there had to be jams for Roly-Polys, and of these in particular I much favoured Raspberry, as for Swiss Sponge Rolls when not using Apricot Purée, and for clapping between Victoria Sponges. So with others as well, I have put together a separate chapter for the Guidance of Others from those tried and tested favourites to which, ever and anon I was adding as the years progressed.

CHUTNEE

This was just one of Dr Watson's concoctions which I was obliged to put up for his solitary delectation.

First you must take 4 large Spanish onions. Chop them very fine, place them in a jar, cover them with wine vinegar (the Doctor desired me to use that malt stuff, but this I confess I could not bring myself to do), tie down with stout parchment (*aluminium kitchen foil, F.C.*) and let lie for seven days. When this period has elapsed take 12 large Pippin apples, peel them, core them and pack down into a stone jar. Add 1 gill of wine vinegar, cover close with parchment and place in a very mild oven until they be collapsed. Stir them around while hot to ensure the collapse is uniform and total then add ½ oz curry powder; 1 oz ground ginger; ½ lb stoned raisins, fine chopped if you please; ½ lb dark pieces sugar; 1 flat, small teaspoon cayenne pepper; 1½ pints wine vinegar. This mixture must be corked down and it must lie for seven days at least. Then mix in the contents of the onion jar and cork down once more for at least one calendar month. Doctor Watson maintained it was not 'at its prime' until one year had elapsed. That Boy and I essayed it after both periods of time and were not impressed.

DR WATSON'S INDIA APPLE CHUTNEE

This, as well as some others, I was required to keep in store for Dr Watson. This duty prevailed even after he was married since, having endeavoured to instruct his own cook, he was sadly disappointed with the results and ever maintained, 'Only Mrs Hudson can make proper Chutnee, at least one to *my* liking,' which I must suppose to have been a compliment.

Preserves

ASSEMBLY

2 lb cored, green cooking apples as tart as may be; 3 breakfastcups wine vinegar; 1 oz chillies; 1 oz garlic; 2 oz shallots, all chopped very fine indeed; 1 oz ground ginger; 2 oz coarse salt; 4 oz mustard seed; 4 oz tamarinds; 12 oz stoned, chopped raisins; 1 lb soft brown (pieces) sugar.

PROCEDURE

Place apples in an unimportant pan with the vinegar and set by the side of your stove till they be collapsed. Turn the pulp into a roomy basin. Mix all remaining prepared items in very thoroughly. Put into small stone jars, tie down with parchment (*aluminium kitchen foil, F.C.*) and store in a dry place. Dr Watson considered this mixture to be always the better for keeping and could seldom be persuaded to take any which was not of at least three months age in a jar.

DR WATSON'S FAVOURITE RAW CHUTNEE

Dr Watson once remarked when emptying the silver-topped glass Chutnee pot which I had put upon the table, 'Capital stuff! A great aid to the consumption of cold meat, eh Holmes?' To which Mr Holmes replied sourly, 'If it happens to be cold mutton my dear Watson, then it is entirely beyond redemption and in married households constitutes, in my considered opinion, *grounds for divorce.*'

ASSEMBLY

1 really large, ripe tomato; 1 Spanish onion of two thirds the tomato's size; 1 green chilli; 1 generous squeeze of lemon juice; 2 pinches salt; 1 rounded eggspoon freshly pounded black peppercorns.

PROCEDURE

Remove the skin from the tomato by plunging this item into boiling water and leaving three minutes, then plunging into very cold water after which the skin will come away. Chop the flesh very finely indeed, and do the same with the peeled onion. Split the chilli lengthwise. Eject all the pips. Chop up as finely as the rest. Put all into a mortar and with a pestle pound with only moderate vigour, adding the lemon juice, salt and pepper. This receipt may be multiplied to match the consumption of the family; but judgement and restraint must always be exercised in this matter to ensure *no waste*!

Author's Note

Rough cut everything. Place in liquidiser or emulsifier. Switch on full, allow four minutes and serve. Sorry Mrs Hudson! *F.C.*

WILD STRAWBERRY JAM

All strawberries are tiresome. Large strawberries defeat any cook if she be so foolish as to employ them for the making of preserves. Even the tiny wild ones, which must only be picked when they are very soft to the touch and actually crush between two fingers if grasped injudiciously, require a little propping up if they are to produce prime results. So here is the way of it.

ASSEMBLY

4 lb wild strawberries; the strained juice of 2 very large lemons; $3\frac{1}{2}$ lb preserving sugar.

PROCEDURE

Place the fruit in a large bowl. Add the sugar. Swill with the lemon juice. Gather up all discarded lemon pips into a muslin bag and, placing them in a small basin, cover them with 4 fluid oz of rain water. Let all rest overnight. In the morning, wash and squeeze the lemon pip bag in the surrounding water to extract every scrap of lemon jelly. Place in the jam kettle, then add the steeping strawberries and their fluid – for by now the sugar will all have melted. Leave on the side of the stove until no grain of sugar sounds against the sides or base of the kettle, then raise to a slow rolling boil. Maintain until the jam darkens. When a drop on a saucer, placed on a piece of cold stone 'sets' in a few moments your jam will be done. Skim away all the ridged scum upon the top surface. Pour the clear jam into small, heated pots or jars – remember that this jam is a luxury – and when completely cold proceed with the coverings.

Begin by towing inner jam covers or small, fitting circles of greaseproof paper, through a saucerful of common brandy. This is invaluable as a preservative and also as a protection from crystallisation. Then cover with parchments and tie down. (*Use outer jam covers or aluminium foil, F.C.*) Store in a very dry place.

WILD STRAWBERRY TART

Set aside 1 lb of wild strawberries. Bake a flan case with My Very Special Melting Crust (see p. 160), baked under a large circle of oiled foolscap (*greaseproof paper, F.C.*) pressed down lightly into the raw paste tart and then filled up with dried beans, or split peas or lentils. Bake in a brisk to medium oven (*one shelf above centre, Gas Mark 5, F.C.*) for long enough to 'set' the pastry and turn the edges a very pale biscuit colour. Withdraw the paper and pulses. Trundle these into an airtight tin. When cold affix the lid and thus waste nothing, but use the pulses again and again for some years to come.

ASSEMBLY

The scum from a 4 lb batch of wild strawberry jam; 1 partially baked flan case; 1 lb of wild strawberries; a squeeze of lemon juice; ¼ lb almond paste.

PROCEDURE

Lay the rolled out almond paste neatly in the base of the baked case. Spread the almond paste liberally with the aforenamed scum. Scatter the wild strawberries over thickly. Moisten with a few flicks of lemon juice. Return to a slow oven (*Gas Mark 3, mid shelf. F.C.*) and leave for twenty minutes. Remove and chill. Paint all over with warmed red currant jelly which by the warming will dissolve to syrup. Leave a while, then decorate with rosettes of whipped cream.

MY BITTER ORANGE MARMALADE

Never a year passes but I do see in the newspapers correspondence from cooks and ladies who are concerned with their own households, complaining of something that went wrong with their marmalades. Some always complain that it is runny, others that it is tough. The letters always follow two or three weeks after the announcement appears in the Ladies Advice Columns stating 'Seville Oranges are now arriving in the shops so it behoves prudent housewives to look to their marmalade making'. This statement is usually supported by one or more receipts.

I have my own. It has never failed to please Mr Holmes, though I cannot abide it myself. Nevertheless, it does not run, though its nature is sorely bitter and leaves *my* mouth a-tingle after partaking of it.

PROCEDURE

Take 12 Seville oranges and weigh them carefully. When the weight has been ascertained allow and weigh off 12 oz of sugar for every pound of fruit. Set this aside. Set ready the grated rind and the strained juice of $4\frac{1}{2}$ good sized lemons. Quarter the oranges. Remove the peel neatly. Throw it into cold water and boil until tender enough for you to pierce the skin-side of one section with the head of a pin. Remove all peel, drain and chill. While this proceeds turn your attention to the fleshy lumps. Remove all pips, place in a basin, cover with $\frac{1}{2}$ pint of cold rainwater and leave them steeping overnight. Remove any white pith which adheres to the flesh quarters. Place pulp and weighed sugar together and let them also steep together overnight. In the morning take up the cooked peel sections, turn them pith-side uppermost and remove the white pith with a very sharp knife then cut into $\frac{3}{8}$-inch strips. Stir these into the steeped pulp. Add the water and the now rather slimy jelly-like substance from the strained pips, stir all and allow to rise with great slowness to a rolling boil. Thus may you be sure every grain of sugar has dissolved before the marmalade reaches boiling point. After this maintain at a slow, rolling boil until quite dark and indeed until a tiny spoonful sets on a test saucer as described for Wild Strawberry Jam on p. 232.

MY MARROW AND GINGER JAM

Select only small, young vegetable marrows with tender skins. Begin by peeling these extremely thinly. Slice the peeled marrows into rounds of just over $\frac{1}{4}$ inch thickness and cut out the central soft pith and immature pips. Dice neatly. Make up a solution of salt* and rainwater by stirring into the rainwater – 1 gallon, 2 piled high tablespoons of grated-down rock salt. Keep this tub in the kitchen that it may remain warm. Drain, rinse in clear water, pat dry in a cloth and then weigh the cubes. Weigh off 1 lb loaf sugar to every pound of marrow cubes. Also measure off 1 pint of rainwater to the same amount of marrow together with $\frac{3}{4}$ oz of well bruised root ginger to every pound of cubes. When all are measured and ready, tie up the bruised ginger in a scrap of muslin and tie a long loop of the string at the end of the bag, securing this to the handle of the pan that the bag may be fished out easily when the jam be done. In the jam kettle or pan place, with the ginger bag, both the water and the sugar and cook slowly to a clear syrup. Then immerse the marrow cubes and simmer gently until these are transparent and tender but on no account let them collapse. When this stage of clarity and tenderness is reached put in the grated rind and the strained juice of 1 good sized

* The salt in the solution helps to draw surplus moisture and any tendency to bitterness from vegetable marrows. *F.C.*

lemon, simmer on for a further fifteen minutes. Stir in 5 fluid oz of gin to every 3 lb of jam, tie down and store as already explained.

Note 1 Some cooks prefer to substitute whisky but not I!
Note 2 I like to add 2 large pieces of ginger-in-syrup, diced small, when jam is finished; but this is a matter for choice.

DRIED APRICOT JAM

Purchase only the very best apricots and work in quantities of 3 lb apricots to 3 pints of weak, strained Indian tea, the thinly peeled rind of 3 lemons, the strained juice of the same and 3 lb of preserving sugar.

Begin by steeping the apricots in the cold tea until these are swollen and soft to the touch. Strain off the tea and wipe the apricots in a clean cloth. Tumble them into the jam kettle and take the precaution of straining the tea thereon *through a fold of fine buttermuslin*, as this will capture and retain any imperfections which may have floated out during the steeping time. Add the lemon rinds, juices and sugar. Set on the side of the stove that the sugar may dissolve perfectly before boiling point is reached. Raise to a slow rolling boil and maintain until a few drops set on a saucer. When this stage is reached, fish out the lemon rinds, pot as usual and tie down when cold.

MY PEACH JAM

This is a drawing-room, afternoon-tea delicacy of great distinction. If served with thin slices of home-made milk bread and the very best butter it will please guests far more than almost any cake.

You must use small, fairly firm peaches. You must skin them by placing them in a bowl and then pouring plenty of boiling water over them. After three to five minutes, lift them out, plunge them into very cold water, wait one minute and the skins will just rub away. Then you must halve them in order to excavate the stones. *This must be done with a silver knife.* When the stones are removed they are slipped inside several folds of clean, brown paper and smashed down lightly with a hammer. Thus you may remove the kernels. Peel them and set them aside. Slice your peach halves into two. Place them in a jam kettle – say 4 lb, cover them with 4 lb of preserving sugar and $\frac{1}{4}$ pint of cold water. Cover with a cloth and leave overnight. In the morning, set upon the stove where it be mild and let the sugar melt completely before coming to a slow, rolling boil. Then boil up and maintain at a strong simmer until a setting test is taken in the manner heretofore described. When this is achieved, skim carefully, set aside the scum for a tart and stir in the white kernels. Withdraw from the heat and let them lie in the jam ten minutes. Pot and tie down as usual.

RASPBERRY JAM

Use 1 lb raspberries to 1 lb sugar and absolutely no water. Proceed in the standard manner, but bruise the fruit somewhat with a wooden spoon in the early stages of heating.

BLACKCURRANT JAM

Cover stripped blackcurrants pound for pound with preserving sugar. In the morning, with well-scrubbed hands, bruise the fruit vigorously to aid the running of the juices therein. Proceed in the standard manner.

RED CURRANT JELLY

Please bear in mind that in giving this receipt I am giving all jelly receipts. The procedure is constant. Only the treatment of some fruits is different so this should be regarded by my readers as the *KEY RECEIPT*. The rest will be very brief and only constitute differences in fruit preparation.

The first constant rule therefore to be absorbed from the onset is that 1 measured pint of strained fruit fluid requires 1 lb of preserving or loaf sugar.

The second is that the fruit, no matter what it may be, must be completely purged of all colour and flavour before the fluid may be considered as ready for straining.

The third must be that the fluid is strained through a Proper Jelly Bag. This container is extremely thick and felt-like in texture. Any false economies such as straining through a piece of clean linen are therefore merely foolish.

The fourth and final one is that *if* a scrap of tested jelly – when suspected to be ready for potting up – does not 'jell' firmly upon a saucer, it is no mortal use imagining that the bulk will do so. Cook must continue with her slow, rolling boil until the jelly 'jells' when submitted to that essential test.

Thus my recommendations run: tumble, pellmell, as many pounds as you desire of red currants into a roomy pan, never bothering to string them, but making sure you have a few totally unripened berries among the rest. Cover them liberally with cold, preferably rain water to 1 inch above the level of the fruit-on-the-stalk when this settles down in the pan. Allow this mixture to come to a rolling boil, whether fairly fast or fairly slow is not of any consequence, for you will continue boiling *until a spoonful of lifted fruit is absolutely colourless and purged*. Now turn all into a jelly bag which has been previously suspended over a proper Jelly Bag Stand and pray remember to place a large container underneath. Leave overnight so that *by its own weight* the purged fruit mess forces every scrap of moisture out of the bag. Measure the container's liquid. Add the sugar as explained and allow this to dissolve over very low heat until every grain of sugar is dissolved. Raise to a slow rolling boil and maintain until you make the 'jell' test. You will observe how the small amount of scum which accumulates will form a ring which gradually widens from around the central, bubbling area to the sides of the jam kettle. Only remove this when you have successfully achieved the 'jell' test. Then pot up and tie down thereafter.

CRAB APPLE JELLY

This is one of the most delicate of all jellies and one with which all poor countryfolk are familiar, since it costs nothing save the sugar. By the Almighty's bounty the fruit festoons the hedgerows upon the weighted branches of crab apple trees in autumn. When these little miniature apples are brilliant-cheeked take them, cut them up roughly, stalks and all, and proceed exactly as for Red Currant Jelly.

QUINCE JELLY

This is the last jelly of the year to be put up, and may be done, on good years, as late as November. Cut up the fruit exactly as for Crab Apple Jelly and proceed exactly as for Red Currant Jelly.

ROWAN OR MOUNTAIN ASH JELLY

The fruit must be picked perfectly ripened. Proceed as for Red Currant Jelly. There are however certain curious results attributed to the partaking of this jelly. My dear father – who certainly was remarkably young-looking for his age – told me that his father and his father before him staunchly maintained that it was due to the eating of the Rowan in jelly form that they retained *all* their masculine vitalities to a Very Great Age. You must judge for yourself if there be anything to it. When I asked Mr Holmes about it he, as usual, had a very great deal to expound. He said it came from Scotland, Switzerland and the Scandinavian countries in particular. He gave me the Irish name 'Quicken' and the Scots one 'Rowan', calling it himself 'Mountain Ash' or *Sorbus Acuparia*. 'As I recall,' he went on, 'it can attain a height of up to sixty feet.' As you may imagine he was obliging enough to write all this down for me in his fine hand, for my poor mind could not retain so much while, of course, standing in his presence. From the notes he gave me I learned that the variety *moravice edulis* has larger fruits and is the one most favoured in France for preserving.

Mr Holmes added a Post Scriptum to the effect that it was also, in common name, referred to as 'Ranty' but admitted ruefully that he was not aware which country so styled it.

He also said, 'You must understand, Mrs Hudson, that from time immemorial this tree has been credited with all manner of mystical and, er, romantical qualities. Certainly it does contain a large amount of *malic* acid, though I am in grave doubts as to whether, as Irish tradition maintains, it is sufficient to corroborate the ancient Irish tradition that 'Quickenberries' will restore the oldest man to the age of thirty and give him back the possession of his full strength in all particulars.' He further wrote, 'Malic acid = $C_4–H_6–O_5$' – whatever *that* may mean.

It was on occasions like this that I appreciated to the full the inestimable privileges of serving so wonderously informed an employer.

LEMON JELLY

This is of great use in imparting a touch of tartness to certain oversweet jellies – using the term 'jelly' in its pudding sense.

For it you must wash, dry and slice up roughly 12 lemons. Remove all pips therefrom. Place the fruit in an earthen container. Cover with 5 quarts fine water and stand for twenty-four hours. Then boil for 2 hours, strain and measure off 1 lb sugar to 1 lb fruit as usual. And so continue to the potting up.

GOOSEBERRY JELLY

Use only very tart, hard gooseberries but see to it that you time your jelly making to synchronise with the full-flowering of the wild elderberry, for then your jelly will become in flavour like the finest muscat grapes. Proceed as for all jelly making, save that when the time comes to raise the mixture to a slow, rolling boil you tie 7 fat elderberry flower heads (for every 4 lb of gooseberries) in a bunch and plunge them head downwards in your jelly to boil for eleven minutes. Remove and proceed as usual.

DAMSON CHEESE

This is another of the preserves which I made every year. When made it should cut like a soft cheese and be quite firm. The end result is delicious, but it takes a long time to make.

PROCEDURE

Put as many stalked damsons as you desire into stone jars, cover them with parchment (*foil, F.C.*) and let them collapse in a slow oven until completely pappy (*floor of oven when in use for other items, F.C.*). Then rub them through your metal colander and stir in over a lowish heat as much sugar as is pleasant to the taste and does not draw the mouth with wryness. Then draw to the side of the stove where the heat is extremely low (*asbestos mat, lowest flame, F.C.*) and there begin by intermittent stirring. This must gradually increase with shorter and shorter periods between until you are stirring continuously. When this stage is reached, be guided by me and draw a very stout canvas or old leather glove over your stirring hand. As the mixture thickens so it begins to bubble and blow over the heat, for all the world – Mr Holmes assured me when he once came into my kitchen and saw me there occupied – like the lava in a volcano bubbling up, popping the bubbles and exploding particles thereby into the upper atmosphere. In this case it will be your stirring hand which is so placed. Therefore I beg of you be careful. On you stir until at length a wooden spoon will stand erect for a second or so before toppling, very slowly towards the side of the pan. At this juncture you will be thankful to learn, all stirring ceases. While you let the cheese stand awhile, you must crack all those tiny kernels, peel them carefully and stir as many as you can persuade yourself to prepare into the mixture before putting it into pots or ornamental moulds. Steep pieces of writing paper, cut to the exact shapes and measurements of your containers, in brandy, lay over the tops, cover with parchment and tie down *the day after potting up*.

Note: Plums and bullaces may be made into delightful cheeses by the same, somewhat laborious process.

TO PRESERVE RUNNER BEANS
(*Sometimes called Scarlet Runners*)

This I learned of my Lady's cook who first taught me the way of it and then left me to put up such beans for winter use when she became infirm.

PROCEDURE

Gather your beans during the first week of October. Take only those which snap when bent. Top, tail and trim down the sides of each one. Slice them fine and pack them very tightly into a stone jar to a depth of 3 inches. Upon the top put a ½-inch layer of coarse-grated rock salt, and repeat until the jar is filled. Finish with a thick ½-inch layer of salt and place a heavy weight upon the top being sure that the weight be laid over a piece of clean parchment cut to fit the jar. (*Foil. F.C.*) Keep in a cool place. When wanted on the following day, put to steep in fresh spring water the afternoon before and be sure to use plenty of this to draw away the brine. Then cook them as you would so for fresh ones but add no more salt. Just finish before taking to table with a generous nut of butter and a good sprinkling of finely chopped parsley heads.

TO PICKLE BEETROOTS

Gentlemen always have a fancy for pickles in one form or another for accompanying cold cuts of meat, game and poultry. I cannot recall ever having put out a home-made pickle jar of any variety that it did not leave the table very nearly emptied. When attempting to pickle beetroots always choose the long variety. Boil them in plenty of unsalted water until the skins rub away easily. This can be up to nearly three hours with really big beetroots. Remove all the skins and then cut up in long fat fingers. Have ready some glass jars and be very sure that they are perfectly dry. Pack in the beetroot pieces as close as may be to the neck of your jars. Into a scrap of muslin place 3 cloves, 6 peppercorns, 3 red chillies and ½-inch of root ginger. Tie all inside the muslin loose, but firm, and do just such a bag for each of your jars. Put one of these bags on top of each jar, then pour on boiling wine vinegar until each jar be brimful. Tie down with vegetable paper (*aluminium foil is easier! F.C.*) and store in a cool, dry place. Not only is this an immensely popular pickle but it may be brought to table speedily for entertaining occasions if it be drained, laid out neat and then dressed with a modicum of cream.

OXFORD SAUCE

It is a fact that both my gentlemen, by whom I mean Mr Holmes and poor dear Dr Watson who suffered much pain with his old wound (and in my private opinion exacerbated this by the strong, highly-spiced dishes in which he delighted) enjoyed my Oxford Sauce! Dr Watson was ever the more liberal in spreading it upon slices of cold ham than was my Master who yet expressed a partiality for it, therefore I always had it to hand as was no more than my bounden duty.

PROCEDURE

Mix 8 oz of the darkest and softest of 'pieces' brown sugar in a basin with 3 oz of made English mustard; 1 oz of course salt; $\frac{1}{2}$ oz of crushed-to-powder peppercorns; 9 fluid oz of the best olive oil. This last you add in drips, beating well between and you likewise incorporate in similar drips 4 fluid oz of red, wine vinegar. Do it well and the resultant sauce is thick and creamy. Pot up, tie down with parchment (*foil, F.C.*) and store in a cool place (*Into little screw-topped jars. F.C.*).

MY PLUMS IN PORT WINE

If my master was very hard-pressed in working upon some particularly knotty problem it was my duty to keep him supplied with hot, strong coffee, sometimes until the small hours of the morning. On one such occasion, when I was well aware that Mr Holmes had eaten nothing all day, and waved away all my suggestions for food, I made a fresh jug of coffee the way he liked it best – in an ordinary enamel jug (please turn to p. 221 for my receipt for same) and I set a small bowl of my Preserved Plums upon the tray, put it quietly at his elbow and tip-toed away. In the morning there were none left! It never occurred to me to make any reference to this matter, but Mr Holmes, on seeing me as he ran down the stairs, deerstalker in hand, cried out, 'Oh, Mrs Hudson I shall be at home for dinner tonight and Mr Hastings will dine too. Can we have some more of those excellent plums of yours with our dinner? . . .' and so saying, he rushed off shouting, 'Billy, follow me!' Billy being the name of That Boy whom he was currently taking everywhere with him.

ASSEMBLY

1 wide-necked bottling jar to hold a quart; about $1\frac{1}{2}$ lb of the very best quality prunes; $\frac{1}{2}$ lb that soft brown sugar sold under the name

'pieces'; a bottle of inferior port of the kind usually labelled 'Fine Ruby' which it certainly is not!

PROCEDURE

Place the prunes in the jar, inserting them loosely and just tapping the jar upon some wood, to settle them. When these reach the shoulder run in the 'pieces' sugar and when this is in, pour in the port, shaking the jar a little until it is filled to the rim. Close down and leave on a dry goods shelf in a cool place for three months, by which time they are ready. I must further observe that for the ordinary person these must be eaten with restraint as they are highly intoxicating. They are excellent for the sweet-toothed if taken, three or four at a time in a small glass dish with some of the port and sugar syrup. First you must stir in some thick cream, which by some curious action of the cream upon the syrup instantly becomes thick. For those whose palates incline to less sweet items serve the prunes (now plums again) by themselves with only sufficient syrup for them not to become dry on the sideboard while awaiting service.

On Writing This Little Book

ON WRITING THIS LITTLE BOOK

THROUGHOUT my labours there have been countless occasions when I have laid down my pen to ease my aching hand, and have, as it were, found myself back at my Duties for my Gentlemen.

At which times I have oft discovered myself back in that sitting-room, or 'Our Sanctum' as my gentlemen called it. It had on occasion been a snowy winter's evening close unto Christmas when I re-lived the drawing across of those heavy curtains as the lamplight fell upon the white pavements beyond the windows. Then I saw again, in memory, the snow laying upon the street lamps like icing upon one of my cakes. The hansoms and horse-buses trotting and lumbering by, their paces slowed by the slippery, skiddy road surfaces. The trembling crossing sweepers in their rags clutching their brooms, their blue chillblained toes curling up in a misery of discomfort. Some crested carriage would draw up outside, that Mr Holmes might leap down upon the pavement, his cloak about him, his cap's long flaps drawn close about his ears to protect them from the cold and, passing him, plodding laden along that pavement, many mufflered men hurrying home after work, their arms filled with Christmas trees, geese and sundry other parcels.

I have lived so many, many moments over again as I have sat in my little cottage writing down my receipts and recalling anecdotes concerning them, that in the doing I have found myself now back again in my warm clean kitchen, talking, as if in reality, to the wraiths of those who were in my care in the past. It has become my present while I have writ this book.

I have seen so clearly Dr Watson sitting before the fire listening to Mr Holmes expounding; and seen the Doctor's hand stealing involuntarily towards that old wound of his which ever seemed to trouble him.

Or I am back again in That Room kneeling to replenish the fire, taking up coals to place thereon with the coal glove I made myself from one of my old red flannel petticoats; mindful as I did so, of Mr Holmes' Sharp Warning, 'Don't forget my cigars are in the coal-scuttle Mrs

Hudson.' Then as I stacked the fire with coals and replaced the withdrawn cigar boxes, I would again glance about me in the flickering firelight as I had done in reality and see as if it were really there again, the flames shining on the polish of the sideboard and on the bottles and retorts of Mr Holmes' chemicals in one corner; lighting up the brasswork on The Safe and on a hundred and more articles of furniture, bric-a-brac, caps, pistols, slippers, books ... oh it was ever a terrible room to dust! handicapped as I was by my Stringent Orders. Mr Holmes was ever drumming into me, 'Pray do not disturb these papers, Mrs Hudson.' It was very difficult; but still the remembering of it conjures up every detail, from that bear-skin rug to the stag-hounds picture – which was forever slipping sideways and I forever straightening it again – even as the good Doctor was forever coming in and stumbling against that octagonal Indian table.

Or again I am a-dusting round the room despite my orders never to lay one finger upon the untidy masses of paperwork. Still, there was dust to shoo from that silver place-card-holder with its cobra at the moment of striking; that sovereign purse with its spring lid; that silver medal from the Afghan war; that little alabaster bust of a Certain Gracious Lady; even that most famous golden snuff-box with the great amethyst upon the lid which no less a Personage than the King of Bohemia did present to my Master. He was likewise forever taking it from the safe and then leaving it about, for which I could do nothing whatever; any more than I could with that Legion of Honour medal, nor the Emerald Pin from Queen Victoria which should have been safe locked away as befitted the great value. Likewise that strange, square Chinese coin which once dangled from the watch-chain of Mr Jabez Wilson; not forgetting also that Ming Saucer, the blue carbuncle ... oh the terrible untidiness frets me almost as much in the recalling of it as it did in the living with it, though my judgement now is clouded by my deep sentiments concerning these objects.

The time I writ out My Tripe and Onions receipt brought back the sharp and horrible memory of the time I was preparing it below stairs at No. 221b when I had to leave off in the procedure, and in memory I was again a-crawling across the room to move that wax bust at the window ... which in its turn recalled to me that frightening time when I did open the door in answer to its ringing, and there did find a huge, coarse Negro a-grinning at me. My heart rose up to my throat as it did upon the *real* occasion. This bruiser demanded to see my Master. When, drawing away in so far as was possible from him I conducted this frightening creature up the stairs and announced him, I then saw again

On writing this little book

as I stood aside, how he set himself in the doorway, his great legs a-straddling and demanded to my two gentlemen who were seated within, 'Which of you two genelmen is Masser Holmes?' Then I closed up the door and went thankfully back to my cookery.

I carried back with me the somewhat pleasanter picture of my two gentlemen at their ease by the fire, with Mr Holmes a-sprawl in his figured dressing-gown, his winged collar and his black stock (of which I had the ironing) with the scarf pin which was one of the valuable gifts made to him to commemorate the success of yet another of his most brilliant deductions.

When I was writing of the teas I gave in my parlour to Inspector Baynes and young Stanley Hopkins, I was reminded of that Other One, Mr Lestrade, whom I never could abide. Though, of course, I never permitted my dislike to reveal itself in the smallest particular – though the sight of his sharp, rat-faced countenance ever did put me out. I thought him foxy, and ferret-like and never once did I ask him to tea in my parlour!

Other little pictures, of matters personal to my care kept popping up like live things as I laboured with my pens. There was for example the Persian slipper into which Mr Holmes shred and stored his tobacco. When I writ about those Mulls and Cordials I could almost swear I smelled the 'baccy' as my employer pulled it; or I was busy with the writing of A Racket and there before my eyes was the jackknife on the mantelpiece transfixing a whole sheaf of unanswered letters.

I can remember too as clear as if it was today when Mr Holmes was said to have died. I straightway put on my best bonnet with the jet upon it, tied up the ribbons with a shaking hand and took me to my chapel to pray. On my way I passed many young men in city dress. One and all had seemed to have conspired together that they did tie black crepe bands around their top hats in mourning for the Great Loss. That was the most terrible time of all! forever linked in my mind with an unfinished batch of bread which never did see its completion all being quite past redemption and forgotten by me when I came home from the chapel.

And now I must speak of Fish. There are some silly rumours about that my Master and the good Doctor never ate fish. This is untrue and quite false. They were Most Particular as to fish's freshness and quality and a trifle pernicketty about the manner of its preparation – which was therefore rewarding to an Honest Cook, when found not wanting – but to say that my gentlemen never ate fish, simply because My Master never spoke of it, is to say Totally False to What was the Facts. Now I do feel better with that off my mind and can pass on to other things.

There is much unsaid concerning my cookery for both my gentlemen, and many other persons and personages too. Mr Holmes did at one time say of me that my cuisine was a little limited; but he taught me much, until, over the years, I think I may safely claim that I had a pretty fair repertory of dishes for the four main meals of any normal day.

Mr Holmes knew so much about food, and indeed about wines, that much brushed off, as it were, upon me. Then, as I was ever eager to learn, and knew well how to listen attentively when once my Master was launched upon one of what Dr Watson called his 'astoundin' culinary disquisitions' adding thereto "Pon my word Holmes, it never ceases to surprise me how much extraordinary knowledge is stored up in that long head of yours!'

Nor did it ever cease to astound me either, but I profited by it, yet was ever marvelling, especially in the early years when Mr Holmes was such a Very Young Man.

In conclusion, I am compelled to own that this little book does not contain ALL my repertory. Oh dear me no! When I had completed what you can read between these covers my nephew advised me to stop, saying, 'Enough is enough, Aunt. We do not want to prejudice the purchasing by some sagacious publisher by making too large and intimidating a manuscript. Such would only increase the publisher's outlay, which, for an unknown writer, could be Highly Prejudicial to an Advantageous Sale.'

So, as I began this little work upon my nephew's advice, so I do conclude also upon it, leaving much unsaid, many anecdotes untold and many receipts still only in my head and in my old copy books which I have ever kept close, detailed and very careful.

INDEX

INDEX

Index

Ale Consoler, 209
Almonds, to brown flaked, 163, 175
Anchovy Toast, 211
Apple Fritters, 158
Apple Stuffing, 78
Archbishop, 211
Artichoke, Jerusalem, soup, 48

Bacon Rolls, 202
Bacon, use of rinds, 23
Baking, to avoid burning, 17
Barley Water, 25
Batters: fritter, 120, 158; pancake, 152
Beadle, 212
Beans, runner, to preserve, 240
Beef: boiled salted brisket, 107; bones, with Mulled Ale, 195; Carpet Bagged Steak, 99; Jelly, 54; Tea, 26
Beetroots, to pickle, 240
Bishop, 210
Black Velvet, 213
Bloaters, grilled, 32
Bones, with Mulled Ale, 195
Brains, Potted Lambs', 119; uses of, 120
Brandy Sour, 214
Bread baking, 23; Pulled, 47; Walnut, 188
Breakfast Cakes, hot, 32
Broth, Remedial, 46
Browning, 18
Bull's Milk, 213
Butter: clarified, 120, 140; to keep cool, 17; to sweeten rancid, 17
Buttered Rum, 209

Cake, to ease from tin, 22
Cakes: Ginger-bread, 181; Macaroon Gâteau, 174; Lardy, 177; Sand, 182; Seed, 185; White Christmas, 183
Capercailzie, roast, 88
Capon, boiled, 90
Cardinal, 212
Carpet, to remove grease, 19
Cheese: Biscuits, 203, to use as savoury, 203; curd, 144; Fondue, 142; Golden Bucks, 202; Hominy, 35; and Onion Pie, 141; Parmesan Balls, 202; Potted Cheshire, 140; Racket (*La Raclette*), 143; Rolls, 141; Stilton, to make, 139; Straws, 201; Welsh Rarebit, 203; Yorkshire Rarebit, 203
Chestnuts, roasted, 133
Chicken: Devilled, 39–40; liver, 198; Pish-Pash, 106
Churchwarden, 210
Chutnee, 230; Dr Watson's India Apple, 230; Favourite Raw, 231
Coffee, to make, 221; syrup, 222
Country Cousin (herb cake), 135
Court-Bouillon, 59
Creams and Jellies, to remove from moulds, 23
Croûtons, 119
Cucumber, to refresh, 21; sandwiches, 183

Devilling receipts, 39–40, 79, 125
Devils upon Horseback, 199
Dough-nuts, 176
Dripping: to clean, 18; Toast, 179
Dumplings, 109

Index

Eel Soup, 52

Eggs: boiled, 33, 67; Fricassée of, 32; Florentine, 34; glaze, 84; poached, 33; to preserve, 23; scrambled, with rice, 37; to test for freshness, 164; and Tomato Ramekins, 34

Fish: Baked Soles, 61; Calcutta Jumble 70; choosing crabs, 57; choosing lobsters, 57; Chowder, 62, fish stock for, 63; faggot, 67; feeding mussels, 23, 58; Lobster Dumplings, 71; Mackerel with Gooseberry Sauce, 67; Oysters in their own liquor, 68; Pie, 65; Pope's Caps (haddock), 197; Potted Shrimps, 63; sprats, 65; strong fish stock, 50; *Truite au bleu*, 59; Turbot with Lobster Sauce, 69; whitebait, to fry, 72; winkles, 58

Flour: seasoned, 217; to make self-raising, 188

Forcemeat, 86

Fowl and Game, to clear small feathers, 21

Fricassée of Eggs, 32

Fritter batter, 120, 158; Madras Fritters, 200

Furniture polish, 20

Gammon, Baked, with raspberry leaves, 40

Giblet soup, 49

Ginger-bread, 181; preparation of tin, 181; storage, 182

Ginger Nuts, 189

Girdle or Griddle Cakes, 187

Goose: to preserve, 79; to roast, 77, 130, 179; Devilled, 79; Goose Pudding, 78

Grouse, to roast, 87

Haggis, 116; Meg Dodd's, 117

Ham: to cook, 95; to glaze, 97; to keep moist, 17; to use slices, 96; Ovals, 198; Special, 97

Hare, Jugged, 91

Hermits (biscuits), 190

Hominy, with cheese, 35

Hotch Potch, 105

Icing, to treat bubbles, 23

Jams and Jellies: Blackcurrant, 236; Crab Apple, 237; Damson Cheese, 239; Dried Apricot, 235; Gooseberry, 238; Lemon, 238; Marmalade, 233; Marrow and Ginger, 234; Peach, 235; Quince, 237; Raspberry, 236; Red Currant, 236; Rowan, 237; Wild Strawberry, 232

Javelle-Water, 19

Kedgeree, 36; Cold Fowl, 37

Kidney and Oyster Pudding, 100

Kidneys, Devilled, 125

King's Peg, 214

Lace, to make string-coloured, 19

Lardy Cake, 177

Lemon peel, to dry, 23

Lemons: to preserve, 18; sauce, 219

Liver: and Bacon, 121; Ox, 121; Chicken's Livers' Toasts, 198

Macaroon Gâteau, 174

Marmalade, Bitter Orange, 233

Mayonnaise, 224; to stiffen, 224

Melting paste, 160, 232

Meringues, to keep, 22; over-browned meringue top, 24

Milk, to avoid burning, 22; Scones, 186

Mirepoix, 84, 220

Mulled Ale, 208; with bones, 195

Mulls, 209

Mussels, to feed, 23, 58

Mustard, 18

Mutton: Chops, 103; Hotch Potch, 105; Navarin, 102; Roast Leg of, 104

Negus, 212

Oatcakes, 38

Onions, Glazed, 134

Index

Orange: Bitter, Marmalade, 233; peel, to dry, 23
Oyster Soup, 45
Oysters, Baked, 196; *see also* Kidney and Oyster Pudding

Pancakes: batter, 152; how to make, 151; Spinach, 200
Parsley Ball, 223
Parsley, to fry, 71, 73, 120, 142
Partridges, to roast, 86
Pastry Paste – *see* Melting Paste, Puff Paste and Savoury Short Paste
Peaches, Brandied, 175
Peas, to cook, 129
Pheasant: Cutlets Pandora, 81; French (*Faisan Souvaroff*), 82
Pigeon Pie, 84
Pish-Pash, 106
Plum Duff, 149
Plums in Port Wine, 241
Pork: baked chops, 109; Faggots, 122
Potato and Cheese Cakes, 131
Potato Soufflé, 130
Potatoes: creamed, 133; proper purée, 131; roast with goose fat, 130
Puddings: Apple Fritters, 158; Apricot, steamed, 154; Bachelors', 163; Black Cherry, 161; Crusades, 163; Fanchette, 159; Italian Pie, 168; Kaiser Wilhelm, 164; Pancakes, 154; Plum Duff, 149; Prince Albert's, 166; Prince Regent's, 162; Queen of, 153; Semolina, 167; Simple Cherry, 161; Six-Cup, 150; Soufflé Surprise, 147; Spotted Dick, 157; Titsy-Bitsies, 154
Puff Paste: origin of, 155; to bake, 22; to make, 156

Rabbit: soup, with sorrel, 47; Scallywag Pie, 123
Raspberry leaves, to dry, 19; with Baked Gammon, 40
Rice, to cook, 37
Rout Biscuits, 191

Salsify, 135
Sand Cake, 182
Sardine Cheeses, 199
Sardines, to remove from tin, 23
Sauce-making: methods, 64; to avoid crusting, 22, 218
Sauces: Apricot, 154; Apricot and Pistachio, 166; Basic White, with Milk and Cream, 218, with Stock and Wine, 217; Brown (*Espagnole*), 84, 220; Butter, melted, 164; Cheese, 66; Devil, 39; Garlic Butter, 218; Gooseberry, 68; Holland (*Hollandaise*), 219; Kaiser, 165; Lemon, 219; Lobster, 69; Mayonnaise, 224; Onion, 105; Oxford, 241; Rum, 162; Shrimp, easy, 64; Spanish, 220
Sausage meat, 21; Topsy-Turvy Pie, 110
Sausages, to cook, 38
Savoury Short Paste: with butter, 197; with dripping, 124
Scallywag Pie, 123
Scones, Milk, 186
Scorch marks, to remove, 20
Scorcher, 208
Seed Cake, 185
Sherry Cobbler, 213
Shrimps, Potted, 63; sauce, 64
Sickroom: abscess, 28; bed table, 24; laundry marking, 24; loosening dose, 24; slipping down in bed, 25; throat cure, 28; toothache, 28
Silver cleaner, 20
Sloe Gin, 207
Slugs, to banish, 21
Snipe, to roast, 86
Soda, not to be used for vegetables, 21
Soufflé Surprise, 147
Soup: Beef Jelly, 54; Beer, 52; Broth, 46; Eel, 52; Giblet, 49; Gravy, 53; Jerusalem Artichoke, 48; Mulligatawny, 50; My Aunt's Hop-Top, 46; Oyster, 45; Rabbit, with sorrel, 47; York Ham Liquor, 51
Spinach, to cook, 34, 134; Pancakes, 200; purée, 134

Index

Starling Pie, 82
Steaming, 149
Stilton cheese, to make, 139
Stock, Strong Fish, 50
Strawberry, Wild: Jam, 232; Tart, 232
Stuffing: Apple, 78; Sage and Onion, 79
Sugar: syrup, 191, 214; to be caramelised, 22; to crush loaf, 24; to treat soft brown, 22
Sweetbreads, Cream of, 118

Toast, to butter, 198
Topsy-Turvy Pie, 110
Tripe, 115
Truite au bleu, 59

Vegetable Colouring, Green, 223
Venison: carving haunch of, 90; choosing, 88; hanging, 89; roasting haunch of, 89
Violets, to revive, 21

Walnut Bread, 188
White Christmas Cake, 183
Windows, to clean, 20
Wine Posset, 210
Woodcock Pie, 85
Wooden kitchen table, to clean, 21